D1479174

Defending Constitutional Rights

STUDIES IN THE LEGAL HISTORY OF THE SOUTH

Kermit L. Hall and Paul Finkelman, *series editors*

Defending Constitutional Rights

Frank M. Johnson, 1918–

Edited by Tony A. Freyer

THE UNIVERSITY OF GEORGIA PRESS

ATHENS AND LONDON

© 2001 by the University of Georgia Press
Athens, Georgia 30602
All rights reserved
Designed by Betty Palmer McDaniel
Set in 9.7/13 Electra by G & S Typesetters, Inc.
Printed and bound by Thomson-Shore, Inc.
The paper in this book meets the guidelines for
permanence and durability of the Committee on
Production Guidelines for Book Longevity of the
Council on Library Resources.

Printed in the United States of America

05 04 03 02 01 C 5 4 3 2 1

Library of Congress Cataloging-in-Publication Data
Johnson, Frank Minis, 1918–
Defending constitutional rights / Frank M. Johnson ;
edited by Tony A. Freyer.
p. cm. — (Studies in the legal history of the South)
Includes bibliographical references and index.
ISBN 0-8203-2285-7 (alk. paper)
1. Equality before the law — United States. 2. Civil rights
movement — United States. 3. Political questions
and judicial power — United States.
I. Freyer, Tony Allan. II. Title. III. Series.

KF4764 .J64 2001
342.73'085 — dc21   00-065795

British Library Cataloging-in-Publication Data available

Contents

Preface

Judge Frank M. Johnson received international recognition for effective resolution of many historic civil rights cases during the 1950s and 1960s, upholding the African American struggle for equal citizenship against the resistance of southern leaders. Yet Johnson's opinions affirmed not only the constitutional rights of African Americans; some of his most important decisions extended the rights of women, white urban voters, college and secondary school students, criminal defendants, prisoners, and the mentally ill. Over the years, Johnson confronted criticism that by addressing the social conflicts arising in their courts, he and other federal judges had usurped the authority of the peoples' democratically elected representatives. As he repeatedly faced protracted resistance from authorities, he accepted invitations from law schools, professional law organizations, and interviewers to present his views regarding the role of law, lawyers, and the Constitution in the American constitutional order. The ideas Johnson expressed on these occasions reveal the mind of a great judge grappling with issues fundamental to maintaining the rule of law. Taken together, these presentations set forth constitutional ideals that add to Johnson's enduring legacy.

Johnson retired from full-time active judicial service in 1991. During his lifetime Robert F. Kennedy Jr., Jack Bass, Frank Sikora, and Tinsley E. Yarbrough published biographical works. Additionally, in 1980 the Public Television program *Bill Moyers' Journal* aired an extensive two-part interview with the judge; and in 1995 Bill Clinton awarded Johnson the Presidential Medal of Freedom. The purpose of this book is threefold. First, I hope to provide general readers, lawyers, and academics access to Judge Johnson's most important constitutional and legal thinking. He published numerous articles on such topics as civil rights struggles, civil disobedience and the rule of law, equal access to justice, the role of the judiciary in the system of constitutional checks and balances, and how lawyers could facilitate social change. These articles, considered in conjunction with the Bill Moyers interview, explain the values and assumptions underlying Johnson's uses of judicial authority. A second purpose of this project is to provide a connected discourse reflecting a judicial consciousness at work. Notwithstanding the claims of critics that Johnson was the quintessential activist liberal judge, the materials collected in this volume evidence core values that are essentially conservative, embodying a view of Americanism based on individual freedom defined in terms of equal opportunity and equality under law. Freedom depended in turn on constitutionally guaranteed rights enforced by an independent judiciary. The central institutional goal to be attained through the entire judicial process was fundamental fairness, maintained by extending access to previously excluded groups through a process of strengthening the incentives for lawyers to represent them.

Finally, Johnson's articles and PBS interview suggest why Americans are so much ruled by judges. Trial judges influence most directly the average American. As early as the 1830s French commentator Alexis de Tocqueville observed that federal judges decided the most important issues involving the nature and limits of governmental power in American society, including conflicts over rights. A tension existed, however, between popular respect for judicial authority and the federal judge's nonelected status, which seemed at odds with American democracy. The historian G. Edward White suggested that this tension was representative of a national judicial tradition. Important works by such scholars as Malcolm M. Feeley and Edward L. Rubin have shown the many sophisticated theories critics and defenders employ to assess this influence. Even so, such commentators as White usually focused their attention on appellate judges, those most removed from popular pressures. Johnson's career is an example, by contrast, of a trial judge who from 1955 to 1979 decided many of the most significant cases in American constitutional history. As an active member of the federal appellate bench between 1979 and 1991 he contributed additional historic opinions. The material collected here makes Johnson's unique contribution readily accessible as a consistent whole and thus understandable as judicial consciousness wrestling with human conflict.

Acknowledgments

It is a pleasure to recognize the individuals and institutions who have helped bring the work to completion. Since I interviewed Judge Johnson in 1990–91, he supported the project. In 1995 I coauthored with Timothy Dixon a history of the federal courts in Alabama, which included a chapter on Johnson. The publisher was Carlson Publishing. In the same year, I published an article in the *Saint Louis University Law Journal* that included much of the same material. I have drawn on these sources extensively in the Introduction and the Conclusion and I thank both organizations for permission to use this material. I am grateful to Bill Moyers for permission to publish the two-part interview with Judge Johnson and to Mrs. Johnson for permission to publish the eight articles.

Throughout the years, the University of Alabama Law School Foundation and the Edward Brett Randolph Fund have provided essential funding. The Eleventh Circuit Historical Society and the Judicial Conference of the United States, Committee on the Bicentennial of the Constitution, were also helpful during the early stages. In this project, as in all my research and writing at the Law School, Dean Kenneth C. Randall has been most supportive. Two law students who provided superb research assistance were Erby Fischer and Vince Carroll. Peter Wonders was also helpful at the start.

I owe a scholarly debt to Johnson's biographers, which is evident from my extensive quotations from their work in the following sections. Also I learned much from Peter Charles Hoffer's, David J. Garrow's, Taylor Branch's, Dan T. Carter's, Juan Williams's, George M. Fredrickson's, and Larry W. Yackle's fine books, again, as evident from my references below.

I am truly grateful to Julia Lewis, Wanda Elliott, and Perin Elliott, whose expert computer skills overcame innumerable difficulties to put the various texts on disk and to prepare a hard copy. Alesia Darling was helpful too. Without the lawyerly assistance of colleague David Epstein the book would very likely have never seen the light of day. I am grateful too for Ellen McDonald's editorial assistance. I appreciate also the support of Kermit Hall, Paul Finkelman, and Malcolm Call and all the University of Georgia Press has done to publish the work. Of course I am responsible for the book's shortcomings or deficiencies. The dedication is to Ruth Jenkins Johnson, the memory of Judge Johnson, and their son James Curtis Johnson.

Tony A. Freyer

Introduction: Johnson's Unusual Origins and Early Career

Frank M. Johnson was a unique figure in American history. Generally, federal judges below the level of the Supreme Court are known primarily in the communities and states they serve; if they achieve national recognition it is for a particular case or series of cases. As a United States District Court judge in Montgomery, Alabama, from 1955 to 1979, Johnson gained a national reputation because of his central role in historic civil rights struggles and other decisions establishing the subordination of state authority to judicial control. Never before had a lower federal court judge done so much to expand individual rights. Appointed in 1979 to the federal appellate court, Johnson decided still more cases that for over a decade influenced the changing course of individual liberty throughout the nation.[1] Many commentators examined Johnson's contribution to resolving the confrontations between such prominent civil rights leaders as Martin Luther King and their opponents, including, especially, George Wallace.[2] Also, legal scholars evaluated the increased authority Johnson employed to expand claims of individual rights.[3] Meanwhile, the U.S. Supreme Court usually upheld, and media coverage almost universally commented favorably on, Johnson's decisions.[4] The following Public Television interview and articles present Johnson's own view of his constitutional role and its broader significance for twentieth-century American history. This introduction provides a biographical context for that material, suggesting how Johnson's early life and career shaped his constitutional ideals into action.[5]

Johnson's future as a judge was shaped by his past. He was born in 1918 and grew up in a family and among a group of people possessing a distinctive heritage associated with a special place. The strength of family bonds and the comparative isolation of the community instilled in Johnson values of independence, self-reliance, integrity, and self-sufficiency conditioned by a sensitivity to personal courage and human frailty. This experience fostered also a profound faith in fundamental fairness, especially involving racial and political minorities. University and legal education broadened Johnson's intellectual capabilities, which were tested to the fullest in a noteworthy criminal trial during his service in World War II. After the war he earned a reputation as a skillful lawyer and active

Republican, preparing him well for a career of public service. In 1955 the Eisenhower administration appointed Johnson to be a federal district judge; at the time he was the nation's youngest federal judge. His appointment coincided with the beginnings of the white South's massive resistance to the civil rights movement, which resulted from the Supreme Court's remedial decree in the *Brown* decision ordering that racial desegregation of the public schools would proceed "with all deliberate speed."[6] Still, comparisons between Johnson and fellow Alabamian Richard T. Rives suggested that, at least initially, family background and the mode of law practice probably most influenced Johnson's attitude toward individual rights.[7]

Johnson's adolescent years and early youth profoundly shaped his instincts concerning right and wrong. Most public assessments, and Johnson himself, emphasized the importance of his Winston County origins. Winston and several neighboring counties in northwestern Alabama were the home of "Mountain Republicans" whose ancestors had resisted secession and who well into the twentieth century retained an independent and unified political influence amid the Democratic majority. Johnson's family lineage included those who not only fought on the Union side in the Civil War but who were respected local leaders, including his great-grandfather James Wallace (Straight Edge) Johnson. According to family tradition, the local community so trusted the elder Johnson's integrity that neighbors often asked him to settle disputes instead of relying on the courts. The community maintained the same trust toward Johnson's father, electing him to the office of probate judge and finally during the 1940s as the only Republican member of the Alabama legislature.

Still, this intermingling of family and political tradition is an incomplete measure of the influence of place. Though Winston County was comparatively isolated and predominantly rural, the Illinois Central Railroad served the area. As a result of the railroad's presence, Johnson acquired an image of individual African Americans which differed from that possessed by most white Alabamians. The fewer than one hundred blacks residing in Winston County lived principally in and around Haleyville, Johnson's hometown until he reached fourteen. Here he played with black children whose fathers worked for the railroad. "They made good money. They lived in nice homes," he later recalled. At the same time, he remembered that his own parents accepted the public and private separation racial orthodoxy imposed but "never did have any racial prejudice, suggestive or overt or any other way."[8] Indeed, Johnson's mother helped to establish the local school for blacks. Thus, unlike most other white Alabamians who identified African Americans with a subservient status consistent with presumptions of white supremacy, Johnson's formative racial image was one that combined legally imposed separation with economic independence, reasonable prosperity, and no formally articulated racism.

The rural, small-town setting influenced Johnson's early family life in other ways. Because Winston County's market position was comparatively marginal, the Johnsons, like many families, produced much of their own food. In addition, as the oldest son in a large family, young Frank Jr. was his mother's principal helper in all aspects of the family's life. "I changed diapers and everything else. Mamma was busy. I helped her everywhere. She never let me cook. I'd bring the wood in, build the fire, I'd help her run that old [hand-cranked] Maytag washing machine," he said. Johnson also was experienced at working with animals and plowing fields. The limited local economy also supported modest educational opportunities, and both of Johnson's parents valued education. His mother taught him to read and spell before he started the first grade; she was a "good teacher" who held "my ear to keep me from moving around and diverting my attention." His parents and his family life thus gave Johnson "a real consciousness that you don't get anything that you don't work for. And you can work and not get much if you don't get an education. And if you want to succeed, you get your education and work hard. You couldn't get it for nothing." [9]

The interdependence between rural environment and family life fostered a profound, though practical, respect for law. Johnson's parents equated personal honesty and responsibility with strict regard for law. "They were very sensitive to their children being honest and not violating the law. You just didn't do it. And they set good examples in that respect all the way back to my grandfather and grandmother on both sides. I don't remember any of them getting into any trouble," he said. Similarly, Johnson's father, for much of the son's youth a local postmaster, "took great pride in the fact" that the annual postal inspections "never [found him] a penny short." [10] In a small community this strict integrity and accountability were integral to maintaining the individual's and the family's respectability. Just as important, perhaps, his parents were firm but understanding during the quite exceptional instances when Johnson found himself on the wrong side of the law. For example, he assaulted one of his father's political opponents for making false accusations about the senior Johnson. His father advised him to plead guilty to disorderly conduct before the local magistrate, and that was the end of the matter. In a similar vein, the sixteen-year-old Johnson came in contact with bootleggers and the temptations of "wildcat whiskey." Fundamentally, the attitude Johnson absorbed from his parents concerning one's responsibility for such conduct was doubtless consistent with the view stated by one of his closest friends: "We never got into any real trouble. We were mischie-vous, but we weren't mean. We didn't do destructive-type things." [11] This attitude blended the belief in moral correctness with a practical appreciation of human nature, tensions inherent in a sense of family pride.

Tensions between moral principle and human nature arose from more en-counters with moonshine whiskey. In the "Free State of Winston" the illegal pro-duction and sale of moonshine whiskey was common. Equally widespread was the direct involvement of local law enforcement and elected officials in the prac-tice. At times, elected authorities protected the moonshiners who voted for their respective party while prosecuting producers who supported the opposing party. As Johnson confronted these moral and legal ambiguities, he instinctively em-braced a faith in equality before the law, due process, and fairness. Discrimina-tory mistreatment of moonshiners, grounded as it was in political prejudice, of-fended Johnson more than violations of the tax code or moral concerns. This consciousness also shaped Johnson's awareness of the connection between unfair treatment and racial injustice. Watching his father handle the duties of a probate judge, Johnson learned respect for elemental procedural fairness. At some level he probably perceived that the basic maintenance of due process was not incon-sistent with the firm, but humane, discipline prevailing in his home.

In any case, Johnson's belief that fundamental fairness and respect for hu-manity were interdependent was already strong by the time he encountered for the first time blatant mistreatment of black convicts. After graduating from high school, Johnson worked carrying the rod for a surveyor's road crew. Black con-vict labor also worked with this crew. Johnson became "sensitized" to the white guards' mistreatment of the black convicts when, "If they tried to escape, or if they were guilty of just blatantly disobeying an order, they'd get a certain num-ber of licks with a whip. And no one would conduct a hearing to determine if it was appropriate or not. I got pretty sensitized to the fact that it wasn't right, that it wasn't just." He never forgot the repulsion he felt. "I was nauseated. That one human being whipped by another with a bullwhip. Nauseated." [12]

Johnson's belief in fundamental fairness also had spiritual and religious roots. Those closest to him knew he was a religious person. "I have some strong, basic religious beliefs," he said. "Doing what's right and wrong to me is a religious be-lief. And doing what's fair instead of unfair to a fellow human being is a religious standard." Johnson prayed privately to God, usually "expressing appreciation, and some of the time asking for help and guidance." There was, nonetheless, a definite separation between the moral principles of the Bible and constitutional or legal principles. He was certain that American law and constitutional principles "should [not] be guided in any way by Biblical principles."[13]

The interplay of family and locale perhaps had its most profound influence through the women in Johnson's life. In the isolated rural setting in which Johnson grew up, women, though working in domestic roles, were independent and strong. According to family tradition, Johnson's great-grandmother Mrs. James Wallace Johnson used a piece of firewood to defend her young grandson Frank Johnson Sr. from a buck deer that came too close to the child. A close friend described Johnson's own mother, Alabama Lang Johnson, as "a lovely lady . . . a woman of strong character, strong morals, strong convictions — the courage of her convictions — a strong, strong woman. And Frank inherited an awful lot of that. He has always shown the courage of his convictions — sometimes to a fault." Johnson married the former Ruth Jenkins, who was from the same locale and, like his mother and grandmother, possessed great inner strength. When Johnson decided to go to the University of Alabama School of Law, Ruth also enrolled at the university. Johnson's mother vigorously supported his wife's decision, saying, "If anybody goes to college, Ruth's going. She's smart."[14] During World War II she served in the navy, attaining the rank of lieutenant junior grade. During the years of conflict and tragedy that eventually engulfed them, they complemented and supported each other. An intimate friend said, "Theirs is a fantastic love story. Ruth provides ballast, security, and the leavening in [Frank's] . . . bread. And sometimes you see Ruth as the one who carries a long hat pin. If the balloon is going to get too big, Ruth doesn't have any hesitancy in puncturing it. It's drop-by-drop, day-by-day constant. Ruth will stay the course, whatever it is." They "disagree philosophically many times on something, but it never gets personal. They've learned to separate their ideas from their personal relationship. Both have teamed to bring out the best that the other had. And ignore the worst."[15]

The qualities instilled by early manhood prepared Johnson for greater responsibilities and independent thought. While still in his early twenties, he supervised about forty men with diverse skills in a construction program under the joint authority of county health departments and the New Deal's Works Progress Administration (WPA). Whites and African Americans worked together in his crews on a nonsegregated basis, receiving the same wage. The effectiveness of this operation strengthened Johnson's conviction that whites' belief in racial inferiority was "hogwash." Sensitive to the fact that most of the black workers possessed little formal education, Johnson found that given "proper guidance, supervision, and incentive" they were nonetheless as "effective in [the] work" as the white workers. Also, he was "impressed how they cared about their families and making a living in an honest way if they got a chance to do so."[16]

Johnson strengthened these administrative and personnel skills when he entered the University of Alabama. He had received his initial education in the Winston County public schools and the Gulf Coast Military Academy; he then attended briefly Birmingham Southern College on a football scholarship before eventually completing a one-year course at a business college in Birmingham. This mixed educational experience fostered Johnson's self-discipline and desire for learning. At the university, however, he confronted "at every turn" the "profound and shocking realization" of his "ignorance." Typically, he worked aggressively to overcome every educational deficiency; feeling challenged by "outstanding professors," he learned "to extricate [him]self from errors in the thinking process that tend to darken one's intelligence and incapacitate a person from listening to and appreciating reason, learned to carefully avoid precipitancy and prejudice and, possibly above all, learned that a person — if he or she is to have a sense of contribution and fulfillment — must be an actor in life and not merely a spectator." As his facility to "reason, meditate, and reflect" grew, Johnson realized that "all one can achieve and all that one fails to achieve are the result of his own thoughts, that a person's weaknesses and strengths are his own — not another's — that these weaknesses and strengths are brought about by himself and can only be altered by himself."[17] Johnson developed and sharpened his intelligence by taking both undergraduate and law school classes at the university.

Johnson's success in law school reflected a blend of intellectual growth and his personal background. Professor Leigh Harrison recalled that at the start of law school Johnson "looked like a country boy when I first called on him, and I was surprised at the way he answered the question. I wouldn't have expected him to do as well as he did." He was "an exceptionally able student who evidently grew up with a sense of responsibility and integrity." Johnson not only grasped quickly and perceptively the "ability to analyze facts and reach a solution based on legal principles," Harrison said, but he also understood clearly that "for a lot of legal problems, there are no precise answers." Johnson later emphasized that Harrison and his other teachers "did not limit their efforts to presenting the law in the traditional manner but challenged me to find truth, justice, common sense, and fairness in our country's law. . . . I learned to think, and through that process, learned to distinguish the true from the false. This is what education is all about."[18]

Intellectual acuity conditioned by life experience shaped Johnson's attitude toward the constitutional law governing race relations. Formative encounters with hardworking African Americans on the railroad in his hometown and as a WPA supervisor, along with the intense repulsion he felt as a result of the whipping of black convicts on the road crews, engendered Johnson's belief that racial segregation was morally wrong. As a law student, this moral conviction in turn influenced his critical analysis of the Supreme Court's sanction of slavery in the *Dred Scott* case and the affirmation of the South's system of racial apartheid through the separate-but-equal doctrine in *Plessy v. Ferguson.* Johnson found Chief Justice Roger B. Taney's denial of the slaves' basic humanity in *Dred Scott* to be "scandalous." Likewise, he thought *Plessy* was "a terrible decision" that could not be the "law under our system of government." He was quite impressed, however, with Justice John Marshall Harlan's lone dissent in *Plessy:* "I think it was one of the finest opinions, even if it was a dissent. It took a lot of courage. And it was obvious that was the law, whether the Supreme Court was following it or not. It had to be the law if the Fourteenth Amendment meant anything."[19]

Johnson's assessment of his legal education and the Court's leading racial decisions was suggestive. Johnson's grasp of what he was taught in law school was sufficiently profound that he graduated first in his class, indicating how deeply Johnson understood what Harrison had taught: that despite the apparent fixity of legal rules and procedures, law was often indeterminate, open-ended, and malleable. Meanwhile, Johnson's family upbringing and home locale fostered character traits combining belief in clear-cut boundaries separating right and wrong; confidence that through discipline and education one could live correctly; the conviction that those in authority should nonetheless treat everyone, including criminals, with fundamental fairness; sensitivity to the vicissitudes resulting from human weakness; and spiritual faith in personal accountability. The intermingling of these character perceptions and a firm grasp of how legal institutions and the Constitution did in fact and ought to function sustained his presumption that a "true" law or constitutional principle existed even if government agencies might at any given time enforce an opposite and therefore "false" rule. Thus Johnson condemned *Plessy* not only because it sanctioned racial separation and a disrespect for individual dignity but also because the system of apartheid it engendered was contrary to the fundamental principles on which the Constitution and America rested, regardless of what the Court had held.

This blend of perspicacity, practicality, and conviction also guided Johnson's view of politics. Like Republicans across the nation and many Democrats in Alabama, Johnson considered much of Franklin D. Roosevelt's New Deal liberalism to be not only socialistic but also an unconstitutional aggrandizement of executive power. Along with many Alabamians, Johnson nonetheless supported the jobs the WPA and other New Deal programs created. Similarly, Johnson understood how his father, the lone Republican in the Alabama legislature, could successfully work with the more progressive National Democratic faction which endorsed Roosevelt's New Deal liberalism in support of economic and social programs benefiting north Alabama and the state as a whole against the generally dominant conservative Democratic majority. In the same vein, Johnson formed friendships with fellow law students who were politically active among the National Democrats associated with future governor James Folsom, such as another future governor, George Wallace. Johnson was also a member of the Pi Kappa Alpha fraternity, whose members included many of Alabama's aspiring or established National Democratic activists affiliated with U.S. senator John Sparkman. Nevertheless, this practical understanding of party politics did not diminish Johnson's propensity to evaluate individual politicians in terms of whether their leadership was ultimately morally consistent with the spirit of America's basic constitutional principles.

Wartime experience reinforced Johnson's character qualities and legal values. He saw combat action in France and Germany; he was twice wounded, receiving a Purple Heart with an oak-leaf cluster and a Bronze Star. Transferred from the war zone to England to serve as a legal officer, he represented the defendants in one of the most publicized military trials of the war. Nine enlisted guards and two lieutenants were charged with brutally treating prisoners at the Litchfield prison. Although inexperienced in criminal trial work, Johnson displayed skill and persistence in his conduct of the case. After lengthy proceedings, Johnson and experienced lead counsel Clinton McGee (also from Alabama) proved that the brutal conditions in the prison were the result of the actions of superior officers, and the principal enlisted man charged in the case received a minimum sentence. At one point an officer testified that Johnson had said that challenging senior officers did not concern him if it was necessary to protect the rights of the accused. During that case, Johnson "filed motions . . . that the U.S. military had never heard of."[20] The Litchfield case demonstrated Johnson's tenacious and creative use of legal process to defend the rights of vulnerable individuals threatened by irresponsible higher authorities.

After the war, Johnson practiced law in the northwest Alabama town of Jasper. The three-man firm's general practice included corporations, probate, criminal work, and public bodies such as the county board of education and county board of revenue. Johnson handled the trial side while other partners advised business clients. From this mix of law practice Johnson learned the financial exigencies of maintaining profitability through fee structures. Winning cases before juries,

Johnson learned how a lawyer could tap the community's instinct for basic fairness; but he also came to understand that courts and opposing attorneys might overcome this instinct by appealing to prejudice and fear. Ultimately, Johnson's success before juries depended on overcoming such tactics, and among the fellow residents of the area he usually succeeded. He also returned to local politics, pushing a ticket-splitting strategy that enabled the Republicans to win an office or two from the dominant Democrats. In addition, Johnson resigned his membership in Rotary and other business groups once he learned that they excluded Jews.

In one case, Johnson proved how local politics and criminal charges could get mixed up. He defended two brothers charged with murdering a county sheriff. The brothers' family, Johnson recalled, "had been in the [moonshine] whiskey business for years, farming on the side."[21] As Republicans, they did not support the local Democratic establishment and the sheriff who was politically involved with the most important banking and political family in the county, which included a long-serving member of the Alabama legislature. A local jury found the brothers guilty. On appeal to the Alabama Supreme Court, however, Johnson proved that the sheriff's allies exercised considerable economic and political influence over the jury selection process. In a four-to-three decision, the state supreme court reversed the conviction on legal technicalities. Eventually the case was dismissed and the brothers went free. Johnson's defense so impressed the two other members of the firm that they offered him a full partnership.

Family and place gave Johnson's values and experience a certain distinctiveness. The mountain Republicanism and strong family heritage identified with his Winston County origins gave Johnson an instinctive grasp of how interdependent were individual responsibility and community values. The Johnson family and its forebears belonged to a political minority; their personal integrity and strength of character inspired their neighbors with sufficient trust and confidence, however, that various members of the family, especially Johnson's father, had active public careers. What balanced minority rights and community interests was the popular instinct for fundamental fairness. As a trial lawyer, Johnson's success before juries depended on an ability to overcome popular prejudices and fears by appealing to this basic instinct. The young Frank Johnson controlled these influences so effectively at a personal level that he rejected the dominant culture's belief in white supremacy and racial segregation imposed by law. Intellectual growth attained through university and law school study equipped him, moreover, with the professional skills not only to become a successful lawyer but also one who often defended underdogs. Pursuing these career goals, he never forgot the lessons learned from his parents and reinforced by his marriage, that often human frailty conditioned moral principle.

Another Alabamian who, during the civil rights struggle, also became one of the few federal judges vigorously defending individual rights lacked Johnson's distinctive origins. Richard T. Rives was a quintessential political and social insider from the heart of Alabama's firmly segregationist black belt, Montgomery. An active and influential National Democrat, he supported New Deal liberalism against the state's generally dominant conservative Democrats, but club memberships and social status clearly indicated that Rives belonged to the state's "Establishment." At the same time, his law firm had a major trial practice that included representing white as well as black criminal defendants and plaintiffs before juries. Unlike other Montgomery firms that shunned defending African Americans and other dispossessed individuals, Rives represented all clients. He resisted the Boswell Amendment, which imposed new devices to keep blacks disfranchised but defended black-belt voter registrars when blacks attempted to defeat the traditional discriminatory methods. Rives explained that what other firms "gained in security they have often lost in the freedom and independence that come from representing many poor plaintiffs, rather than a few rich defendants." On the federal Fifth Circuit Court of Appeals his respect for fundamental fairness set Rives apart. He was both "no radical. . . . [and] a tradition-minded . . . [New Deal] Southern Democrat," wrote one incisive observer: "At the same time, Rives was never committed to segregation as an item of faith, and he was a passionately fair man." The evidence of this in his years of practice was clear, and Rives maintained that this attitude came from his father. For him and for the judge, "it was 'just an innate idea of what's right and wrong.'" Thus the interplay between the beliefs acquired from his family and his atypical jury trial practice, which included outsiders and the dispossessed, enabled Rives to become one of the very few southern federal judges who "rose above the received values of his [social and regional] background and established himself as one of the most courageous judges in our times." [22]

The characteristics Johnson and Rives shared were noteworthy. The locales from which each man came differed, as did their social status and partisan political affiliation, but these differences were more profound in appearance than in substance. The National Democratic leadership often supported Johnson's father as the lone Republican in the Alabama legislature, primarily because of shared economic and political values and associations inherent in the New Deal liberal consensus, to which Alabama's conservative Democrats were not party. Moreover, while both the state's National Democrats and the Eisenhower Republicans were relatively moderate on race, at least for Alabama, Rives's and Johnson's unusual personal rejection of white supremacy was due more to the influence of family than to political values or interests. Nevertheless, the most conspicuous common experiences between the two men were their law practices. Unlike most Alabama lawyers, Johnson and Rives not only represented poor and minority clients before juries composed of all white middle-class males, but they usually also won. Success reinforced the faith in fundamental fairness both men learned from their parents. Ultimately, however, this faith was inseparable from reliance on the institutional autonomy associated with the independent judiciary and the adversarial process itself.

Johnson became a federal judge through ordinary politics, but the consequences of his appointment could not have been predicted. The active Republican partisanship of Johnson and his father, the personal connections the young Johnson had with Republican U.S. attorney general Herbert Brownell and Alabama's National Democratic faction, the election to the presidency of the first Republican in twenty years, and the Supreme Court's growing support for civil rights converged to bring about Johnson's appointments, first as U.S. district attorney and then as federal district judge. Neither the Eisenhower administration's moderate support for civil rights nor the inconsistent decisions of other Alabama federal judges who came from either Republican or National Democratic backgrounds suggested how distinctive would be Johnson's judicial career. His actions as U.S. attorney revealed a willingness to follow an independent path. Once he became a judge, Johnson's contribution to the Montgomery bus boycott case indicated that such independence would be the norm. Yet like Judge Rives, Johnson pursued a distinctive course because the values and experiences rooted in his family origins and legal career enabled him to use judicial independence and the adversarial process to achieve the basic outcome of fundamental fairness.

The combination of lawyerly acumen and Republican activism won Johnson an appointment as the United States attorney for northern Alabama. In 1944 and 1948, Johnson's father actively supported New York governor Thomas Dewey as the Republican Party's presidential candidate. Frank Johnson Jr. was a Dewey loyalist too. During the 1948 campaign he met Warren Burger, Richard Nixon, and Herbert Brownell, Dewey's campaign manager; at the time too, Alabama's politics were split between the supporters of the more progressive National Democrats and the third-party Dixiecrats who defended racial segregation. Governor James Folsom and his floor leader in the Alabama legislature, George Wallace, were politically aligned with the state's National Democrats. Of course,

Dewey lost in 1948, but Brownell also managed Dwight D. Eisenhower's successful campaign in 1952, a campaign Johnson worked for actively in Alabama. Appointed Eisenhower's attorney general, Brownell chose Johnson to be U.S. attorney for northern Alabama with the support of the new assistant attorney general, Warren Burger. On race and various post–New Deal economic issues, the Dewey-Eisenhower Republicans in Alabama were closer to the National Democrats affiliated with Senators Sparkman and Lister Hill, so the state's all-Democratic congressional delegation supported the selection of Johnson in 1953.

As U.S. attorney, Johnson demonstrated further the qualities that made him such an effective trial lawyer. Usually, U.S. attorneys administered the office, delegating to staff lawyers most of the trial work. Johnson, however, handled most trials himself. At the same time, he significantly improved the office's administrative efficiency. He also learned how to use the FBI's investigative resources. This commitment to trial advocacy and administrative effectiveness coincided with the judicial approach of the northern district's two federal judges, Seybourn H. Lynne and H. Hobart Grooms. Under Lynne's leadership especially, the northern district of Alabama was recognized as among the best administered courts in the nation. Johnson displayed independence, however, declining to follow the court's standard regard for plea bargaining. Johnson knew that prosecutors often plea bargained for a "lighter sentence than there should be just to avoid the work of prosecuting a case, or because of friendship with another lawyer, or political considerations."[23] His experience in law school, as a legal officer in the army, and during private practice convinced him that it was through a trial that justice was found.

Johnson's facility for equating justice with trial due process was clear in a peonage case. The owner of a black funeral home in Sumter County, Alabama, sent Johnson a photograph of a brutally beaten and mutilated African American man's corpse. An accompanying letter claimed that whites had whipped the man to death. Johnson ordered an FBI investigation. The resulting evidence showed that on their plantation in Sumter County, a family named Dial cooperated with local officials to entrap blacks in a debt system which the Dials exploited to maintain a captive labor force. The black man whose photograph Johnson received had tried to escape. Using dogs, the plantation owners tracked the man down, "brought him back and beat him with a bullwhip—and killed him." The Dials' counsel was the "best criminal defense lawyer in the South at the time." Nevertheless, Johnson skillfully brought out testimony that beatings were a common occurrence on the Dial farm. The furious defense attorney called a recess and privately rebuked the testifier for admitting to something "bad" about the Dials. The testifier told the lawyer that "whuping a nigger ain't bad in Sumter County."[24] The jury returned verdicts of guilty.

The peonage case coincided with the Supreme Court's decision of *Brown*. Johnson's ability to win guilty verdicts from an all-white jury for whites' brutality against a black man impressed Brownell. Clearly, *Brown*'s holding overruling *Plessy*'s separate-but-equal doctrine in public education undercut the constitutional legitimacy of segregation, threatening massive resistance from the white South. Brownell not only strongly favored *Brown*; he also interpreted the peonage verdict as indicating a willingness among most southern whites to obey the Supreme Court's decision. Judge Lynne, on the other hand, predicted that Johnson had a historic destiny because he would be the "last United States attorney . . . in the South to get a conviction for slavery, now that the Supreme Court's decided this *Brown* case."[25]

Success as U.S. attorney paved the way for Johnson's selection as a federal district judge. Trying cases before Lynne and Grooms "impressed" Johnson that the federal district court was "a very important place and a federal judge had tremendous authority and discretion. That's when I got interested in it. But getting interested in being a federal judge won't do it. You have to be where lightning strikes."[26] Even so, Johnson's future was tied to *Brown*. After the 1954 decision, the Court waited a year to formulate its implementation order of the same name. Brownell and the Justice Department perceived that the federal courts would bear the brunt of enforcing the decree the Court finally handed down in May 1955. During the same year, federal district judge Charles B. Kennemer of Alabama's middle district suddenly died. Inevitably, choosing a replacement was inseparable from the tensions surrounding *Brown*'s enforcement. Consistent with the tradition that judges should be selected from the areas in which they lived, Republicans and Democrats put forward candidates from Montgomery and south Alabama. Since *Brown* made civil rights a more volatile issue than ever, however, Brownell wanted Johnson in the middle district because he had demonstrated a firm willingness to defend the rights of all, regardless of race.

Other factors worked in Johnson's favor. State Republican Party leaders selected Johnson because he and his father had been loyal to Dewey and Eisenhower. They may also have been aware that Kennemer was living in north Alabama when Herbert Hoover appointed him to the middle district in 1931, making residence a less important factor in the appointment process. Meanwhile, Johnson was acceptable to the state's National Democrats, including Senators Lister Hill and John Sparkman, because he and his father were aligned with Governor Folsom and opposed to Alabama's Dixiecrat faction. Some of the National Democrats' inner circle had known and trusted Johnson since his university years and Pi Kappa Alpha days. Finally, the lifetime judicial appointment removed Johnson from future political contests against National Democratic candidates.

Ultimately, however, the determining factor was that Brownell wanted Johnson. Johnson's prosecution of the Sumter County peonage case demonstrated an ability to subordinate the express issue of race to the larger concern for humanity and fundamental fairness. This quality was consistent with the Eisenhower administration's moderate approach to enforcing the school desegregation orders *Brown* spawned. Eisenhower himself had publicly expressed doubts about the wisdom of the *Brown* decision, so the administration's civil rights policy depended primarily on the discretion of federal judges. When two eastern Texas communities refused to desegregate public educational institutions, the federal government did nothing because the federal courts left matters in the hands of local officials. Somewhat later, the government intervened directly to enforce the lower court's desegregation order in Little Rock only after the Justice Department's secret negotiations with Arkansas governor Orval Faubus failed and violence erupted. Thus Brownell probably realized that Johnson's appeal to fundamental fairness rather than racial justice per se in the peonage case corresponded to the government's reliance on moderate judicial discretion in civil rights suits generally.

Nevertheless, resistance to *Brown* became so extensive that Johnson could not avoid exercising expanded judicial discretion. Lynne's prediction that white public opinion in Alabama and the South generally would harden against civil rights was prophetic. In local and state government, as well as in the congressional delegations, southern elected officials defended racial segregation and denied the authority of federal intervention, particularly through the federal courts. State and local authorities' defiance fostered brutal treatment of civil rights supporters; it also encouraged private terrorist attacks against nonviolent civil rights activists such as Martin Luther King Jr. and Medger Evers. The fundamental institutional fact was, however, that public officials in Alabama and other southern states virtually never resisted to the point of going to jail. Instead, these leaders politically exploited the federal courts, blaming them for actions which in fact resulted from the officials' own opposition and refusal to comply with constitutional principles. As a result, they gained local political advantage but also forced increased federal intervention.

Thus federal judges enforced constitutional principles creatively or indirectly permitted law and order to disintegrate. Shortly after Johnson received unanimous Senate confirmation, Judge Grooms faced mob disruption resulting from Autherine Lucy's enrollment at the University of Alabama in Tuscaloosa. When Lucy first sought admission, Grooms granted a court order that overcame the university's racially exclusionary policy. But within days, continuing harassment compelled university officials to suspend Lucy to ensure her safety and "the safety of the students and faculty members."[27] Lucy's National Association for the Advancement of Colored People (NAACP) lawyers, Thurgood Marshall and Arthur Shores, filed suit seeking readmission, alleging that university officials and the mob had conspired to force her out. In court, however, they could present no evidence supporting the conspiracy charge. The university then formally expelled Lucy for making false claims, and Grooms upheld the university's action. Reportedly, Grooms admitted to Marshall and Shores in private that threats against his wife and two young children made a ruling in Lucy's favor increasingly dangerous. Grooms, like Johnson a Republican appointed by Eisenhower, received no help from the president, who said he hoped federal action could be avoided.

The Autherine Lucy confrontation and Grooms's response revealed the magnitude of the desegregation struggle to Johnson. He saw that federal judges were not insulated from threats, nor could they count on formal support from the executive. More particularly, he realized the scope of the discretionary authority of a federal judge. Grooms had used his authority courageously, yet ultimately conservatively, initially defending Lucy's constitutional rights but then affirming her expulsion by the university when violence erupted. Unintentionally, Grooms's conservatism suggested to the public that disorder and violence could prevail over constitutional principle, but the wartime Litchfield trial and various Alabama cases involving political or racial minorities convinced Johnson that skillful and creative uses of legal process could protect individual rights despite public antagonism.

As Johnson performed this judicial role over nearly four decades, his Winston County origins shaped his personal style. The judge approached everyone with courtesy and respect, but no one could miss his seriousness of purpose and disdain for pretentiousness. He preferred the solitude of fishing or working in the wood shop back of the family home to the gregariousness of high society. With his wife, law clerks, and close friends, however, he had a sense of humor that drew on his rural small-town roots. He conveyed larger meanings through country stories, like that involving the owner of a contrary mule in Winston County. Unable after repeated efforts to train the mule, the owner took him to a professional. After the two men reached an agreement and the owner was about to leave, the trainer took a two-by-four and with it slammed the mule on the side of the head. Shocked, the owner said that he wanted the mule trained not dead, to which the trainer replied that he "was just getting the mule's attention so it understood who was in charge." In the Public Television interview, Johnson used this story to explain why he resorted to unusual remedial orders in response to defiant political leaders like George Wallace. Thus the lawyers who came to Johnson's court, whether it was to represent their clients or merely to seek advice on the legal issues arising from his decisions, encountered a personality that combined intellectual acuity, wisdom, folksy good humor, and understated yet unquestioned authority.

Johnson gave the Moyers interview and wrote the following articles explaining the values and assumptions underlying his uses of judicial discretion. Consistent with his origins and family background, Johnson's core values were essentially conservative, embodying a view of Americanism based on individual freedom defined in terms of equal opportunity and equality under law. Freedom depended in turn on constitutionally guaranteed rights enforced by an independent judiciary. Johnson's view of independence extended the parameters of discretionary authority to flexible procedures and forms of remedial relief that combined social science theory with a practical understanding of human nature and politics, including the resistance of public officials. The basic purpose to be achieved was judicially arbitrated fairness, which enlarged access to previously excluded minorities by strengthening the incentives for lawyers to take their cases. Thus neither the federal judiciary's institutional autonomy nor creative injunctive remedies were sufficient in and of themselves to overcome the inertia or outright defiance of public authorities. The active role of lawyers was indispensable.

Johnson's public commentary suggests a legacy that transcends the times in which he lived. By his retirement to judicial senior status in 1991, Johnson had successfully defended civil rights and liberties over four decades of change. His most famous decisions grew out of the African American struggle for equal citizenship under the Constitution and the white South's segregationist defiance. As the years of direct racial confrontation receded, he decided many other cases that expanded the rights of women, college students, criminal defendants, indigents, prisoners, and the mentally infirm. During the 1970s litigation on behalf of the latter two groups, especially, required overcoming public authorities' failure to maintain even the most minimal constitutional standards in state institutions. Johnson's years of service on the federal appellate court beginning in 1979 coincided with a growing ambivalence in American society toward rights claims.

Generally, there was an expansion of rights consciousness to include new groups, such as the disabled and homosexuals; at the same time, a contraction in rights claims occurred in such fields as affirmative action and the administration of the death penalty. Near the end of Johnson's active judicial tenure he wrote articles affirming the necessity of maintaining broad access to the judicial process by providing incentives for the legal profession to defend the rights of all in the name of the Constitution. Ultimately, he believed, the revolution in rights that had taken place in his lifetime was what was most right about America. When Johnson died on July 23, 1999, at age eighty, few Americans had done as much to preserve that faith.

Tony A. Freyer

Part One

Bill Moyers Interviews

Judge Johnson (1980)

Moyers's interview presents clearly and insightfully Johnson's reflections on his role in the civil rights struggle. The discourse between the two men locates the conflict within the mid–twentieth century American South's racially segregated society and institutions. Johnson articulates his historic contributions to ending segregation in terms of several key points. First, he describes southern white society and how his own distinctive family background contrasts with it. Next, he characterizes white public officials, particularly George Wallace, as pursuing a resistance strategy that sought and won short-term political gain by compelling federal enforcement of constitutional rights. A variation of this strategy Johnson calls the Alabama "punting syndrome," whereby state authorities declined to address deplorable, even tragic, conditions in mental health institutions and prisons until the federal courts ordered them to do so. Johnson's constitutional rationale for his actions in these confrontations is based on a traditional American judicial philosophy growing out of the powers and authority the Constitution grants federal judges. He thus explains his decisions with reference to his unusual personal background and a standard American philosophy of judicial power.

The interview occurred at a meaningful time in Johnson's own life and at a turning point in the nation's postwar rights revolution. In 1977 President Jimmy Carter nominated Johnson to be director of the Federal Bureau of Investigation. Shortly before the confirmation process was concluded, however, Johnson underwent heart-related surgery, whereupon he withdrew his name from further consideration for the position. After Johnson's complete recovery, Carter nominated him to serve on the Fifth Circuit Court of Appeals and Senate confirmation followed in July 1979. The Moyers interview took place a year later. These changes in personal life and position, especially the removal from daily trial court work, provided Johnson with a new standpoint to reflect on his tumultuous twenty-four-year career as a federal district judge. The interview coincided, too, with the aftermath of an era in which the South's defiance of federal authority resulted in African Americans winning formal constitutional equality. But racial conflict persisted in clashes over policies to remedy continuing racial discrimination through affirmative action and to achieve further public school desegregation by court-ordered busing. Meanwhile, the federal courts had enlarged constitutional rights guarantees for women and other groups. Thus the Moyers interview provided unique insight into the constitutional ideals guiding Johnson's leading role in bringing about a transformation in the nation's rights consciousness.

Judge — The Law and Frank Johnson

Bill Moyers' Journal
Air Date: July 24, 1980

[*Tease*]

JUDGE FRANK M. JOHNSON: People in the South are unique. They're law-abiding. They have—they may not like it, but if they become convinced that something is the law of the land, then they're inclined to obey it, and it hurts them to disobey it. I'm talking about the majority of the people. I'm not talking about the exception. And I realize that a good many people here in this section of the country were dissatisfied with some of the constitutional decisions that I found it necessary to make, but at the same time, through the years, I don't think there's any question about it, that I gained a reputation among a large majority of the people in this section of the country, that Judge Johnson's tough. Judge Johnson will rule the way he sees the Constitution, but there's always one thing—he's always fair. And that's the only reputation that a judge can hope to get. And that's the only kind of a reputation he ought to want.

[*Interior, Judge Frank Johnson's courtroom in Montgomery, Alabama*]

BILL MOYERS: In this courtroom in Montgomery, Alabama, more epic civil rights cases were decided in the last twenty-five years than in any other courtroom in America. They were decided by a judge some called the most hated man in the South, but a man who has earned an enduring place in our history for his courage and wisdom. His decisions changed the face of the South and helped to bring about a new American revolution. Tonight, in the first televised interview he has ever granted, I'll talk with Judge Frank Johnson, known around here as simply Judge. I'm Bill Moyers.

[*Bill Moyers' Journal opening*]

[*Film montage of the South from ante-bellum days through the civil rights movement to the present day*]

MOYERS [*voice-over*]: You have only to scratch the surface of memory to recall the times when life in the South, still referred to as ante-bellum, was slow and segregated. Rural blacks lived in unspeakable conditions seldom broadcast to the world beyond. In towns and cities, blacks were confronted with daily reminders of laws and customs that kept them separate and unequal. Most were constantly denied their constitutional rights, thus were powerless to bring about change. The poet Langston Hughes captured the frustrations of his people when he wrote in the '50s, "Get out the lunch box of your dreams, bite into the sandwich of your heart, and ride the Jim Crow car until it screams, then like an atom bomb, it bursts apart." It burst apart in 1955 when a forty-two-year-old seamstress named Rosa Parks refused to give up her seat on a city bus in Montgomery, Alabama, to a white man. She had, perhaps unwittingly, detonated the civil rights crusade. From that chilly December day on, action and reaction combined to create an inexorable pattern of petition, violence, and change that lasted nearly two decades. Boycotts, marches, rallies — they all brought hatred, anger, violence, and demagoguery. As black frustration and resentment changed to protest, the worst of prejudice exploded across the South. In the midst of all the passion and turmoil, a quiet Southern judge, a Republican from the Free State of Winston County, turned the tide of white resistance with a stream of decisions that upheld the claim of blacks to their civil rights. President Eisenhower brought him down from the hills of northern Alabama to sit as a federal district judge in Montgomery. It was 1955. He was just thirty-seven, the youngest federal judge in the country. Fate placed Frank Minis Johnson Jr. in the nerve center of confrontation and change. To give you an idea of his impact on the South and the nation during his twenty-four years on the district bench, this is how he responded to the challenge. He declared segregated public transportation unconstitutional (*Browder v. Gayle*, 1956). He ordered the integration of public parks (*Gilmore v. City of Montgomery*, 1959), interstate bus terminals (*Lewis v. Greyhound Corporation*, 1961), restaurants and restrooms (*U.S. v. City of Montgomery*, 1962), and libraries and museums (*Cobb v. Montgomery Library Board*, 1962). He required that blacks be registered to vote (*U.S. v. Alabama*, 1961), creating a standard that was later written into the 1965 Voting Rights Act. He was the first judge to apply the one man–one vote principle to state legislative apportionment (*Reynolds v. Sims*, 1964). He abolished the poll tax. He ordered Governor George Wallace to allow the civil rights march from Selma to Montgomery (*Williams v. Wallace*, 1965). He ordered the first comprehensive state-wide school desegregation (*Lee v. Macon County Board of Education*, 1967), was the first to apply the equal protection clause of the Constitution to state laws discriminating against women (*White v. Crook*, 1966). He established the precedent that people in mental institutions have a constitutional right to treatment (*Wyatt v. Stickney*, 1971), a sweeping breakthrough in mental health law. His order to eliminate jungle conditions in Alabama prisons is the landmark in prison reform (*Pugh v. Locke*, 1976). In 1969 Richard Nixon considered Frank Johnson for an appointment to the Supreme Court. Southern Republicans vehemently objected, and the appointment was blocked. President Carter nominated Johnson in 1977 to head the FBI, but the judge withdrew a few months later after major surgery. Last year, after almost a quarter century as a district judge, Johnson was elevated to the Fifth Circuit Court of Appeals. We spoke in that courtroom in Montgomery where his momentous decisions had been made. Tonight, the first part of our conversation.

MOYERS: When you were appointed to the bench, one of the newspapers in Alabama referred to you as "a furriner."

JOHNSON: A foreigner. That's true.

MOYERS: They said the feds had gone all the way up to the damn Yankee territory of Alabama —

JOHNSON: North Alabama.

MOYERS: — to north Alabama to bring a Yankee down to —

JOHNSON: Imported him.

MOYERS: Imported him down to Montgomery, which is the old capital of the Confederacy.

JOHNSON: Cradle of the Confederacy.

MOYERS: Cradle of the Confederacy. What did they mean when they said "the damn Yankee territory of northern Alabama"?

JOHNSON: Well, northwest Alabama was inhabited back in the early 1800s by a lot of Andrew Jackson's people, the men that came with him down to fight the Creek Indians. And land in Tennessee at that time was selling for $2, $3, $4 and $5 an acre. Land in northwest Alabama was selling for five and 10 cents an acre. And they bought small farms, and they brought their families, and they settled in the northwestern part of the state. They not only brought their families with them, they brought their attitude toward government. And the people up there have been referred to in many instances as Jacksonian people, Jacksonian Democrats. I think that they envision themselves as adhering to the Andrew Jackson philosophy of government, and the Republicanism didn't grow up in northwest Alabama until the Civil War.

MOYERS: What happened after that?

JOHNSON: The Civil War?

MOYERS: How did the Republicans get established in northern Alabama?

JOHNSON: Well, the people that adhered to the Jackson philosophy had a fierce loyalty to the national government. I expect probably the most dramatic example of that is a resolution that they passed in Winston County—

MOYERS: That's where you were born?

JOHNSON: That's right. And raised, in Winston County. I grew up there. The sentiment in Winston County and that entire area was for neutrality. They did not want the state of Alabama to secede from the Union. And they adopted a resolution on July 4, 1861, to this effect, "We agree with Jackson"—meaning Andrew Jackson—"that no state can legally get out of the Union, but if we're mistaken in this, and a state can lawfully and legally secede or withdraw, being only a part of the Union, then a county, any county, being a part of the state, by the same process of reasoning, could cease to be a part of the state." And then they continued, "We think that our neighbors in the South made a great mistake when they attempted to secede and set up a new government. However, we do not desire to see our neighbors in the South mistreated. And therefore, we're not going to take up arms against them. But, on the other hand, we're not going to shoot at the flag of our fathers, Old Glory, the flag of Washington, the flag of Jefferson, the flag of Jackson. Therefore, we ask that the Confederacy on the one hand, and the Union on the other, leave us alone, unmolested, that we may work out our political and financial destiny here in the hills of northwest Alabama." And that's a part of my heritage. That's the reason they—the people here—I think jokingly more than anything else, made reference to my being a foreigner and being imported.

MOYERS: Is that why they call Winston County the Free State of Winston?

JOHNSON: That is true. That is true. After this resolution, they passed a formal resolution, the same day, seceding from the state of Alabama.

MOYERS: What happened practically? Where—what happened to it in the Civil War?

JOHNSON: Very few eligible men—by eligible, I mean those that were fit for war duty—joined the Confederate forces. Over 90 percent of the men in Winston County and surrounding counties—Winston probably took the lead in all of this—refused to go. The Confederacy sent what they called press gangs in to arrest them and force them and take them and impress them into Confederate army service. A lot of them fled, hid in the hills and in the caves. And many of them were pushed to the point that they went through what was then the underground and joined the Union forces. And some of my forebears joined the Union forces.

MOYERS: But some also fought on the Confederate—

JOHNSON: They did. They did.

MOYERS: Did you ever feel divided loyalties?

JOHNSON: Oh, no. No. Never. The division, insofar as the Civil War is concerned, never played any strong part in discussions in our home. We always had an intense pride in being Americans. We had intense loyalty to our central government. But I never felt like I was torn between two ideologies, and I don't think either of my parents did.

MOYERS: So long [sic]we look back to the Civil War, back to those days when—the Glorious Defeat, one author called it. Do you think that's over, that for all practical purposes, that's no longer the definitive memory in the mind of the South?

JOHNSON: Well, you still see tags on automobiles of the old Confederate veteran with his whiskers and his walking stick, and he says, "Hell, I ain't forgot." [They laugh] You still see rebel flags at public gatherings, particularly football games. You still have people that wave the Confederate battle flag, but I don't think seriously the conflict to which you made reference, the Civil War, plays any part in our society at this time. I don't envision that it will in the future. Of course, not many people down here refer to it as the Civil War. They refer to it as the Northern—War of Northern Aggression. Some of them refer to it, and most people refer to it, as the War Between the States. They refuse to acknowledge that it was a civil war.

MOYERS: What do you think that growing up in Winston County did for you? I mean, somebody wrote of you that they think that your code of what's right and wrong was very much molded by your upbringing in Winston County. "All the people up there," he said, "have a strong sense of frontier justice."

JOHNSON: I think that's true. I don't think there's any question about it.

MOYERS: What was frontier justice?

JOHNSON: I think my regional background had a very, very decisive effect on my approach to dispensing what I consider to be justice, and attempting to, through judicial decisions, thwart actions that I considered unjust. People in that section of the country have a fiercely independent attitude and personality. They have an intense respect for the individual and the individual's rights. They believe in a person's dignity, and they believe each person is possessed of and is entitled to integrity. They believe that without regard to race, creed, color or ideology. "Every man's his own man" is a real basic philosophy. I came here with that, maybe most of it unconsciously ingrained in me.

MOYERS: It's amazing how a small pocket of an exceptional mentality can thrive surrounded by a conformist mentality, and have such an impact ultimately on the society of which it was not a part.

JOHNSON: Well, if you knew — if you knew the individual strength of the ordinary citizen up there in the hills, you'd understand it. They're strong people. They're a loyal people. They're a highly intelligent people. A lot of them aren't well-educated, but some are now. But —

MOYERS: Your great-grandfather, I think, was named Straight Edge Treadaway.*

JOHNSON: That's right.

MOYERS: How'd he get that name?

JOHNSON: Well, carpenters use that expression when they want to draw a straight line. Draftsmen use that expression if they want to draw a line that's absolutely straight, that doesn't deviate, one way or the other. So, they put the straight edge to it and draw it. And that's how he got his nickname.

MOYERS: What was he?

JOHNSON: He became sheriff. He was the first Republican sheriff in Fayette County after the Civil War, elected by the people. There were that many Republicans there at that time.

---

*According to Jack Bass, *Taming the Storm*, 8–9, it was Johnson's great-grandfather James Wallace Johnson who went by the name Straight Edge.

MOYERS: And they considered him a fair sheriff—

JOHNSON: Oh, yes.

MOYERS: Called him Straight Edge.

JOHNSON: Yes, sir. Absolutely.

MOYERS: That name stuck with you all these years—

JOHNSON: Yes, it did, the nickname.

MOYERS: Well, Charles Lamb wrote, "Lawyers, I suppose, were children once." What do you think your childhood—what values do you think your childhood gave you that are important to you today?

JOHNSON: Well, I think the value of approaching life with the idea that you get what you earn. You earn no more and no less than that to which you're entitled. You find very few people up in that section of the country that inherited anything. They came to the hills without anything. They had only what they were willing to work for. I expect that plus a strong sense of fair play and a respect for the individual's dignity served me in great stead as a lawyer and as a judge.

MOYERS: I'm told that there used to be a sign at the county line in Winston County—I don't know whether it was on the Winston County side or the other side—that said, "Nigger, don't let the sun set on you here." How did that—How did you escape that poison infecting your own sense of things?

JOHNSON: Well, I've heard about that. If that sign existed, I never saw it. It did not represent and it does not represent the large majority of the attitude and the thinking of those people in that section of the country. So, I wouldn't say that it was necessary that I escaped that attitude, or that I had to take some kind of action on my part to keep from being imbued with it. It just was not a predominant attitude.

MOYERS: For years, your father was the only Republican in the state legislature in Alabama.

JOHNSON: That's true.

MOYERS: And you spent your whole life in this—much of your whole life in this courtroom rendering decisions that were very unpopular in this part of Alabama. What does it take for your father as the only Republican and for you as an uncompromising judge—What does it take to go it alone?

JOHNSON: Well, I think there's a basic fallacy in that question, Bill. I've never thought that I was going it alone. As a federal judge, I operated as a member of the federal judiciary. I operated as an officer of the United States. I operated with an intensely loyal group of people constituting the supporting personnel of the court, the United States marshals, the United States attorneys, Federal Bureau of Investigation, the Secret Service, court clerks, probation officers. And aside from that, my wife and I have made a tremendous number of friends in this section of the country since we came down here, and friends whose friendship we prize very highly.

MOYERS: But your decisions were very unpopular. You know that.

JOHNSON: They were unpopular to a large — Some of them were unpopular to a large segment of the population. No question about that. People in the South are unique. They're law-abiding. They have — They may not like it, but if they become convinced that something is the law of the land, then they're inclined to obey it, and it hurts them to disobey it. I'm talking about the majority of the people. I'm not talking about the exception. And I realize that a good many people here in this section of the country were dissatisfied with some of the constitutional decisions that I found it necessary to make, but at the same time, through the years, I don't think there's any question about it, that I gained a reputation among a large majority of the people in this section of the country, that Judge Johnson's tough, Judge Johnson will rule the way he sees the Constitution, but there's always one thing — he's always fair. And that's the only reputation that a judge can hope to get. And that's the only kind of a reputation he ought to want.

MOYERS: But weren't you ostracized —

JOHNSON: A judge that decides cases in order to curry public favor, or decides cases in order to keep from incurring public disfavor, doesn't have any business being on the bench, whether you're going through the kind of a social revolution that we've been through the last twenty-five years in this country or not.

MOYERS: It's hard for a federal judge to do that, that often, and in fact, law scholars point out that over the years, the federal district judges, coming as they do from a particular part of the country serving in that part of the country, often nominated through their participation or association in the politics of that part of the country, have generally tended in the history of our judiciary more to reflect popular sentiment in that region than any other judges. And yet, here you were in Montgomery, and of course, you were from northern Alabama, rendering these decisions that were helping to create the social upheaval. Did Montgomery ostracize you and your family? I've heard the stories —

JOHNSON: A portion of the people in Montgomery — no question about that. But a large portion of them didn't. We never suffered from any ostracism that — to which we may have been subjected. It's hard to — and I've said this before — but it's hard to ostracize someone that does their own ostracizing.

MOYERS: What do you mean?

JOHNSON: I mean that before I became a judge — I liked to choose my own friends. I liked to go my own course. Social functions were a burden. I'd rather be out fishing in a fishing boat than at the Phantom Ball. And it's hard to ostracize someone that —

MOYERS: That likes to fish.

JOHNSON: It is, it is. Absolutely.

MOYERS: But there were fire bombings, crosses burned on your lawn, bags of hate mail. Your mother's own house was fire bombed while she was on the second floor.

JOHNSON: Dynamited.

MOYERS: Dynamited.

JOHNSON: That's right.

MOYERS: I mean, that's pretty expressive hostility. Did it make you angry?

JOHNSON: Why, of course. Of course, makes me angry, like — the same way that if I was driving an automobile down the road and some drunk came and ran me off the highway. That would make me angry.

MOYERS: Yes, but the fire bombing —

JOHNSON: This was closer.

MOYERS: That was very targeted.

JOHNSON: It was.

MOYERS: It was very deliberate.

JOHNSON: Absolutely. It did make me angry, but I could not, and I hope that I did not, let that influence me in any decisions that I made.

MOYERS: Well, no one has ever said that it did, but I just wondered how you —

JOHNSON: The boys who burned the cross in my front yard — of course, I recused myself in that case. Judge Rives handled it.

MOYERS: And what happened?

JOHNSON: I recommended to Judge Rives that he put them on probation, and he did.

MOYERS: Why?

JOHNSON: Well, they were misguided, and I didn't suffer by the cross being burned in my front yard. They were demonstrating. They were expressing themselves. In an illegal way, to be sure, but it didn't harm me. It burned a patch of my lawn, but —

MOYERS: But your mother could have been killed —

JOHNSON: Absolutely. Absolutely.

MOYERS: Did you think, "This is the last straw"?

JOHNSON: No, no. And neither did she.

MOYERS: She sounds like a marvelous person. What was her name?

JOHNSON: Alabama.

MOYERS: Alabama. That was her name?

JOHNSON: Oh, yeah, sure. Her name's Alabama. She's still living.

MOYERS: Is she alive? Alabama Long.

JOHNSON: That's right. Alabama Long Johnson.

MOYERS: Did she stay with you through all those years? I mean, did —

JOHNSON: You mean, philosophically? Oh, my goodness, yes. I could do no wrong. So did my father.

MOYERS: Well, what did she think when that — when her home was dynamited, and she was sitting in there? What did she say to you?

JOHNSON: Well, nothing much. Mother is pretty cool. She didn't have too much reaction. The newspaper reporters were there and the FBI and—, "Miz Johnson, don't you want to go somewhere and spend the night?" Says, "Absolutely not. They're not going to run me away from my home. I'm staying right here." And she did. They boarded up some windows, swept up the glass, picked up the chandelier in the dining room—the force of it swept all the way through the downstairs, tore the carport up, but Mother is a pretty strong character. She was widowed then. My father had already died. We put FBI agents out there, put marshals out there. They were more of a nuisance to her than anything else. She said, "When are you going to take them away? They bother me at night opening and closing doors and shining flashlights around my house." So, I expect her attitude caused [sic] me from being upset. I was a little upset that they weren't able to discover who did it and apprehend those that did it.

MOYERS: Have they ever?

JOHNSON: No, they have not.

MOYERS: Would you have recommended probation, as you did for the—

JOHNSON: No, no, I sure would not have. That had the potential for extreme violence. It wasn't just merely a method of expressing their dissatisfaction with some of my decisions. There's no question but that it was directed toward me. My father's name was Frank M. Johnson, and he was listed in the telephone book. I took my listing out of the book the first two or three nights they kept me awake, way back in 1956 when we first entered the *Browder-Gayle* case desegregating public transportation—

[*Film montage of events relating to desegregation rulings of Judge Johnson*]

MOYERS: [*voice-over*] Judge Johnson's baptism on the bench couldn't have been more significant. In the early 1950s, segregation in Montgomery's public facilities, including its municipal bus system, was legally mandated. On December 1st, 1955, a black woman named Rosa Parks, holding a bag of groceries and tired from a long day of work as a seamstress, took a seat in the first row behind the crowded whites-only section of a Montgomery bus. Two white men boarded the bus on Cleveland Avenue. The driver called out, "Niggers move back." Most obediently gave up their seats. Rosa Parks did not. All conversation stopped. No one moved. It was a moment that would change forever the social traditions so deeply ingrained in the South. Rosa Parks' protest gave local black leaders the constitutional challenge they had been seeking, and the cause needed to mobilize their community. From their ranks emerged the pastor of a local Baptist church, a twenty-seven-year-old named Martin Luther King Jr. A few days after Rosa Parks' arrest, he organized the blacks' boycott of the Montgomery bus system that was to last a year. It was the first large-scale mobilization of black protest, the spearhead of the civil rights movement, the origin of the era of passive resistance. The laws that separated blacks and whites on the buses were given legitimacy in a Supreme Court decision, *Plessy v. Ferguson*. It created the separate but equal doctrine in transportation cases. In 1954, the Supreme Court rejected that doctrine in its historic *Brown v. Board of Education* decision, but it applied only to the area of education. Judge Johnson, as part of a three-judge panel, concluded, "There is no rational basis upon which the separate but equal doctrine can be validly applied to public carrier transportation within the city of Montgomery."

[*Interior, Judge Johnson's courtroom*]

MOYERS: Wasn't this the first case to extend the Supreme Court's decision of 1954 beyond schools?

JOHNSON: That is true. The interesting thing about *Browder v. Gayle* and the thing that prompted Judge Lynne to dissent in that case — it was a three-judge case — the thing that prompted Judge Lynne to dissent was that the Supreme Court of the United States had decided *Plessy v. Ferguson*. *Plessy v. Ferguson* factually was on all fours with this case. It involved public transportation, and the Supreme Court said that separate but equal is constitutionally acceptable insofar as public transportation is concerned. *Plessy against Ferguson* had not been discussed in *Brown*. *Plessy against Ferguson* had not been overruled by the Supreme Court. So, that made *Browder v. Gayle* very unique, not only for the reasons that it's the first case that extended the rationale of *Brown against Board of Education*, but it was probably the first time in the history of this country that a district court has ever overruled a decision of the Supreme Court of the United States. Of course, we perceived, and it was evident to us, that there was a doctrinal trend in judicial decisions, not only by the Supreme Court, but by some of the other federal appellate courts throughout the country —

MOYERS: A doctrinal trend?

JOHNSON: A doctrinal trend that rendered *Plessy against Ferguson* no longer viable. And *Brown against Board of Education* was a major part of that doctrinal trend.

MOYERS: What was the key element in your own mind in deciding, in effect, to overrule the Supreme Court and to order the desegregation of Montgomery buses?

JOHNSON: Justice Harlan's dissent in *Plessy against Ferguson*. And he said—he was right all the time—he said there's no place in our Constitution, that our Constitution will not tolerate segregation of the citizens on the basis of race in any public facilities.

MOYERS: When you agreed with that, and made that decision with your other colleague on that three-member panel, were you aware of the social upheaval that was about to be visited upon this—

JOHNSON: I don't think so. I don't think so. I—Of course, I didn't study about that, and I really wasn't concerned about it, but I don't think that it ever occurred to me that there would be an adverse reaction to a court saying to the people that you cannot tell the black people that are citizens—and they're not second class citizens. People that argue that they are not entitled to full constitutional rights just can't read the Constitution. We made them citizens in the 13th and the 14th and the 15th Amendments to the Constitution. And when you say they're not entitled to full rights, then you do not accept the provisions of those amendments to the Constitution. It didn't occur to me that there was a large segment of the people in this country that would resent a judicial decision that was based on that concept.

MOYERS: When did it become aware to you that that was an enormously unpopular decision, at least locally?

JOHNSON: Well, I think it was enormously unpopular all over, because every state in the South had segregated public transportation facilities. So, *Browder against Gale* not only affected Montgomery, it affected state statutes in Alabama. It stood for a case from a three-judge court, a bee-line directly to the Supreme Court of the United States, and that's the only route that you can take one of those cases—it doesn't go to an intermediate appellate court. I think that it gave concern to the state authorities, and municipal authorities throughout the South. It was evident almost immediately that there was a tremendous adverse reaction to the action that we had taken.

MOYERS: Anybody call you and say, "My God, Johnson, you don't know what you've done." Or, "Do you know what you've done."

JOHNSON: Well, they didn't put it in those words.

MOYERS: How did they put it?

JOHNSON: For public television consumption? [*They laugh*] I'll let you read some of my mail. I don't think I was subjected to the vilification. I don't think I was subject to the feeling of hate comparable to that which Judge Rives was subjected. Judge Richard Rives and I are the ones that decided that case. Judge Rives had grown up here in Montgomery. He had practiced law here in Montgomery. He was one of the most able — recognized as one of the most able lawyers in the South. President Truman appointed him to the federal bench. He'd been on the bench about four years when I came on in '55. He helped swear me in, in this courtroom. But Judge Rives' roots were here. He was one of them. He wasn't a foreigner that had been imported from the hills in north Alabama. And it was said by several people, and probably in the newspapers — I think I recall — here in Montgomery, "Well, we didn't expect any more out of that fellow from up at north Alabama, but Richard Rives is one of our own, and we did expect more out of him, and he's forfeited the right to be buried in Confederate soil." And that's how strong it was.

MOYERS: When you were discussing that case in your private chambers, after it had been argued —

JOHNSON: The junior member of the court votes first. The senior member of the court votes last. That's followed throughout the system. That's to keep the senior member from influencing the junior member in his vote.

MOYERS: And you voted first?

JOHNSON: So, Judge Rives says, "Frank, what do you think about this case?" "I don't think segregation in any public facilities is constitutional. Violates the equal protection clause of the 14th Amendment, Judge." That's all I had to say. It didn't take me long to express myself. The law was clear. And I might add this, Bill, the law to me was clear in practically every one of these cases that I've decided where race was involved. I had no problem with the case where we outlawed the poll tax, charging people to vote. I had no problem with the museums, the libraries, the public parks, or any public facilities. The law will not tolerate discrimination on the basis of race.

MOYERS: When you said this to Judge Rives, who voted with you or you two voted together, what did he say? You said, "Segregation is wrong, Judge."

JOHNSON: No, I didn't say "segregation is wrong." I said "state imposed segregation in public facilities is unconstitutional."

MOYERS: And what did he say?

JOHNSON: I didn't take a moral position. I never have taken a moral position in any of these cases.

MOYERS: Wait a minute. What's the difference between —

JOHNSON: Well, segregation being wrong is my moral concept of what's right and what's wrong and that's not the approach that a judge takes when he's deciding constitutional cases. He cannot impose his own sense of morality or superimpose it on a constitutional provision. Of course, it's true that — I think it was [Justice Benjamin] Cardozo that said that a judge should be impartial and should view these cases with complete impartiality, but he sees the case through his own eyes, and in that sense, I expect every judge decides cases to some degree on his concept of what he sees to be right and wrong. But that's not the judicial approach that I've always taken in these cases.

MOYERS: You really try to separate the —

JOHNSON: My feeling of morality, my feeling of what's right and wrong? Absolutely. I've decided cases in a way that ran contrary to my feeling of morality.

MOYERS: Because you felt the law —

JOHNSON: Absolutely. Absolutely.

MOYERS: But, in interpreting the law, don't subconscious forces, your own experience in Winston County, your own forebears being the free citizens of the Free State of that county . . . ?

JOHNSON: There is no question, and that's the reason I made reference to Justice Cardozo's statement. There is no question but that when I'm looking and trying to interpret a constitutional provision or a legislative provision, or any law that comes under my scrutiny, I see that law through my own eyes, and that means I see it and I interpret it, and I evaluate it according to my past experiences and according to my heritage, which includes, in part, my regional background, my upbringing.

MOYERS: But not as a moral crusader?

JOHNSON: Absolutely not.

MOYERS: Not trying to—

JOHNSON: Absolutely not. A judge cannot be, if he stays within his role as a judge, be a crusader.

MOYERS: Well, what did Judge Rives say to you?

JOHNSON: Well, when it came Judge Rives' time to vote, he says, "I feel the same way."

MOYERS: And that was it.

JOHNSON: Absolutely. Sure. Sure. Well, I don't guess we deliberated over ten minutes at the outside.

MOYERS: History seems to require more dramatic moments than that.

JOHNSON: There are rarely ever any dramatic moments in a judge's conference room. It's a cold, calculated, legal approach.

MOYERS: Have you read Harper Lee's wonderful novel, *To Kill a Mockingbird?*

JOHNSON: Sure.

MOYERS: There's a figure in *To Kill a Mockingbird*—a lawyer, named Atticus Finch—

JOHNSON: That's right.

MOYERS: And Atticus Finch is the symbol of the judge, the lawyer in the South that has so long been honored. An incorruptible individual who stands against the passions of his times, even against his own sympathies and biases to do what he knows is right. And the interesting point to me about Atticus Finch is that the people in that community, who ostracized him for defending a black man, wanted him to do the right thing. Now, I think there may have been Southerners who wanted you to do the right thing, but they were angry as hell because you did. And it's that contradiction that I wish you would try to explain to me.

JOHNSON: I doubt if there's any explanation that I could give for what you term a contradiction. I think a large part of what gives the appearance of being a contradictory reaction arises out of the fact that many state and county and municipal officials understood what they were required to do. They understood what they were prohibited from doing, when they measured it against constitutional requirements. But, they did not feel that they could do that or fail to do that, whichever it was, and continue to live in their community. So, they punted their problem to the federal court.

MOYERS: Punted?

JOHNSON: Punted, that's an expression that I started using back several years ago. And they knew what the decision would be. Practically everyone involved in the case, and certainly the lawyers knew what the decision would be, but you had a political approach that gave them an opportunity to holler "Federal court infringement, judicial usurpation of states' rights," and then they go back and say, "Well, we have the decision now, and it's a federal court order and we're required to implement it. We're required to abide by the law. We're required to desegregate our schools. We're required to desegregate our bus stations, we're required to desegregate our state penal facilities." Let me read you what one writer said about that.

MOYERS: In other words, the elected official needs the federal court both as a scapegoat and as an agent for doing what he knows is necessary.

JOHNSON: Absolutely. Absolutely. And that's the point. Neal Peirce made it in his book on *The Deep South States of America*. He wrote of Alabama, and this is not unique to Alabama, but he was writing about Alabama at the time. He said, "There was no state in the country in which the federal courts were intruding themselves so deeply into the basic governmental process, but perhaps none in which their interference was more justified, because of the inaction and reaction of state government." "We holler about the federal courts having too much power," State Attorney General Bill Baxley said, "But if you have states' rights, you also have states' responsibilities. The state refused to face up to its responsibilities time and time again. We abdicated our power." So that gives rise to probably the appearance that there was some contradiction in the attitude that people had, "We're angry because you did it, but we're glad that you did it, because it needed to be done." Now, the ordinary citizen out in the state did not realize what was happening.

MOYERS: What do you mean?

JOHNSON: Well, they didn't realize that state officials knew that it was the law. They didn't realize that the state officials knew that the Constitution required them to take some action, or forbade them to take some action. They didn't realize that the state officials were punting their problems to the federal court knowing what the outcome was going to be. They listened to the political speeches about judicial infringement, judicial usurpation of states' rights or functions, and that's the only part of it that they got. That's the only part of it they absorbed.

MOYERS: What surprises me, looking back over the last twenty-five years, is that when the Supreme Court in 1954 made its judgment in *Brown v. Board of Education*, those judges on that court assumed compliance and cooperation on the part of lower courts and citizens. And the Court got little of either. Now, how does—how do you think the Court misjudged the reaction to those decisions?

JOHNSON: I'm not sure they did misjudge the reaction. They discussed in *Brown II*, the '55 decision, that this will cut across the social fabric in certain sections of this country more than others, that there will be problems in various sections of the country that are different from those problems in other sections. That it will take longer to implement this decision in some sections of the country. And they discussed all of those things, and that's what prompted them to put the implementation of *Brown* back on your trial judges and your district judges throughout the country. And that's what prompted them to say, "We will not order the implementation of *Brown* overnight. We will not give you any certain deadline. We will not require its implementation within six months or a year, but we'll require that you proceed with deliberate speed." And those were the words of the Court. With deliberate speed, to devise plans for implementation and achieve full implementation.

MOYERS: How did you—

JOHNSON: I doubt seriously if the Supreme Court thought that, as it has been said, that there would be more deliberation than speed in certain sections of the country, which certainly there was. But when you consider the tremendous task that the trial judges, the district judges on the federal level, had to implement *Brown v. Board of Education* in sections like Alabama and Mississippi and Georgia and North and South Carolina, then I do not think the time that it took was necessarily unreasonable. Looking at it as a whole. In some instances, it was. In other instances, it was fairly rapid.

MOYERS: Do you think, in retrospect, Judge, that perhaps putting so much of the burden of desegregation on the schools was the wrong way to go about overcoming the effects of all that history?

JOHNSON: No. Where should the burden be, if it shouldn't be on the school officials? The people that operate the schools have the primary duty to operate them within what's permissible from a constitutional standpoint. That's what they're there for. And that's where the duty belongs. And that's where I always attempted to put it.

MOYERS: Well, you never liked busing as a tool of desegregation very much, did you?

JOHNSON: No, no I did not. And I rarely ever used it, because when you start busing children, particularly those in the elementary schools, you are putting the burden of desegregating on the children, instead of putting the burden of desegregating or eliminating the dual school system on the school officials where it belongs. When you make a child, or children, in a school system get up at five o'clock in the morning and stand on the side of the road and wait for a bus to haul them 10 or 15 miles, past schools to which they were formerly eligible to go, then I think you're doing tremendous damage. There were a hundred different means that you could use other than busing small children. And a little ingenuity and study and a lot of cooperation on the part of school officials — once you got their attention.

MOYERS: Once you got their attention.

JOHNSON: Sure. Like you heard the story about the mule trainer, haven't you?

MOYERS: I'm not sure.

JOHNSON: The man — mules — everyone in Winston County knows that mules are the most stubborn characters in the world. This fellow had a mule he couldn't train. When he told it to giddy-up, why, the mule would stop. But when he'd tell it to whoa, the mule would get up. You'd tell it to gee, it would haw. You'd tell it to haw, it would gee. He finally decided he had to take it to a mule trainer, and he did. He took it across the county, left it, and told the man what he wanted. The man said, "Sure, I think I can train your mule," says "leave your mule here, and come back in 30 days." The man started to walk off that owned the mule, and the mule trainer picked up a singletree, a piece of wood about three feet long, you know what a singletree is.

MOYERS: Sure.

JOHNSON: So he knocked the mule in the head with it. The mule fell to his feet, and the owner of the mule says, "I wanted you to train my mule. I didn't want you to beat him to death." And the man says, "Well, I haven't even started training your mule." He says, "I'm just trying to get his attention." [*Moyers laughs*] So, I did have to use some pretty drastic means to get the attention of some of the school boards. I gave them deadlines. I gave them some plans that were specific and simple to understand. Third and fourth grade children could have read them and understood them. And I didn't leave them any squirming room when I was in the process and the stage of desegregation of trying to get their attention. Once I did, once I did, I found that generally most school board members genuinely attempted to implement the court orders. They did it—well, Montgomery school system is one of the largest in the state. We did it without any disruption in public education. We did it with the preservation of the public school system. We have some private schools where whites have fled, but very, very few. Not what was predicted. These decisions that were so controversial back when I entered them, some of them were, and I readily acceded that a while ago. But they've become accepted now. People in Montgomery, Alabama, or people in Alabama, people throughout the South—I don't think very many of them would go back to where we were before the public accommodations law was implemented. They wouldn't make black people go to the back door of a restaurant. They wouldn't make them drive with their children along the public highways without having a restroom to go to, or without having a restaurant to go to, or without having a motel to stop in. We've passed that point. I don't think there are many people in this country that would want to go back. The decisions that I entered guaranteeing those rights, and making certain that they were accorded, did meet with some public disfavor. But the people that met or demonstrated or felt that resentment, have changed. I had a man the other day that served in John Patterson's cabinet, stopped me on the street—

MOYERS: Governor John—late Governor, former Governor John Patterson?

JOHNSON: Former Governor John Patterson who—

MOYERS: —was a real segregationist.

JOHNSON: —outsegged George Wallace and beat him in 1958. I believe that was the year. Wallace said that "he outsegged me," meaning that he cried *black* or *nigger*—to use the expression—louder than I did. That's the way he defeated me. This member of his cabinet, who was a defendant on a good many of these cases, stopped me on the street, says, "Judge, I want to tell you that you were right, we were wrong." He says, "I don't want to die without having told you that." So, the resentment has passed. It no longer exists.

MOYERS: Back when I first became aware of you, in the '60s, when I was on the White House staff concerned with civil rights legislation, I thought that Abraham

Lincoln would have found delicious satisfaction in a Republican judge in the South, a hundred years later, fulfilling so many of the things he let loose as the first Republican president. Did that paradox ever occur to you?

JOHNSON: No. No, it didn't. I have not spent any time trying to evaluate my performance as a federal judge, or my impact as a federal judge. I hope to some day, but I haven't had time to do it up to this point. Since you mention Lincoln, I expect he would have gotten a tremendous kick out of the fact that I've kept one of his quotes on my desk under a paperweight for twenty-five years.

MOYERS: Which one?

JOHNSON: It goes something like this. "I intend to do right, or I have done right. I've done what I consider to be right, and I intend to keep doing so until the end. If the end brings me out all right, what's said against me will amount to nothing. If the end brings me out wrong, what's said—ten angels swearing I was right would make no difference." Great quote.

MOYERS: Do you think the end's going to bring you out all right?

JOHNSON: Oh, I think it already has. I think it already has.

MOYERS: Judge, we've covered a lot of territory in this first hour. Let's come back next week and finish this, and talk about the '60s and the '70s, and the law today. Fair enough?

JOHNSON: Great. Great. I would enjoy that.

MOYERS: From Montgomery, Alabama, this has been a conversation with Judge Frank Johnson. I'm Bill Moyers.

Judge — The Law and Frank Johnson, Part 2

Bill Moyers' Journal
Air Date: July 31, 1980

[*Tease*]

BILL MOYERS: I'm Bill Moyers. Last week at this time, I began a conversation with a man who's left a lasting impact on our times. His name is Frank M. Johnson Jr., but down South, he's known simply as Judge. In this hour, we return to Montgomery, Alabama, to complete that conversation.

[*Bill Moyers' Journal opening*]

[*Film montage of the South from ante-bellum days through the civil rights movement to the present day*]

MOYERS [*voice-over*]: You have only to scratch the surface of memory to recall the times when life in the South, still referred to as ante-bellum, was slow and segregated. Rural blacks lived in unspeakable conditions seldom broadcast to the world beyond. In towns and cities, blacks were confronted with daily reminders of laws and customs that kept them separate and unequal. Most were constantly denied their constitutional rights, thus were powerless to bring about change. The poet Langston Hughes captured the frustrations of his people when he wrote in the '50s, "Get out the lunch box of your dreams, bite into the sandwich of your heart, and ride the Jim Crow car until it screams, then like an atom bomb, it bursts apart." It burst apart in 1955 when a forty-two-year-old seamstress named Rosa Parks refused to give up her seat on a city bus in Montgomery, Alabama, to a white man. She had, perhaps unwittingly, detonated the civil rights crusade. From that chilly December day on, action and reaction combined to create an inexorable pattern of petition, violence and change that lasted nearly two decades. Boycotts, marches, rallies—they all brought hatred, anger, violence, and demagoguery. As black frustration and resentment changed to protest, the worst of prejudice exploded across the South. In the midst of all the passion and turmoil, a quiet Southern judge, a Republican from the Free State of Winston County, turned the tide of white resistance with a stream of decisions that upheld the claim of blacks to their civil rights. President Eisenhower brought him down from the hills of northern Alabama to sit as a federal district judge in Montgomery. It was 1955. He was just thirty-seven, the youngest federal judge in the country. Fate placed Frank Minis Johnson Jr. in the nerve center of confrontation and change. To give you an idea of his impact on the South and the nation during his twenty-four years on the district bench, this is how he responded to the challenge. He declared segregated public transportation unconstitutional (*Browder v. Gayle*, 1956). He ordered the integration of public parks (*Gilmore v. City of Montgomery*, 1959), interstate bus terminals (*Lewis v. Greyhound Corporation*, 1961), restaurants and restrooms (*U.S. v. City of Montgomery*, 1962), and libraries and museums (*Cobb v. Montgomery Library Board*, 1962). He required that blacks be registered to vote (*U.S. v. Alabama*, 1961), creating a standard that was later written into the 1965 Voting Rights Act. He was the first judge to apply the one man–one vote principle to state legislative apportionment (*Reynolds v. Sims*, 1964). He abolished the poll tax. He ordered Governor George Wallace to allow the civil rights march from Selma to Montgomery (*Williams v. Wallace*, 1965). He ordered the first comprehensive state-wide school desegregation (*Lee v. Macon County Board of Education*, 1967), was the first to apply the equal protection clause of the Constitution to state laws discriminating against women (*White v. Crook*, 1966). He established the precedent that people in mental institutions have a constitutional right to treatment (*Wyatt v. Stickney*, 1971), a sweeping breakthrough in mental health law. His order to eliminate jungle conditions in Alabama prisons is the landmark in prison reform (*Pugh v. Locke*, 1976).

[*Interior, Judge Frank Johnson's courtroom in Montgomery, Alabama*]

MOYERS: [*voice-over*]: In 1969 Richard Nixon considered Frank Johnson for an appointment to the Supreme Court. Southern Republicans vehemently objected, and the appointment was blocked. President Carter nominated Johnson in 1977 to head the FBI, but the judge withdrew a few months later after major surgery. Last year, after almost a quarter century as a district judge, Johnson was elevated to the Fifth Circuit Court of Appeals. We spoke in that courtroom in Montgomery where his momentous decisions had been made. Tonight, Part 2 of our conversation.

MOYERS: What have you learned in your own part in that process about human nature, upon which the law ultimately rests and for which it grows? I mean, someone wrote of Frank Johnson that "His willingness to do the right thing has led him on a long odyssey into the dark side of the human spirit. The history of his cases is a history of the state as outlaw and of the savagery which that fact has inevitably fostered." What have you learned about human nature in all these years on the bench?

JUDGE FRANK M. JOHNSON JR.: That dramatizes it, of course. And it was probably intended to dramatize it. I think the strongest feeling that I've gained from handling all of these cases, fraught with tension and fraught with emotion, and they all were — we're talking about the civil rights cases now, we're not talking about the majority of the litigation I handled, which is just run-of-the-mill litigation — but, is a strong feeling of respect for the American citizen, whether he's a southerner or regardless of what section of the country he lives in. That, if you can impress him that this is a legal principle, this is something that is the law of the land, then they may do it grudgingly, they may do it hesitatingly, but they will do it. They will do it.

MOYERS: You're saying that human beings don't change their nature, but they certainly change their perception of their nature once they're convinced that there is a higher law, a higher order to which they must correspond?

JOHNSON: I believe that the majority of the people in this country will agree that the judicial decisions of the Supreme Court of the United States and the other courts that have been created by Congress, including the district courts, from the time of *Marbury* — and that's the first one that established the supremacy of the Constitution of the United States insofar as other government bodies, including the states, were concerned — from that time until the present time, will all agree that these judicial decisions stand as monuments that memorialize the strength and the durability of the American government. And they are proud of their judicial system as an integral part of their government.

MOYERS: You really do believe in the face of all that you've seen down here?

JOHNSON: I do. I've come out of all of these with a strong feeling to that effect.

MOYERS: The supremacy of the law?

JOHNSON: Absolutely. And a willingness on the part of the people to accept it.

MOYERS: Young people often ask me, since they know I'm a southerner, "Through all that period leading up to Judge Johnson's decisions, where was the mind of the South? Where was the law? And you know, they remember Bull

Connor [*stills of Bull Connor, protestors being firehosed*]—Bull Connor was the police commissioner of Birmingham who gave the orders to turn the fire hoses on children, and to use attack dogs on children marching for school integration—remember Bull Connor saying, "Damn the law down here, we make our own law." And the question, because that was true for so long, is, "Was it the law all those years, the function—not of some higher reality that you've described as being the federal perception—not of some higher reality, but of social norms and political power used for repressive ends." And that's what in the southern history bothers so many people and remains inexplicable to them. And the question that seems to perplex us all, those of us who think about the South and its history, is simply, how did this great evil, segregation, racism, how did it get so deeply embedded in our part of society?

JOHNSON: Well, I don't think the feeling of racism or desegregation or whatever you want to call it, or the strong feeling that we must maintain segregation is unique just to the South. I think that it exists in other sections of the country, but here in the South, probably it is based upon fear of the unknown, fear of what will happen if the blacks do achieve equal rights, what will happen if the blacks secure the right to vote, to hold public office, to sit on juries, what will happen if black people attend our public schools with our white children? And I think probably that's the greatest thing that caused it to maybe be ingrained to start with, and certainly to cause people to resist congressional enactments and court decisions that were designed to eliminate racism in our society.

MOYERS: Fear of changing a way of life that had persisted for so long?

JOHNSON: Certainly, and fear of what would happen to them from an economic standpoint. What will happen when it's necessary to compete against black people for jobs? What will happen when it's necessary to compete against them for political positions? What will happen to the social structure that we have, that we prize so much, when blacks get social equality.

MOYERS: George Wallace, your old nemesis, still governor, was waving his own stick around trying to get the attention of the bench and the public and the press, and saying, "Frank Johnson is going way beyond what those robes entitled him to do. He's running the schools, he's running everything in this state. He's going out beyond the law to try to bring about these changes." And he was fairly successful with the ordinary voters of Alabama. Do you think that—

JOHNSON: He capitalized on it, politically.

MOYERS: Do you think this progress—Do you think progress would have come sooner if it hadn't been for George Wallace, or if he hadn't been there, would there have been someone else?

JOHNSON: I think there would have been someone else. They might not have been as vitriolic as George Wallace was.

[*Film package: George Wallace*]

MOYERS [*voice-over*]: Wallace was indeed vitriolic in those early days of the 1960s. A stubborn, guileful, race-baiting politician who obstructed the path of integration at every opportunity. He harangued the federal government for its intervention.

GOV. GEORGE WALLACE: And anybody who says the Civil Rights Bill is good, and any party who talks about what a good bill it is, and we gonna work for it, and so forth, they're talking about a bill that is—was endorsed in 1928 in every aspect of it by the Communist Party, who says it's the best bill ever introduced. Now, I ain't never heard the Communist Party recommend anything good for the United States of America. But that's the bill—[*the crowd roars*]

MOYERS [*voice-over*]: The federal judiciary in general.

WALLACE: The federal court system, and I get my words from Jefferson and Jackson and Abraham Lincoln and Franklin Roosevelt who said worse things about 'em than I do, and if they said 'em, I can say it, too—the federal court with few notable exceptions, is a sorry, lousy, irresponsible outfit in this country—[*the crowd roars*]

MOYERS [*voice-over*]: The federal judiciary in general.

WALLACE: Judge Frank M. Johnson's order to admit six of the twelve students at the close of Tuskegee High to Shorter, and six to Notasulga, is an order of spite. The action of this federal judge is rash, headstrong, and vindictive. This action is unstable and erratic.

MOYERS [*voice-over*]: When he was elected governor in 1962, this is how he began his term.

WALLACE: In the name of the greatest people that have ever trod this earth, I draw the line in the dust and toss the gauntlet before the feet of tyranny, and I say segregation now, segregation tomorrow, and segregation forever. [*the crowd whoops and yells*]

[*Interior, courtroom*]

MOYERS: Do you remember hearing that, or hearing about it?

JOHNSON: Oh. I did hear it. I heard it on the radio.

MOYERS: What did you think?

JOHNSON: I don't know whether I gave it too much thought. I crossed these bridges when I came to them. I tried not to anticipate what would happen. I tried not to dodge from shadows. I guess I thought, "Well, here we go again." Patterson had just left office, and we had a good desegregation case while Governor Patterson was in office. And I guess I says to myself, "Well, here we go again."

MOYERS: You knew George Wallace at the University of Alabama, didn't you?

JOHNSON: We went through law school at the same time, yes.

MOYERS: What was he like then?

JOHNSON: George Wallace was a strong follower of Franklin Roosevelt—

MOYERS: New Dealer?

JOHNSON: —and the New Deal concepts. He and I [*insert: photo of Wallace and Johnson in law school*] had many debates about socialism, governmental control of public utilities, the TVA. I was absolutely against any governmental control of public utilities. It violated my concept of what the federal government should be doing. But George was probably the most liberal student in the law school at the University of Alabama, and he was for a good number of years after he got out of the legislature. He was Jim Folsom, Governor Folsom's campaign manager for south Alabama, and Folsom's one of the most liberal governors that the South had. Even up till now.

MOYERS: Well, how do you explain what happened? What finally made George Wallace what he was?

JOHNSON: George saw the handwriting, he saw that race was going to be something that he could use to his political advantage, and he was shrewd, and smart, and capitalized on it. George Wallace was a great politician. You could never underestimate George Wallace. He would land on his feet regardless of how far you threw him up, or what position he was in when you threw him. He's a professional politician, the best I've ever seen.

MOYERS: Do you think he believed all of that hate he was spouting and —

JOHNSON: I don't think so. No. I never did believe that he believed it. He doesn't believe it now. He acknowledges that he doesn't believe it now.

MOYERS: A lot of people believe that the first real clash between the two of you back in 1959 was just what he needed to win the governorship after he'd lost it the first time in 1958. And in fact, that he came to power partly because of that incident. I'd like to review that story.

JOHNSON: All right.

MOYERS: It's 1959.

JOHNSON: Right.

MOYERS: George Wallace has been defeated in 1958 as a candidate for governor. He's still a circuit court judge, and he's impounded, withheld, the voting records that the Civil Rights Commission wants in order to study discrimination in the South. And you've threatened him with contempt of court if he doesn't turn them over to the Civil Rights Commission. Is that a synopsis of it?

JOHNSON: That's not quite the posture. The Civil Rights Commission was created by the Congress, given authority to subpoena and examine voting right records not only in Alabama, but throughout the country. They came to Alabama first. They subpoenaed the records from Barbour County and Bullock County, two of the counties in then Judge Wallace's circuit. The act provided that if the subpoenas are not honored, that the Civil Rights Commission is to apply to the district judge wherein there then functioning to enforce the subpoena. So, George Wallace impounded the records from the registrars in each of those counties. He told the Civil Rights Commission that "I will not give them to you. If you send any FBI agents down here, I'll put 'em in jail. If any Civil Rights Commission employees come down here, I'll put them in jail." And he made all of these fiery speeches on television. And I issued an order directing that he produce the records of both counties for inspection, examination by the representatives of the Civil Rights Commission. He held some news conferences to the effect that he would not do it. I issued a show cause order as to why he shouldn't be found guilty of contempt of court, and gave him maybe ten or fifteen days — I don't recall how long I gave him — to show cause, in writing. In the meantime, from the time I issued the contempt order until the date he was supposed to show cause, he slipped around in the courthouse in Barbour County and made most of the records available to the representatives of the Civil Rights Commission. He did it at night time, and I made those findings, and those findings are part of the court record.

MOYERS: He did it clandestinely?

JOHNSON: Oh, yes, absolutely.

MOYERS: And he was doing this because he didn't want to go to jail—

JOHNSON: Well, he wanted to go to jail for a little while—

MOYERS: For a little while—but he was afraid that you would put him up for a long time.

JOHNSON: I told him if he didn't produce the records like I'd ordered him to, I'd pop him in jail for as long as I could.

MOYERS: All right, now, let me examine that, because the story is that while all this was going on, he sought a meeting with you, that he wanted to come to your house to work out something. And that he came to the house—

JOHNSON: That's true.

MOYERS: —and he knocked on the door. Now—

JOHNSON: That's true.

MOYERS: The story is that when the door opened, there he was holding his coat over his head—

JOHNSON: That's true.

MOYERS: It was true?

JOHNSON: That's true.

MOYERS: He didn't want the neighbors to know that he was calling—

JOHNSON: He didn't want anyone to know. [*Laughing*] That's the way George operated.

MOYERS: What did he say?

JOHNSON: What did he say? He says, "Judge, my ass is in a crack. I need some help." That's to quote him verbatim.

MOYERS: Verbatim.

JOHNSON: My wife was in the bedroom, she heard him say it. I said, "George, come on in. I made some coffee." He had had a mutual friend call me and tell me he was driving over a hundred miles to see me, and I had some coffee for him. And we had a cup of coffee, and that's when he asked me if I'd send him to jail "just a little," it would help him politically.

MOYERS: And—

JOHNSON: I told him no. If he didn't comply with my order, I'd send him to jail for as long as I could.

MOYERS: George thought—George Wallace thought you could send him up for three years, but under the law, how much time could you have given him?

JOHNSON: Well, it depended on whether I proceeded with contempt under the Civil Rights Act, and I think it had a maximum of thirty or forty or fifty days. Or whether I proceeded under the General Contempt Statute, and I could have sent him up for six months.

MOYERS: That's how he wanted the best of both worlds. He wanted to be able to say he defied your court, but at the same time he wanted to give them to the Civil Rights Commission.

JOHNSON: Sure, and he did. And when I made the findings that he had complied even though surreptitiously and deviously, and discharged him from being in contempt because he hadn't complied, that's what gave rise to his cry that he made famous that "Anybody that says I didn't defy the federal court, anybody that says I didn't back 'em down, is an integrating, scallywagging, carpetbagging liar."

MOYERS: Namely, Frank Johnson.

JOHNSON: Well, sure. But everyone that studied the record and everyone that knew the situation, knew that George Wallace had slipped the records to them.

MOYERS: And yet was able to say he had defied the federal government.

JOHNSON: He sold it to a large segment of the people in Alabama that he absolutely duped and hoodwinked.

MOYERS: He needed you, didn't he? He needed you as a scapegoat?

JOHNSON: Oh, of course. He needed anyone as a scapegoat.

MOYERS: Just like any demagogue.

JOHNSON: Sure. I was just in a place that he could use.

MOYERS: And yet you must have despised everything George Wallace was up to — defying the law, arousing passions.

JOHNSON: Of course, absolutely. Absolutely. I despise the fact that he was using the people in the state of Alabama for his own political gains. That he was lying to them, that he was misleading them, that he was promising and holding out hope that he knew he couldn't give them. Did that in the Macon County case. Led people to believe that they never would have to desegregate their schools. George couldn't have believed that.

MOYERS: The irony strikes me that George Wallace — George Wallace had the voters, he had the notoriety, he had the ambition, and he had the guile, but in the end, it was an unelected federal judge who altered forever the face of the South.

JOHNSON: Well, I think people eventually came to the realization that the decisions that Judge Johnson's been making are not all bad. The decisions that Judge Johnson's been making have not destroyed us like we were told they were going to do. They haven't destroyed our institutions like we understood. Our daughters haven't been raped because of these desegregation orders. I think they realized they had been duped, just to put it bluntly. And most of them know now that they had been.

MOYERS: You know, Judge, it's rather remarkable when one thinks about it, and bear with me on this because it's a long litany. But either singly or as a member of a three-judge panel, you desegregated Alabama schools, you desegregated the buses, the bus terminals, the parks, the museums, the mental institutions, the jails and the prisons, the airports and the libraries. You ordered the legislature to reapportion itself, and when it refused, you drew up the first court-ordered legislative reapportionment in history.

JOHNSON: I gave them ten years to do it before I did that.

MOYERS: You changed the state's electoral system and voter registration procedures. You abolished the poll tax before the Congress ever acted. You were the first judge to put — in the South — the first judge to put women on your juries. You changed the system of taxation in Alabama. You took over the administration of the prisons and the mental institutions. And when I read that litany, I think of something Lyndon Johnson said to some of his friends, the night after the march from Selma to Montgomery was over, he said, "You know, I wouldn't have to be president if my name were Frank Johnson instead of Lyndon Johnson." [*Johnson laughs*] Now, did you ever think about having that much power? More power to accomplish in the South than the governor of Alabama, and even the president of the United States.

JOHNSON: Federal judges are given lots of power. They were given that power deliberately. You have federal judges that are appointed during good behavior for life, so to speak. That insulates them from any outside pressures so that they may act impartially and they may act courageously, and when they accept an appointment as federal judge, they implicitly agree with their government that "if I'm appointed federal judge, if I'm given this role, lifetime appointment, tenure in office, if I'm given these insulations from outside pressures, then I will act courageously and I will decide these cases impartially." More specifically in response to your question, it never occurred to me that all of this litigation was coming. I took these cases case by case. All of them didn't come at one time. You've talked about civil rights litigation over a period of twenty-four years.

MOYERS: It's quite a body of work for one man.

JOHNSON: Well, it was interesting. And in retrospect, it was worth it.

MOYERS: It raises the question —

JOHNSON: It was very fulfilling and rewarding as far as I'm concerned.

MOYERS: —gets us right to the heart of one of the most profound controversies in the land today. And in the history of the judiciary. And that is the heart, the question of judicial activism. Judicial interventionism. Judges beginning to get involved in so many aspects of our lives that they have become, according to some critics, the dominant force in our lives. It's what, you know, the most harsh critics have called "an imperial judicial oligarchy, a ruling class accountable to no one." And I'm just wondering if you don't think there isn't some merit to George Wallace's notion that a nonelected federal judge has no business running a state's prisons, tax systems, mental institutions and schools?

JOHNSON: Well, I'll answer the last part of that question first. I do think a federal judge has no business running state institutions such as prisons and schools and mental institutions. But the state has defaulted in those areas, or the federal judge wouldn't find it necessary to step in. But I haven't stepped in to the point that I've run, in the popular sense of the word, any of the institutions. I've imposed minimum standards that it was necessary for them to comply with, in order to eliminate the constitutional problems that necessitated federal court intervention to start with. Federal courts have not engaged in what I consider unwarranted judicial activism. In all of those decisions, and the decisions in the main, with a very few exceptions, they are discharging the constitutional duty that's imposed upon them. De Tocqueville put it in a very good way when—

MOYERS: The Judge always comes with his precedents.

JOHNSON: —he wrote this, the French historian. He came over here and studied our constitutional system. He said, "The American judge is brought into the political arena independent of his own will. He only judges the law because he's obliged to judge a case. The political question which he's called upon to resolve is connected with the interest of the parties, and he cannot refuse to decide it without abdicating the duties of his post." And then he said this, "The peace and prosperity and the very existence of the Union"—talking about our Union—"are invested in the hands of the judges. Without their active cooperation, the Constitution would be a dead letter. The Executive appeals to the court for assistance against encroachments of the Legislature. The Legislature demands their protection from the designs of the Executive. They defend the Union from the disobedience of the states. They defend the states from the exaggerated claims of the Union. The public interest against the interest of the private citizen." And it should be added that the courts, the federal courts, defend the interests of private citizens against the government.

MOYERS: Well, I concede that historical—that history, Judge. It's been an argument ever since the first day, as you said. But the reason you've become controversial, and judges like you—you're not alone in this—has been because you've moved into what the scholars call structural reform, whereby a judge tries to reorganize a bureaucracy in the name of constitutional values which he believes have been threatened. In particular, I'm thinking of *Newman v. Alabama*, in which you actually took over responsibility for the state prison. And *Wyatt v. Stickney*, in which you took over the mental hospitals. And the question is, had the Constitution been so interpreted that way in the past, so that a federal judge actually assumes the administrative power over a state agency?

JOHNSON: We've moved from litigation that was involved with property rights and capitalism, to litigation that's involved with human rights and civil rights.

The people in this country have become conscious of the many, many, additional governmental controls that are imposed upon them —

MOYERS: Regulatory society.

JOHNSON: — in the environment, in every aspect of life, and they seek refuge in the federal courts. I don't mean governmental controls imposed just by the federal government. I mean, by the state government. Litigation is no longer a bipolar thing between two parties. It's class action, it's brought to vindicate the rights of classes. Our federal procedures have been changed to recognize and even, in proper circumstances, encourage class action litigation. The class action litigation such as you mentioned for the prisoners, challenging the conditions in the Alabama prison system. The *Newman* case was one that alleged a deprivation of medical care and treatment. *Pugh against James* was one that alleged 8th Amendment violations because of the general conditions in the Alabama prison system. *Wyatt against Stickney* was one that alleged, on behalf of the class of over five thousand people, deprived of their liberty through civil proceedings in the state of Alabama and incarcerated in state mental institutions for treatment purposes, that they were not receiving treatment. And so, they raised constitutional issues. They presented them to the federal court, and there's no way for a federal judge to discharge his oath of office if he tells those people, "I'm going to award you some damages for the things that they've done to you in the past." That's not much solace to a prisoner that doesn't have a decent or safe environment. Award a mental patient damages for what they've done to him by depriving him of treatment in the past, won't get him anything in the future. So, the litigation has not stayed the type that asked for redress for past wrongs.

MOYERS: Which is the traditional way.

JOHNSON: That's right.

MOYERS: Two parties come together and you say, "You were wrong, pay this person accordingly."

JOHNSON: The litigation now seeks prospective relief. It seeks the elimination of conditions that exist. And most of these cases, they aren't particularly interested in damages. You rarely ever have a claim for damages where — in a case like the prison suit or the mental health suit. And so, the judge is confronted with this new type of litigation, and there's no way to — and he shouldn't — attempt to dodge it.

MOYERS: In both cases, you said, conditions in the mental institution and conditions in the hospital were intolerable. When you looked into them, what did you find?

JOHNSON: Well, I found that in the Bryce facility, located in the Tuscaloosa area, which is the largest for mental institutions in the state of Alabama, over five thousand people had been committed there for treatment for their mental illness. They had been committed by the courts of the state of Alabama. They'd been deprived of their liberty for the purpose of giving them treatment. And the evidence showed that they weren't getting any treatment at all, they were being warehoused. And so, the constitutional issue was presented. Were they entitled to treatment? And I held, as a basic principle before we ever got into the type of relief that they may have been entitled to, I held that people that are committed through a state civil proceedings and deprived of their liberty under the altruistic theory of giving them treatment for mental illness, and then warehousing them, and not giving them any treatment at all, strikes at the very core of deprivation of due process. And that they were entitled, if they are deprived of their liberty for treatment purposes, then they're entitled to some treatment that is medically and minimally acceptable. They're not entitled to the best treatment, and I emphasized the word "minimally," and I used it in that.

MOYERS: But what criteria did you use? I remember Judge David Bazelon of the Court of Appeals —

JOHNSON: He was exactly right.

MOYERS: — in Washington. He said that his criteria for intervention goes far beyond just minimum standards of justice and fairness, and he said his test was a gut reaction to a situation, which, he said, "Does it make you sick?" Now, when you went into those prisons and into those mental institutions, did it make you sick?

JOHNSON: I've never been in a prison. I've never been in a mental institution. I didn't find it necessary to go there.

MOYERS: Well, how could you —

JOHNSON: I did not want to get a gut reaction. I did not want to base my decision on any emotional feeling I might get from visiting those places. I wanted to base it on the evidence that was presented in the court where — in an adversary proceeding, where both parties had an opportunity to present evidence and be heard.

MOYERS: And the evidence—

JOHNSON: And the evidence in this case, in the state mental case, was overwhelming that they weren't getting any treatment, they were being warehoused.

MOYERS: Well, how—

JOHNSON: You had sixteen hundred people out of five hundred [sic] that wouldn't benefit from any treatment at all, that were taking space in this mental hospital. They were geriatrics. The only thing that they were suffering with was the ravages of old age. They should have been in a nursing home. You had a thousand of the five thousand that weren't mentally ill at all. They were retardates, that should have been in an institution for retarded people, and subjected to some program designed to habilitate them.

MOYERS: And you didn't need to go there to discover that?

JOHNSON: Absolutely not. I needed *not* to go there. A judge shouldn't go visiting a place that he has under scrutiny in a lawsuit, and base his decision in whole or in part on what he's observed, unless he's going to submit himself to cross-examination. He should do it on the basis of evidence that's presented during the adversary proceeding. And so, I've been criticized for not going to Bryce Hospital. I've been criticized for not visiting the penitentiaries. But that's not the approach, in my judgment.

MOYERS: How did you determine what appropriate relief consisted of? I mean, the court order you issued from that bench was incredibly comprehensive. It covered everything from the amount of space allotted to each patient, the number of toilets, the frequency that each patient had to be bathed, down to requiring that toothbrushes be provided and toenails cut.

JOHNSON: Federal judges are trained in the law. They're not penologists. We're not psychiatrists. We're not educators that can run schools, yet we've entered school orders setting forth in detail what your faculty ratio should be, and what your pupil ratio should be, what kind of a facility you should have. If you had an ideal situation, you would have these cases decided by, in the penitentiary, penologists. In the mental institutions, psychologists and psychiatrists. In the school cases, by educators. But federal judges have the job of doing it. But we have a tremendous number of aides, and we don't fly blind in these—we have experts. For instance, in the *Wyatt-Stickney* case I had experts — that's the mental health case — come to this court and testify from that witness stand from all over the United States, ranging from the, — Karl Meninger, from Topeka, Kansas, to psychiatrists and psychologists and mental institution experts from California to Maine. And I based my decision and I based these minimal standards on their testimony.

MOYERS: You said in your ruling, "A state is not at liberty to afford its citizens only those constitutional rights which fit comfortably within its budget." And the question arises, if a legislature refuses to appropriate money, what power does a court have to make it?

JOHNSON: Well, to answer your question as it's asked, a federal judge cannot make the legislature appropriate money. There are many alternative means, though, by which a federal judge can enforce his order. He has contempt power, by those that are charged with operating the institution. He can close the institutions. He can say to the state of Alabama, "Well, it's fine that you're operating a mental institution," or "It's fine that you're operating a prison, but you cannot operate it and continue to violate the constitutional rights of those that you've incarcerated there. You either have to comply or close your facility." That's a drastic measure. But some courts have done it, to a certain extent. You have the authority to appoint receivers to take over and run the institutions, and attempt to do it in a more efficient manner and more effective manner, and eliminate these egregious wrongs that exist, that form the basis for these decisions. These orders were not entered in an attempt on my part, and they're not entered, as far as I know, on an attempt on the part of any federal judge, to make hotels out of these prisons.

MOYERS: That's what George Wallace said.

JOHNSON: Oh, yeah. But —

MOYERS: So, what did you say to George Wallace when he said that you want to run a hotel?

JOHNSON: Well, I said, putting a quadriplegic in a bed and not changing his bandages for thirty days, and letting maggots get in his sores, is not running a hotel. Putting a man that cannot control his bowels on a board instead of letting him lay in a bed, making him sit on a board until he falls off two days before he dies, is not running a hotel. Stopping things like that is not creating hotel conditions, is what I said.

MOYERS: He said you wanted Utopia. You and all the other men in robes who kept trying to dictate to the state really were after Utopia.

JOHNSON: The federal courts are not omnipotent and they're not tyrannical, and those that criticize the courts on that theory are just absolutely wrong, and they don't understand the history and they don't understand the constitutional restrictions that federal courts operate under. We can't go out and just reach out and get cases. We can't—and we're restricted from issuing advisory opinions. The only time we can rule is when there is a genuine case or controversy be-tween litigants that have standing to bring it. We do not make the facts that form the basis for the litigation.

MOYERS: Which is higher, the conscience of the people or the conscience of the court?

JOHNSON: Well, they shouldn't be any different. They shouldn't be any differ-ent. They should be the same. Court opinions can—on a short run—be en-forced against the will of the people. On a long run, there's no way to enforce them against the will of the people. If they violate the conscience of the people, they won't stand. For court decisions to be effective, they must be accepted by the people. And that's the reason at the beginning of this discussion that we've had, I attempted to emphasize that people have accepted *Brown against Board of Education*. People have accepted cruel and inhuman treatment cases, such as *Pugh against James*. And deprivation of medical attention such as the *Newman* case. And treatment for them and habilitation for the mentally ill and retarded, they've accepted that and they're proud of it. They've accepted the implementa-tion of *Brown*, and the people, I submit to you, in this section of the country, and I'm not just talking about Alabama, are proud of the fact that we have, with a minimum amount of disruption, implemented a case that cut across the social fabric to the extent that that case did.

MOYERS: But you said, "I'm not a crusader." I've read other statements you've made, when you said, "I don't make the law. I don't create the facts. I interpret the law." But pragmatically, when a judge interprets an old law in a new way, he's actually making new law, isn't he?

JOHNSON: I wouldn't think so. The Constitution of the United States—and we're talking generally, and we have been, about cases involving constitutional questions—the Constitution of the United States has five thousand words in it. It's a bare outline that we refer to as our charter of government. It takes interpre-tation on the part of judges, and on the part of courts, to make the Constitution a document that preserves rights now. It may have been construed most restrictively and literally at that time and covered most, if not all the questions presented. But there's no way to construe the Constitution of the United States literally at this time, and make it a document that has any viability. And if that's called judicial activism, then I submit that it's something that's necessary in our form of government, unless we want to spend all of our time amending and enlarging and changing the Constitution.

MOYERS: Let's see if we can — if I can understand it more graphically by looking at a particular case, a very important decision you made back in the early '60s when Martin Luther King and his followers were preparing to march from Selma to Montgomery, now a celebrated historical episode in the life of our country. I remember sitting in the White House with the president and his advisers, waiting for your decision. The word out of Montgomery that—was that you were taking your time, that you weren't sure you were going to grant the marchers the right to march. And then there was that incident at the bridge, when the marchers were beaten by some of the authorities here —

JOHNSON: State troopers.

MOYERS: State troopers.

[*Film package: Selma march, 1965*]

MOYERS: [*voice-over*]: In the winter of 1965, Martin Luther King chose Selma, Alabama, to be the target of a massive voter registration drive, to expose and eliminate the barriers blacks faced in the expression of the 15th Amendment right to vote. To dramatize their battle, to find a national audience, King called for a massive march from Selma to Montgomery, Alabama's capital. Governor Wallace issued an order forbidding the march. They went anyway. What happened next at the Pettus Bridge needs no explanation [*State troopers stampede the marchers*].

[*Interior, courtroom*]

MOYERS: And then you came down with your judgment, and you allowed the marchers to proceed from Selma to Montgomery. And by your own admission, that decision "reached to the outer limits of what is constitutionally possible." And you said in your ruling, and I'd like to quote it, "It seems basic to our constitutional principles that the extent of the right to assemble, demonstrate and march peaceably along the highways and street in an orderly manner" — and here's the phrase — "should be commensurate with the enormity of the wrongs being protested and petitioned against." Now, your critics ask, if Frank Johnson had not personally felt that the wrongs were enormous, would not the demonstrators have lost their First Amendment rights?

JOHNSON: No. Not at all. I did not issue that opinion, I did not write those words before having a hearing and taking evidence. The purpose of the proposed demonstration, and it was a demonstration, was to attempt to secure a redress for grievances that had existed over many, many years in Alabama. That is, the deprivation of the right to register and vote insofar as blacks were concerned. The evidence in that case showed that in some counties in Alabama, there were 113 percent of the eligible white people registered to vote. There were 2 percent, or 3 percent, or 4 or 5 or up to 6 percent, of the eligible black people registered to vote. It shows that in Macon County, for instance, there were over 100 percent of the white people registered to vote, entitled to vote, but in a county where you have a large percentage of black people with college degrees, some with doctors' degrees, some with several college degrees, all failing the examination that the registrars were giving them as a test, as a precondition to registering them to vote. You had a situation in Selma where, when they lined up to vote, some of them had been subjected to electric cattle prods. Some of them in the state that I was familiar with from having handled voting cases in many counties in this section of the state had been required to write Article 2 to the Constitution of the United States. Whites were not given any similar test. So, you had a wholesale deprivation by the authorities representing the state of Alabama in this section, of an entire race of people that wanted to secure a right that was basic to their citizenship.

MOYERS: Why, then, did you wait several days before granting the permission to give the rights? Because there was doubt in Washington after a while — twenty-four, thirty-six hours — that you might decide in their favor. That some people were even saying, "I don't believe he's going to grant the right to the march."

JOHNSON: No. No. A judge doesn't go to court with one opinion written out in this pocket, if he decides that way, and one written out in this pocket, if he decides that way. He has to hear his evidence. He has to evaluate it. He has to write it. Decisions of this import should not be rendered orally. They should be in writing and they should be well-documented as far as legal authority is concerned. And it takes a day or two for even the speediest judge to act.

MOYERS: And you decided that this record of discrimination against blacks in voting, the removal of which was the object of the march, was so great, so grave, that they were justified in marching from Selma to Montgomery?

JOHNSON: Absolutely. If the deprivation had been restricted to maybe fifty or a hundred people, not over an extended period of time, and this theory of proportionality—and that's what it was. The right to demonstrate and redress, a petition for redress for your grievances should be in proportion to the wrongs that you're petitioning against, that you're trying to dramatize. If it had just been deprivation of a hundred people to vote, it wouldn't have justified a march from Selma to Montgomery, Alabama. If some black person had been fired by the state as an employee solely because of his color, that wouldn't have justified any demonstration of this magnitude. But this, as I said a while ago, was a deprivation that concerned the whole black race in the state of Alabama, and it had been long, and it was a grievous form of discrimination.

MOYERS: There's an interesting case you decided just two years ago, the first time it had ever been decided that a black institution was found to have discriminated against whites. That was made right here in this courtroom. It was against the Alabama State University—

JOHNSON: That's right.

MOYERS: —which is an all-black school.

JOHNSON: Well, not all-black, predominantly black. It was established as an all-black school.

MOYERS: And you decided that—

JOHNSON: It's been desegregated to some extent now.

MOYERS: And you decided that it had been discriminating against whites. Tell me about that case.

JOHNSON: Well, the case was presented through the pleadings. A group of white faculty members hired a lawyer and filed a lawsuit as a class, claiming that the black administration at the University—Alabama State University—had discriminated against them on the basis of their race. Some people referred to it as a reverse discrimination case. There's no such thing as reverse discrimination. It's just plain, old discrimination, whether the whites do it to the blacks, or the blacks do it to the whites. And the evidence reflected that there had been discrimination against the white faculty members on a wholesale scale, and I so found. And enjoined them from doing it in future. I required that they make some monetary awards to compensate for—or partially compensate for what they had been—had been taken away from them.

MOYERS: Did blacks —

JOHNSON: Same kind of case that I've entered a dozen times against white schools. Blacks got incensed, just like the whites get incensed when a ruling comes that they don't like. Sure, I got letters, telephone calls. I got publications in the black newspapers about that judicial activist sitting on the bench down there in Montgomery, Alabama, about that lawyer that engages in exercise — I mean, that judge that engages in the exercise of arbitrary power. And — same old, song, same old dance. [*laughs*]

MOYERS: Did it affect you?

JOHNSON: Course not. Course not.

MOYERS: So, in the last analysis, old question, old debate — do we have a government of laws or a government of men?

JOHNSON: Well, we have a government of laws. Judges decide cases according to the law. True, as we said a while ago, judges interpret the law. They interpret the laws through their own eyes. They pour what's necessary into an empty vessel, as Judge [Learned] Hand said. But they still are not imposing their own sense of morality on the people or the litigants when they decide this case. They're imposing what they determine to be the morality required by the Constitution of the United States, and that's the role of the judge.

MOYERS: There's no job like it, is there?

JOHNSON: No. There isn't.

MOYERS: Could you have done anything else — would you like to have done anything else?

JOHNSON: Oh, if I could go back and choose, I'd go the same route. The same route. I've enjoyed it. It's been most fulfilling.

MOYERS: Thank you very much, Judge Frank Johnson.

JOHNSON: Thank you.

Part Two
Judge Johnson's
Articles

This section of the book includes eight lectures Johnson gave between 1966 and 1990. The last delivered piece was "What Is Right with America"; it summarizes the judge's core beliefs more formally than the PBS interview. Delivered the year before Johnson retired to judicial senior status, the lecture also represents a mature reflection on the meaning of a judge's life. The seven other articles were published in professional legal periodicals and present Johnson's views concerning constitutional issues he addressed at high points throughout his career.

These eight articles examine more formally the themes Johnson addressed in the Moyers interview. The first piece, published in 1966 during the civil rights struggle near the end of Alabama governor George Wallace's first term, considers the bearing official defiance of federal court authority had on the lawyer's ethical obligation to preserve the rule of law. Two years later Johnson incorporated these issues into a penetrating assessment of civil disobedience, articulating a conservative justification for a limited course of action in order to diffuse social discontent engendered by genuine injustice that certain democratically chosen leaders perpetuated. Johnson employed these constitutional ideals to analyze changing rights claims during the 1970s. His historical case study published in 1970, tracing the course of public school desegregation over sixteen years following the Supreme Court's 1954 Brown decision, explains in graphic terms why social change achieved through litigation resulted in an ambiguous victory. In the three pieces published in 1975, 1976, and 1977 respectively, Johnson adapts his constitutional ideals to a defense of creative equitable remedies in cases where elected officials abdicated their authority, fostering inhumane and even tragic conditions for mental health patients and prisoners. Again, Johnson's ideals blend a traditional view of the role of the federal courts in the Constitution's separation of powers, the belief in the lawyer's ethical responsibility to represent the rights claims of poor and weak groups, and the conviction that a judge's implementation of these principles will strengthen Americans' faith, which, in turn, will preserve social order. The public lectures Johnson gave in 1989 and 1990, shortly before his retirement from active judicial service, presented his most focused statement of a constitutional faith. The first appealed to University of Alabama law students to maintain the access of all individuals and groups to the judicial process. The second urged the state's lawyers to consider how much the postwar rights revolution had been a source of national strength and justice against the failing forces of Cold War totalitarianism.

The Attorney and the Supremacy of Law

I Georgia Law Review 38 (1966)

This article identifies the fundamental duty of the attorney to consistently uphold the supremacy of the law. This is a duty to safeguard the faith that Americans have in their courts. Not only is the attorney to keep controversial political matters and individual opinions out of courts but he or she is to "Cease irresponsible criticism and substitute a program of constructive analysis and elucidation" (40). That same duty extends to social and political leaders. The context for Johnson's admonishment follows accordingly: "It is the sacred and unique responsibility of the legal profession to quietly illuminate the path of reason and to loudly proclaim the supremacy of the law, especially during a time when a brutal attack is being launched against such fundamentals of a democratic society as the administration of justice by impartial courts, and the consensus of acceptance and respect for judicial decisions."

By 1966 Johnson had gained a national reputation for fair and effective handling of significant civil rights confrontations, including the Montgomery bus boycott (1956), the desegregation of public parks (1959), the desegregation of public libraries and museums (1962), the Freedom Riders (1961), statewide public school desegregation (1963), ending racial discrimination in voter registration requirements (1961), the abolition of the use of the poll tax to disfranchise black voters (1966), overturning racial discrimination in jury selection (1966), and, above all, the Selma-to-Montgomery voting rights march (1965). Martin Luther King Jr. commended Johnson as a man of justice, while George Wallace and other southern leaders repeatedly attacked him as an agent of federal coercion. Socially, in Montgomery the Johnson family was isolated. Even so, as the nation embarked on a decade of anti–Vietnam War protest, urban racial unrest in northern cities, and student demonstrations, Johnson's national recognition grew because of his often precedent-setting decisions beyond the field of racial struggle. In 1962 he ordered the nation's first legislative reapportionment according to the standard of one person, one vote, giving urban and suburban voters fairer electoral representation in state legislatures. Four years later he overturned the exclusion of women from juries. Less well known was his repeated affirmation of requiring the states and federal government to extend to poor and indigent defen-

dants the criminal procedure guarantees of the Bill of Rights. Johnson's decisions influenced provisions of the federal Criminal Justice Act of 1964, in which Congress wrote into law new criminal procedure rules as a result of leading opinions of the Supreme Court under Chief Justice Earl Warren. Thus Johnson was a federal district judge of national stature by the mid-1960s, and the experience that brought him to this point shaped the ideas he presented concerning the lawyer's unique role in maintaining the supremacy of law.

A modern attorney is constantly reminded that the art of legal advocacy—the practice of law—is a profession and not a business. For this reason, an attorney's daily performance must meet certain professional standards. For example, all attorneys must fulfil their (1) duty of public service—often without remuneration,[1] (2) duty as an "officer of the court" to assist in the administration of justice, discharged by sincerity, integrity, and reliability at all times in dealings with the court,[2] (3) duty in a fiduciary capacity to clients,[3] (4) duty to colleagues, which must be characterized at all times by fairness, candor, and understanding.[4] However, in addition to these enumerated duties, the attorney must consistently uphold the supremacy of law. This fundamental duty is the bedrock upon which the legal profession is based. Today, more than ever before, the importance of the supremacy of law should be reexamined and perhaps reemphasized.

The lawyer has played a major role in the history of the world, especially in the development and administration of government. For the most part, he has borne his full share of responsibility in safeguarding life and liberty and in promoting peace and happiness. This has been particularly true in America. Lawyers have served as draftsmen of constitutional documents, legislators, executives, judges, advisers, defenders of the people, and also as quiet practitioners who have molded public opinion and hence, in large measure, regulated the life of their times. These lawyers were average men with human failings, but they were devoted to their country and made great contributions to its traditions. Both the lawyers of yesterday and today inherited the same traditions and principles of the common law, the supremacy of the law, and the inestimable benefits of a free and independent judiciary. These principles, born in the minds of tolerant, patient lawyers, became the pattern for the traditional American lawyer.

During the same period of growth, the courts as a free and independent judiciary were the great source of law and protection for the individual and his property. Consequently, the people of America have learned to have faith in their courts and pride in their judges. Most lay citizens cannot understand jurisdictional problems or legal procedures; nevertheless, the individual citizen has confidence in the law. He knows that oppression has its limits; that no agency or power can transgress him or his property except by judgment of a duly constituted court applying the law of the land; that for any wrong there is a remedy under the Constitution and laws of this country. Judges will be appointed and will pass away. One generation rapidly succeeds another. But regardless of who comes and goes, the courts and the law they dispense — with the assistance of a qualified Bar — remain supreme. Strong in traditions, consecrated by memories, fortified with the steadfast support of the profession that surrounds them, the courts have existed independently of the men who have served upon them. In this manner have our courts become symbols of the supremacy of the law.

In light of these great traditions and institutions, what is the present day obligation of the attorney to the concept of the supremacy of the law? Surely it is to keep the courts always unsullied and free from the pressures of men, to keep them out of controversial political strife and ambitions, and to submerge individual opinions and pride. However, today this is not enough. During a time when government is seen either as the embodiment of power or as the embodiment of justice; during a time when over our world hangs the dread uncertainty arising from ideologies that seek to destroy our form of government — and with it, of course, our system of law — more is required of every attorney.

All good judges welcome constructive criticism as an invaluable aid in improving the process and substance of judicial decisions, and certainly there is an obligation on the attorney to constantly appraise and evaluate the judicial process. However, in recent years, some of this criticism has not only been devoid of good taste but even worse, has been bred by ignorance of the precise questions presented to and decided by the courts. This criticism has failed to consider that courts do not create the issues presented to them and that, in defense and explanation of their decisions, judges cannot engage in popularity contests. The judge must, regardless of the temptation, remain objective and detached. Therefore, judges are necessarily vulnerable, and cannot respond even to unjust and unfounded criticism and condemnation. Therefore, as a part of his duty to maintain the supremacy of the law, the lawyer owes an obligation to the courts, if not to the individual judges, to cease irresponsible criticism and substitute a program of constructive analysis and elucidation. This is mandatory if the profession is to merit its position of leadership; if it is to continue in its traditions. The present concern of lawyers must be for something more fundamental than any one de-

cision or any group of decisions. It must be for the proposition that the law in the
United States is supreme. It is this obligation on the part of trial lawyers that Section 1, American Bar Association Canons of Ethics, recognizes when it states:

> It is the duty of the lawyer to maintain towards the Courts a respectful attitude,
> not for the sake of the temporary incumbent of the judicial office, but for the
> maintenance of its supreme importance; judges, not being wholly free to de-
> fend themselves, are peculiarly entitled to receive the support of the bar
> against unjust criticism and clamor.[5]

A typical example of a State Bar Code of Ethics on this subject is:

> The respect enjoined by law for courts and judicial officers is exacted for the
> sake of the office, and not for the individual who administers it. Bad opinion
> of the incumbent, however well founded, cannot excuse the withholding of
> the respect due the office. . . .
>
> The proprieties of the judicial station, in a great measure, disable the judge
> from defending himself against strictures upon his official conduct. For this
> reason, and because such criticisms tend to impair public confidence in the
> administration of justice, attorneys should, as a rule, refrain from published
> criticism of judicial conduct. . . .
>
> Courts and Judicial officers, in their rightful exercise of their functions,
> should always receive the support and countenance of attorneys against unjust
> criticism and popular clamor; and it is an attorney's duty to give them his
> moral support in all proper ways. . . .[6]

Performance of the lawyer's highest duty presents a direct, current challenge
to the entire legal profession, especially since some lawyers, a few judges, some
public officials, and certain leaders of sociological movements manifest a continuing disregard of the principle of supremacy of the law and constitutional processes. The lawyer must condemn the conduct of those leaders, both political
and social, who are busily engaged in the frustration of the law for personal gain.
The attorney of integrity has a positive duty to intercede when persons with public responsibility make a mockery of law by prostituting legal process and stultifying the forms of law in defiance of their sworn duty to uphold the Constitution
and the laws of the land. That same duty is required when some of the powerful
leaders in the social field, reinforced by a multitude of blind followers, engage in
demonstrations that inevitably foment violence and preach moral defiance of judicial decisions designed to protect the rights of all citizens. In both instances,
these persons are motivated by personal gain, be it economic, social, or political,

without regard for the rights of fellow citizens, constructive efforts by government and the courts, or the supremacy of the law.

It is the sacred and unique responsibility of the individual members of the legal profession to quietly illuminate the path of reason and to loudly proclaim the supremacy of the law, especially during a time when a brutal attack is being launched against such fundamentals of a democratic society as the administration of justice by impartial courts, and the consensus of acceptance and respect for judicial decision.

The lawyer should remember that the man who defies or flouts the law is like the proverbial fool who saws away the plank on which he sits, and that a disrespect or disregard for law is always the first sign of a disintegrating society. Respect for the law is the most fundamental of all social virtues, for the alternative to the rule of law is violence and anarchy. To those not versed in the law, the lawyer must proclaim that the heart of our American system rests in obedience to the laws which protect the individual rights of our citizenry. No system can endure if each citizen is free to choose which laws he will obey. Obedience to the laws we like and defiance of those we dislike is the route to chaos. In times of riot and disrespect for judicial decisions, the lawyer must speak. To remain silent is not only a violation of his oath but is tantamount to cowardice and is a grievous injustice to the free society which men of law, by conscience and sworn duty, are bound to maintain. The voice of moderation must be heard above the cries of the far left and far right. Although these extremes talk of social and political freedoms, individual liberties and states rights, they are driven by fanaticism. They invariably espouse democracy, but do not begin to understand its very heart: supremacy of and respect for the law—whether we like it or not.

> A people may prefer a free government, but if, from indolence, or carelessness or cowardice, or want of public spirit, they are unequal to the exertions necessary for preserving it; if they will not fight for it when it is directly attacked . . . in all these cases they are more or less unfit for liberty; and though it may be for their good to have had it even for a short time, they are unlikely long to enjoy it.[7]

In my opinion, the principles and traditions of the American lawyer require that his voice be raised at this crucial time in support of the never-ending struggle to maintain the supremacy of the law.

Civil Disobedience and the Law

XLIV Tulane Law Review 1 (1969)

This article may be considered one of the most important Johnson ever wrote. Published by three different law reviews over the course of 1968–69, against the background of the assassinations of Martin Luther King Jr. and Robert F. Kennedy, urban riots and student shutdowns of universities, and the violent disorder of the Chicago Democratic Party Convention of 1968, the article states forcefully Johnson's philosophy concerning the boundary between unlawful and legitimate protest. In classic form it presents the quintessential conservative justification for civil disobedience.

To give substance to his argument that limited, peaceful civil disobedience may be compatible with the rule of law in those few instances where individuals or groups have been long denied their fundamental constitutional rights, Johnson drew upon his own decisions. In particular, he examined the controversial equitable decree which enabled the Selma-to-Montgomery voting rights march to go forward in March 1965. Martin Luther King's agreement to follow Johnson's order put the force of the federal government behind the march, undercutting the obstruction and violence Wallace's defiance had spawned. Even Johnson's strongest supporters found such wide-ranging judicial intervention in a protest action to be problematic. Nevertheless, the outcome was the historic Voting Rights Act of 1965.

Not only cases, however, informed the ideas Johnson's article developed. In April 1967, a year before he published the article for the first time, a bomb damaged a portion of Johnson's mother's home. Mrs. Alabama Johnson narrowly missed being seriously injured or even killed. Undoubtedly, the bomber, who was never apprehended, mistook Mrs. Johnson's home for that of her son, who lived nearby. A month after the attack Johnson's face appeared on the cover of Time *magazine; the accompanying story identified him as a judge whose courageous decisions had shaped the victories of civil rights leaders like King against Wallace and other opponents. By contrast, in 1969, when two other law school journals published the article, Johnson's fellow Alabama Republicans publicly denounced him before President Richard Nixon as "too liberal" to be appointed to the U.S. Supreme Court. Thus the context that informed Johnson's assessment of civil dis-*

obedience had personal as well as public consequences, but, as the repeated presentation of the article suggested, he remained as committed as ever to maintaining his constitutional ideals.

[As *a Southern Federal District Judge, Judge Johnson has had occasion to observe at close range both sides of the question of civil disobedience. At the height of the unrest last spring, Judge Johnson delivered the following address at the* Tulane Law Review *Annual Banquet, April 14, 1969. His discussion of the responsibilities of the lawyer in reconciling the inherent inconsistencies underlying this contemporary problem should be of particular interest to readers of the* Tulane Law Review.]

I am pleased to be here with you members of the Tulane Law Review Association and your guests. Most of you are probably aware that federal judges rarely make statements other than in the courtroom or in judicial opinions. This is as it should be because it is nearly impossible for a judge who has been largely removed from the political and business world — in order to more nearly maintain an impartiality necessary to the performance of his duties — to say anything publicly that will not be interpreted as an official position or judicial attitude. I have usually made an exception to this rule when invited to speak to lawyers and especially to law students.

My topic — Civil Disobedience and the Law — seems particularly appropriate since so many of you are at once students and lawyers. The 1960's have witnessed the development of protest movements which may well give the decade its name. To be sure, this nation has witnessed other periods of discontent, other outbursts of moral indignation, and more than occasional fits of violence. Yet, the movements of the 1960's seem distinctive. One distinctive feature, of course, is the prominent role assumed, largely for the first time, by the American student. Another and increasingly disturbing feature of these movements has been the tendency toward "emotionalism" — by which I mean emotion divorced from reason. Lawyers, both as members of the Bar and as responsible citizens, of course, have accepted the principle that the law is supreme and the responsibility of maintaining the principle as a working idea in this country. To those of us committed to that principle, emotionalism presents a special problem and a special challenge. We might respond initially to that challenge by noting the emotionalism surrounding the phrase "civil disobedience." I do not suggest that the phrase has a precise meaning, but it does seem clear that unrestrained and ill-considered ad-

vocacy of civil disobedience by its proponents has led to the loss of public support for certain aspects of the protest movement that would otherwise be acceptable by American standards. Moreover, it has unfortunately led some well-
intentioned participants into the wrong view that clearly illegal acts would be
immune from punishment. On the other hand, sweeping condemnation of all
protest as anarchy has tended to drown out responsible criticism of protest methods by those who sympathize with some of the goals of the protesters. The upshot
has been increased intolerance and polarization of opinion — two great enemies
of the rule of law.

At the outset, I think it is important to note that many of the issues involved
are not, strictly speaking, legal issues. For example, to the questions "When may
I disobey the law?" and "When ought I to disobey the law?", the law has a clear
and straightforward answer: "Never!" Justice White has made this point quite
precisely:

> Whether persons or groups should engage in nonviolent disobedience to laws
> with which they disagree perhaps defies any categorical answer for the guid-
> ance of every individual in every circumstance. But whether a court should
> give it wholesale sanction is a wholly different question which calls for only
> one answer.[1]

As a United States District Judge, I have had occasion to make a similar statement:

> There is no immunity conferred by our Constitution and laws of the United
> States to those individuals who insist upon practicing civil disobedience un-
> der the guise of demonstrating or protesting for "civil rights." The philosophy
> that a person may — if his cause is labeled "civil rights" or "states rights" — de-
> termine for himself that laws and court decisions are morally right or wrong
> and either obey or refuse to obey them according to his own determination, is
> a philosophy that is foreign to our "rule-of-law" theory of government.[2]

Nevertheless, there are circumstances where it is clear that the moral duty to
obey the law ceased. Even lawyers were justified, if not morally obliged, to counsel, and engage in, disobedience to the racial laws of the Third Reich. Similarly,
the laws in the Stalinist Soviet Union ordering the genocide of the kulaks were
devoid of any moral obligation that they be obeyed.

It would be a mistake to conclude from what has been said, however, that disobedience of the law is justified, provided only that it is disobedience in the
name of higher principles; strong moral conviction is not all that is required to
turn breaking the law into a service that benefits society. Civil disobedience is

simply not like other acts in which men stand up courageously for their principles. Civil disobedience necessarily involves violation of the law, and the law can make no provision for its violation except to hold the offender liable for punishment. It is this fact which accounts for the delicate ambivalence of President Kennedy's position at the time of the Negro demonstrations in Birmingham. He gave many signs that, as an individual, he was in sympathy with the goals of the demonstrators. As a political realist he probably knew that these goals could not be obtained without dramatic actions across the line into illegality, but as Chief Executive he could give neither permission nor approval to such actions.

I cannot propose a set of principles that will generate automatic answers to the questions: "When may I disobey the law?"; some guidance can be given, however. One thing that lawyers can do is to make and to expound to the public certain basic distinctions. The vast majority of the protest movement in this decade has been not only legal but affirmatively protected by our constitutional guarantees of freedom of speech and freedom of assembly. Most protest has involved totally obedient, nonviolent challenges to law or state policy, such as distributing pamphlets on segregation or in opposition to the war in Viet Nam, programs on voter registration, parades and picketing under permits where they are required. The Selma-Montgomery march is an example of a completely legal protest, since it was not held until the court approved the details of the planned demonstration.[3] This distinction is scarcely one that need be belabored to members of the legal profession. Yet in the current emotional climate it has been a point obscured to the public and to the protesters.

Of course, it is not always easy to decide what is protected speech or assembly and what is disobedience of law. The general principles are clear, however. In the early stages of the direct action cases, the Supreme Court frequently gave the demonstrators protection, but the decisions were not put squarely on First Amendment grounds.[4] Later, as the protesters became diffuse in their aims and careless in their methods, the Court became less willing to protect their activities.[5] Instead, it would seem that the Court's efforts became directed at elaborating the distinction between speech and action.[6] The recent draft-card burning case, *United States v. O'Brien*,[7] in which the issue of symbolic speech was raised, also seems to indicate that approach. But it is important to recall that a great deal turns on the precise circumstances of the protest. It matters a great deal whether the protest is by an individual or by a large group. It matters where and when the protest is to be held. Justice Harlan recently suggested in *O'Brien* the familiar legal principle of availability of alternatives.[8] Thus it would appear that conduct otherwise unprotected may be legal if it is the only means of communicating with a significant audience. I would also suggest that the principle of proportionality has relevance here. In the Selma march case, I had the occasion to state:

> . . . There must be in cases like the one now presented, a "constitutional boundary line" drawn between the competing interests of society. This Court has the duty and responsibility in this case of drawing the "constitutional boundary line." In doing so, it seems basic to our constitutional principles that the extent of the right to assemble, demonstrate and march peaceably along the highways and streets should be commensurate with the enormity of the wrongs that are being protested and petitioned against. In this case the wrongs are enormous. The extent of the right to demonstrate against these wrongs should be determined accordingly.[9]

The notion of testing the law is not an unfamiliar concept. The law in many cases is uncertain, governed only by broad principles, or what the philosophers refer to as "open-textured concepts." Those who practice law know that sometimes a lawyer advises making a deduction from an income tax return when it is not clear whether it is legal or not in order to determine its legality. Although there is occasionally a more orderly procedure available, e.g., a ruling by the Commissioner of Internal Revenue, we probably would not view these people as law breakers if their actions were later proved illegal. It has been suggested that when persons appeal over the head of the state to the laws of the nation by asserting and vindicating the Constitution, they are impliedly submitting to rather than defying the rule of law.[10] If there is no violence and the violation does not interfere with the rights of others, there is much to be said for that argument.

Having made some distinctions to the lawful side of civil disobedience, we may now appropriately consider distinctions to the unlawful side. One should observe first that while civil disobedience does imply violation of the law, it does not necessarily involve violence. There is no legal or moral justification for the rioting, burning, looting and killing that have occurred in such cities as Los Angeles, Detroit, Chicago, Newark, Kansas City and Washington. Understandable, perhaps; justifiable, never. And, of course, all of us feel nothing but revulsion at the senseless and brutal killings of President Kennedy, his brother Robert, Dr. Martin Luther King, or of Medgar Evers, Schwerner, Chaney, and Goodman in Jackson and Neshoba Counties, Mississippi, or of Viola Liuzzo, the Rev. Mr. Daniel and the Rev. Mr. Reeb in Lowndes and Dallas Counties, Alabama. These acts are not the assertion of rights; they are not to be justified under the guise of civil disobedience; they are nothing more than the infliction of gross wrongs upon innocent citizens; they are insurrections against government. Participants in such activities, and those who by their inflammatory and defiant statements possibly incite such activities, disregard utterly and completely the supremacy of any law other than the law of the jungle.

Although both necessarily involve violation of the law, it is appropriate to keep in mind that civil disobedience of the law and evasion of the law are usually to be distinguished. Civil disobedience is usually thought of as open violation of the law under a banner of morality or justice accompanied by at least a theoretical willingness to accept the appropriate punishment. Those who make moonshine whiskey in some parts of the country are usually merely law violators trying to conceal their violations, even though some of them doubtless feel that it is unjust for the United States to prosecute them for such activity. Those who believe that the taxing of income is contrary to natural law and therefore surreptitiously refuse to record their income should not be put in the same category with Thoreau, who announced to all the world his refusal to pay what he considered an illegal and unjust tax and willingly went to jail for that refusal.[11]

By the process of distinguishing away what it is not, we now approach a useful notion of the concept of civil disobedience: An open, intentional violation of a law concededly valid, under a banner of morality or justice by one willing to accept punishment for the violation. To this might be added one more refinement, one which distinguishes a civil disobedient from a revolutionary, *viz.*, that a civil disobedient is one who generally speaking obeys the law and may be said to usually recognize its supremacy. In other words, civil disobedience is directed at changing the existing legal order. A revolutionary, on the other hand, directs his law-breaking at the total eradication of the existing legal system.

It is this concept of civil disobedience, then, that I have suggested earlier cannot be condoned by me in my capacity as a federal judge. The law cannot as a matter of law officially recognize a right of civil disobedience. It is this concept which I understand Thoreau, Gandhi, and, at least in the early years, Dr. Martin Luther King to have advocated. And, unless they were speaking and advocating for no reason other than political purposes, it appears to have been the belief of Governors Ross Barnett, John Patterson, and George Wallace.

Having conceded as a moral matter that in certain extreme circumstances civil disobedience may be justified, I cannot distinguish my position qualitatively from the position reflected in the actions of those mentioned above. This may be one of those situations, however, where a quantitative difference becomes a difference in kind. This is said because I take the writings and the utterances of Thoreau, King, and Wallace on this point as an attempt to redefine obligation to law in terms of an individual right, or perhaps an individual duty, to determine whether a law is just or unjust and to obey it if it is considered just and to disobey it if it is not. The advocates of this position do not, as I understand them, offer any qualifying principles which limit the situations in which an individual has a right to disobey the law. With no qualifications, of course, George Wallace, to be consistent, must acknowledge that Dr. King had a right as an individual to violate what Dr. King considered to be unjust laws, and Dr. King should have acknowledged the same right to George Wallace. And the radical students who forcibly and illegally take over college buildings cannot consistently criticize, in the name of the law, the administration's denial of due process (e.g., failure to give fair notice and grant a hearing) in throwing them out of school.

It is submitted that those of us who attempt to act and think consistently must have grave misgivings about an unqualified doctrine that an individual has the right to violate any law he determines to be unjust. Such doctrine is morally unsound and practically foolish. While morality and law are not coexistive, the rule of law is a necessary condition for the exercise of individual morality in a social context. Embodied in the notion of the rule of law are basic principles of fair dealing among men, widely agreed upon, which govern the situations in which men's interests and ideals conflict. Embodied in law are principles that protect individuals from the exercise of another man's morality. Embodied in law are principles which provide a degree of flexibility for the exercise of one's own morality, free from the interference of other individuals or the state. Under the rule of law, these principles apply, prima facie, to everyone.

The unqualified doctrine that an individual has the right to disobey any law he determines to be unjust is simply a more sophisticated way of saying that a man is entitled to take the law into his own hands. It means government by force, not by law. It means might makes right. In short, while such an unqualified doctrine may find short-run justification in protesting or preventing a single injustice, it is actually extremely shortsighted because it destroys the condition for our full development as moral beings — the rule of law.

Therefore, I am sure it has become obvious why the unqualified doctrine is practically foolish for those who now advocate it, namely, minority groups such as militant blacks, radical students, and die-hard segregationists — all groups with unorthodox ideas and limited access to the levers of power. A society where each man decides which law to obey has really reverted to anarchy, or, in other words, to a state of nature. We all recall that Hobbes described life in a state of nature as "solitary, poor, nasty, brutish and short."[12] He might have added as a corollary that it is nastiest and shortest for those of weak body and strong principle. It is only under the rule of law that moral heterogeneity can peacefully flourish.

If one must reject both the extreme that civil disobedience is never justified and the extreme that an individual has the right to disobey any law he determines to be unjust, how do we determine which are those rare circumstances in which civil disobedience may be morally justified? Again, I can offer no panaceas, but can only point to a few benchmarks. Thinking should begin, I believe, with an almost irrebuttable presumption that civil disobedience is not justified. Indeed, proof beyond a reasonable doubt, proof to a moral certainty, is required before we take any such steps. This almost irrebuttable presumption finds its justification in American constitutional democracy. We might even define the American system as one designed to provide alternatives to civil disobedience. Majority rule is a key feature of this system. Elaborate institutions have evolved to ensure that majorities are indeed majorities. But there are definite limits on the substantive powers of the majority; basic standards of due process and equal protection regulate the exercise of those powers. In addition to substantive shelter, minorities in America are ensured the fundamental political freedoms of speech, press, and assembly which make it possible for them to become tomorrow's majorities. Finally, one must observe that these principles of government are more than pious admonitions to the wielders of power. Enshrined in a living Constitution, these principles are given the force and majesty of law through the operation of our unique institution of judicial review.

What has been stated here, you will be quick to point out, are the ideals of our constitutional democracy. In practice, in actual accomplishment, we may find considerable shortfall. Courts may be biased, elections rigged, legislators bought, or the police hostile. Our history does reflect all too frequent examples of such shortcomings. But with only the rarest of exceptions, the shortcomings of individuals have not created serious unresponsiveness in our institutions over long periods of time. And I submit that a serious, extensive, and apparently enduring breakdown in the responsiveness of our institutions must be a necessary condition of justified civil disobedience. In recent history, only the persistent and flagrant denial of the rights of our Negro citizens in certain sections of our country could be cited as an example of this kind of breakdown.

I would also suggest that a pragmatic evaluation of the consequences of particular acts of civil disobedience should be made. One should consider the risks that a peaceful act of disobedience may erupt into violent confrontation. One who is responsible for violence loses all possible justification for civil disobedience. One should also consider whether the act of disobedience will foster disrespect for law in general. Civil disobedients often do not intend to foster disrespect, but their actions can have and have had that effect. This is particularly true where the provocation is obscure and the disobedience general and unfocused.

Pragmatically speaking, basic principles must be at issue, the provocation must be extreme, and the evils likely to endure unless most vigorously combated.

These pragmatic considerations suggest that in terms of moral justification we note the difference between the practice of civil disobedience by large dissident groups as a tactic of political protest and civil disobedience by an individual as a private assertion of personal conviction. In the latter situation, there is virtually no risk of violence and the effect on attitudes toward law likely to be slight. Indeed, there is a tradition in this country of deferring to the mandates of the individual conscience. The Free Exercise Clause of the First Amendment and the provisions for conscientious objectors in the selective service laws are prime examples of this. And it is in this sense that we inherit a tradition of civil disobedience from men of the moral stature of Socrates, Jesus Christ, and St. Thomas More.

That essentially concludes my discussion of what civil disobedience is and when it may be or may not be morally justified. It has necessarily dealt in broad, general principles. It might be useful now to attempt to apply at least some of these principles to concrete situations.

Most of you will recall the events surrounding the Selma to Montgomery march in March of 1965. At that time in Alabama a number of Negro groups were holding voter registration drives, and in connection with these had staged rather large public demonstrations for the purpose of encouraging Negroes to register to vote and to protest generally discriminatory voter registration tactics in Alabama. As the evidence in *Williams v. Wallace*[13] was to reflect, the demonstrators were subject to an almost continuous pattern of harassment, intimidation, and occasionally brutal mistreatment by Sheriff Jim Clark and his "possemen" and by Alabama State troopers under the command of Colonel Albert Lingo. This conduct was climaxed by the severe beatings and tear gas treatment administered at the Pettus Bridge in Selma, Alabama.

A class action seeking judicial protection of the right to assemble peaceably without unlawful interference was brought in the federal court. The plaintiffs' application for a temporary restraining order was denied because it was sought without notice to or a hearing for the defendants and no irreparable injury was shown. The plaintiffs, however, were restrained from further attempts to enforce their rights of peaceable assembly until the court could judicially determine the rights of the plaintiffs. A hearing was set two days thence. Governor LeRoy Collins, President Kennedy's representative who was sent to Alabama and who reported directly to the White House on the matter, informed the court that Dr. Martin Luther King felt that an imminent march was essential and that he considered disregarding the restraining order. As you know, he did not, and after a hearing the court ordered the defendants to permit the march to be held and to affirmatively protect the marchers. The moral impact of the march, which was to produce the Voting Rights Act of 1965,[14] would have been greatly diminished if the court order had been violated.

The violent confrontation between police and demonstrators at the Democratic Convention in Chicago can also be discussed with the above principles in mind. It seems clear that a substantial number of the Chicago demonstrators were interested only in peaceful expression of their dissent.[15] Various groups applied for permits to demonstrate. Many Chicago officials were unwilling to permit demonstrations — even those subject to reasonable restrictions on time, place, and manner.[16] But it should also be noted that once the demonstrators were refused permits, much of what they did subsequently was in violation of the law. I cannot justify the civil disobedience in these circumstances. While the refusal to grant permits may have been unjust, it hardly constituted the requisite breakdown in the responsiveness of our institutions.[17] The spectacle in Chicago seems to me more than [casually] related to the emotionalism which has been so prevalent in this country.

Considerable emotionalism was also generated by a recent case in the Middle District of Alabama, *Brooks v. Auburn University*,[18] which involved a scheduled speaking appearance by the Reverend William Sloane Coffin Jr. at Auburn University. The evidence at the trial clearly reflected that the students were principally interested in a peaceful exercise of their First Amendment right to hear, but responsible officials again took a narrow and unfavorable view of the scope of First Amendment protections. The Auburn students, rather than resorting to civil disobedience, adopted the commendable procedure of exhausting their internal remedies and then coming to federal court. Auburn was ordered to permit the Reverend Mr. Coffin to speak and to furnish facilities, and the speech was held without incident. Many of these points were lost in the emotional climate that surrounded the case. An overwhelming majority of the press and public in Alabama were convinced that ordering Auburn to permit the Reverend Mr. Coffin to speak was undermining the authority of the university president and opening the floodgates of anarchy. A local newspaper rather candidly urged that censorship was preferable.

Finally, it must be observed that the trend toward the use of disruptive and violent action as a means of protesting felt grievances causes concern that goes beyond its immediate effect on the campus or community environment. Some of the grievances protested seem to be real; while others are quite trivial; but that is largely beside the point. One problem is frequently that the means of protest are out of focus with, and out of proportion to, the grievances alleged. Moreover, some of the protest seems to be taking the form of indiscriminate attacks on the "system." In some instances these attacks have even become assaults on our "system" of constitutional democracy. For example, in the case of *Johnson v. City of Montgomery*,[19] school officials of Alabama State College requested the Montgomery, Alabama, Police Department to arrest a group of students for disrupting classes and conducting a sit-in in the office of the president of the college. The students were demonstrating for the purpose of expressing their grievances against alleged denials of academic freedom and for better physical facilities at the college. On being requested to refrain from such conduct, they refused. After arrest, the students sought to remove their criminal prosecutions to the federal court upon the theory that their arrest and prosecution deprived them of equal civil rights. In ordering the cases remanded to the state court for prosecution, the general legal principles applicable to all who practice civil disobedience were held applicable to the on-campus conduct of these students. The court wrote:

> . . . [T]he evidence in these cases supports the finding at prior to the time any arrests were made, the law enforcement officers of the City of Montgomery made timely and fair requests of these petitioners to cease their illegal conduct. The requests were not based on any policy of racial discrimination. There was and is no attempt on the part of the City of Montgomery authorities, by these arrests and prosecutions, to deny any of these petitioners any right or privilege secured them by the Constitution and laws of the United States. When arrested, the petitioners were engaged in illegal conduct and had, under the circumstances leading up to and surrounding their actual arrests, reached the point of being of an aggravated nature.
>
> . . . These petitioners and others so inclined must come to recognize that judicial processes are available for the purpose of protecting their constitutional rights in this district.[20]

Within a single week last spring, the press reported that 200 protesters forcibly took Harvard's University Hall, that a mass sit-in had occurred at a Stanford University laboratory, and that student protesters on the New Orleans campus at Southern University forced the closing of the school. These student protesters must be made to realize that there is no constitutional immunity conferred upon such conduct. When individuals engage in the type of unlawful conduct that this appears to be, the enforcement of penal ordinances and statutes may "chill" that conduct, but there can be no legitimate complaint as to the "chilling" effect. They must be made to realize that deterrence of that which society has a right to prevent has always been, and I trust always will be, recognized as a legitimate function of city, state, and federal penal statutes.

Lawyers bear special responsibilities in any society built upon the rule of law. Perhaps nowhere are those responsibilities as great as they are here in the United States. In this country, lawyers are not only legal technicians, but also the principal source of social generalists. Thus, this important issue of civil disobedience, which is more a matter of political and moral wisdom than it is of technical law, imposes special responsibilities on lawyers as individuals, as members of firms, and as members of professional groups.

In combatting emotionalism and demagoguery, lawyers have an educational function with respect to laymen. They must clarify and illumine the distinction between the constitutionally protected rights of expression and violation of the law. They must make clear that the law does not recognize a right of civil disobedience and that violators must expect to be punished.

Lawyers must also be vigilant in keeping our institutions responsive to claims of injustice and voices of dissent. If they succeed in this, the condition for justifiable civil disobedience will rarely, if ever, exist. Finally, lawyers must expend their energies in eliminating injustice through legal channels, lest the victims thereof take to the streets. Chief Justice Warren recently counseled sagely:

> I am certain of only one thing, though the principles which have sustained us in preserving individual liberty will be as valid as ever — the techniques of yesterday cannot be the techniques of the future. The legal profession, like all professions, must move with the times and be a part of the times.
>
> Our Constitution and laws are, in the last analysis, only meaningful when lawyers have the courage and zeal to stand up in court and assert them. Unless one trained in the law and fearless in advocacy takes on the causes of justice, those causes are forgotten.[21]

Lawyers, therefore, face a special challenge in this period of emotionalism: To fulfill the finest traditions of their profession by directing their efforts in support of the continuing struggle to maintain the rule of law.

School Desegregation Problems in the South: An Historical Perspective

54 Minnesota Law Review 1157 (1970)

This was an address delivered before the University of Minnesota Law Forum, April 17, 1970.

In this article Johnson describes at length the history of school desegregation in the South (particularly Alabama) and identifies the many problems that attached to that process. The article gives a step-by-step account of the process of desegregation: the various responses that the Alabama legislature had to the Brown I *and* Brown II *decisions and the many lower federal court decisions that followed are cataloged. The actions of Governor Wallace are also described. The first part of the article describes the process in general; the second part explains the process through the lens of a particular case that came before Johnson:* Lee v. Macon County Board of Education, 221 F. Supp. 1211 (M.D. Ala. 1963). *The central theme of the article is the persistent resistance by much of the leadership in the South to the process of desegregation. The article documents this process extensively with a general historical account, then specifically recounts the history of the Macon County case.*

Johnson's historical assessment of southern public school desegregation was timely. For a decade following the Brown II *decision of 1955, the Supreme Court adhered to its standard of "with all deliberate speed," which encouraged the sort of local defiance initiated by Arkansas governor Orval Faubus in the Little Rock case of 1957–59. It was Alabama's Governor Wallace, however, who perfected defiance as a political strategy in the Macon County desegregation case, beginning in 1963. Not until the Supreme Court sanctioned greater federal administrative intervention to compel compliance with desegregation decrees in 1965 did Wallace and other southern leaders shift their strategy from active resistance to condemnatory rhetoric only. Accordingly, as Johnson noted, the number of desegregated schools in Alabama went from less than 1 percent in 1965 to 90 percent in 1970. In addition, Johnson observes, the chief threat to this success was that whites fled desegregated schools. Although this "white flight" represented the end of state-imposed racial separation identified with Jim Crow, it nonetheless engen-*

dered the sort of voluntary or de facto segregation prevalent throughout the North and West. Thus, whites left racially mixed public schools, either by sending their children to private "academies" or by changing residence to areas where few or no blacks lived. Even so, Johnson recognizes that in desegregated schools where the proportion of whites remained above 60 percent, significant white flight was less likely to occur, and thus the benefits of desegregation would become apparent. In order to maintain this delicate balance, Johnson opposed busing remedies in favor of judicial orders that permitted neighborhood schools and other desegregation plans that took into account residential patterns. Generally, Johnson's approach left Alabama with higher levels of desegregation than most other Deep South states.

I was pleased to accept the invitation of the University of Minnesota Law Forum to be with you and to speak to you today. Most of you are probably aware that federal judges rarely make public statements outside of the courtroom or judicial opinions. This is as it should be because it is virtually impossible for a judge who has been completely removed from the political and business world — in order more nearly to maintain an impartiality necessary for the performance of his duties — to say anything that will not be interpreted as an official position or judicial attitude. I have usually made an exception to this rule when invited to speak to university and college groups and especially to law students.

My topic — School Desegregation Problems in the South — is particularly appropriate because so much of the progress accomplished in the field of school desegregation has been brought about through the efforts and courage of lawyers and young people. The recent Supreme Court decisions and President Nixon's statement have made this topic a timely one as well.

When the Supreme Court handed down its unanimous decision in *Brown v. Board of Education*[1] (*Brown I*), no one had given much thought to the problem of implementation. Argument had focused on whether segregated schools were inherently unequal and on the circumstances surrounding the adoption of the Fourteenth Amendment in 1868. The Court asked for further argument on the nature of the relief to be granted, saying:

> Because these are class actions, because of the wide applicability of this decision, and because of the great variety of local conditions, the formulation of decrees in these cases presents problems of considerable complexity.[2]

Surely one of the great understatements in the literature of the law!

The questions propounded by the Court indicated that the Justices were considering several alternative approaches in May of 1954. The Court asked whether a decree should be entered permitting Negro children to attend forthwith the schools of their choice or whether the Court could "in the exercise of its equity powers, permit an effective gradual adjustment to be brought about from existing segregated systems to a system not based on color distinctions?"[3] Assuming the gradual approach were taken, the Court asked, should the Supreme Court formulate detailed decrees; if so, what specific issues should the decrees reach; should the Court appoint a special master to hear evidence with a view to recommending specific terms for such decrees, or should the Court remand to the courts of first instance with directions to frame decrees? On May 31, 1955, the Supreme Court delivered its opinion on how and when desegregation would be required, adopting the now famous "all deliberate speed" formula.[4] The key features of the decision were:

> All provisions of federal, state or local law requiring or permitting such discrimination must yield to this [Brown II] principle. Full implementation of these constitutional principles may require solution of varied local school problems.... [T]he courts will require that the defendants make a prompt and reasonable start toward full compliance with our May 17, 1954, ruling. Once such a start has been made, the courts may find that additional time is necessary to carry out the ruling in an effective manner. The burden rests upon the defendants to establish that such time is necessary in the public interest and is consistent with good faith compliance at the earliest practicable date.[5]

The cases were remanded to the courts which had originally heard them because those courts, owing to "their proximity to local conditions and the possible need for further hearings,"[6] could best perform the judicial appraisal of the good faith of the school systems' proposals for the "solution of varied local school problems," which might arise in the full implementation of the Brown I principles. Although the Court twice made it clear that desegregation was not to be blocked because of disagreement with constitutional principles which required it, the Justices clearly expected cooperation and compliance from both the local school boards and the lower courts. There are some who believe it received precious little from either. I would like to describe to you some impressions of the Fifth Circuit's experience with school desegregation litigation, and, more particularly, my experiences in the Alabama statewide case—Lee v. Macon County Board of Education.[7]

The first thing which impresses the student of school desegregation in the

Deep South is the slowness with which it has proceeded. No Negroes attended white primary or secondary schools in Alabama until 1963. The record elsewhere was little better. When resistance finally began to crumble, the meager result of massive litigation was tokenism. In the 1963–64 school year, the eleven states of the Confederacy had 1.17 percent of their Negro students in schools with white students. In 1964–65, the percentage doubled, reaching 2.25 percent. In 1965–66, with increasing pressure from the Fifth Circuit, a few district courts, and the Department of Health, Education and Welfare (HEW) Guidelines, the percentage climbed to 6.01 percent. The border states had a higher percentage of desegregation, but Alabama, Louisiana and Mississippi still had fewer than 1 percent of their Negro students attending schools with white students. By 1965, 56 percent of the South's school districts had desegregation policies but only about 11 percent of the total Negro enrollment attended desegregated schools. In 1966, 97 percent of the school districts were in official compliance with the HEW Guidelines or under court order, but the actual attendance of Negroes in formerly all-white schools was less than 16 percent for the border and Deep South states.

There are many reasons for the long delay between the declaration of the right to attend desegregated schools and its implementation. The profound disagreement of most regions of the Deep South is probably the most important single factor. School board members, regardless of their personal feelings, were pressured to resist by their constituencies. Opposition to "Washington" and the federal courts soon became political issues, and unscrupulous politicians quickly learned to exploit the problem instead of attempting to deal with it. The political aspects of this problem were aggravated by the disenfranchisement of the Negroes until recently.

For example, the Board of Education in Little Rock had prepared a stair-step integration plan for the Arkansas capital before any litigation had begun. The federal district court rejected a challenge to the plan brought by Negro parents who argued that the plan was too drawn out. When it came time for the entrance of the Negro students into Central High School in the fall of 1957, Governor Faubus stepped in to block their admission. The furor that was unnecessarily created led to a severe setback for desegregation and the defeat at the next election of those incumbent members of the Board of Education, not to mention Congressman Brooks Hays, who had voted for the desegregation plan.

Resistance took many forms; some were spectacular, like sending state troopers and governors to stand in schoolhouse doors. Others were mere bombast, like the interposition and nullification resolutions passed by several state legislatures.[8] Of some effect, certainly, was the pressure applied by the white commu-nity against Negro parents and children who brought legal actions and tried to exercise their right to attend desegregated schools.

The Alabama Legislature was particularly active. That august body did not even wait for the *Brown* decision, but took notice of the pendency of the cases in the Supreme Court and in a Joint Resolution, adopted September 21, 1953, ap-pointed an interim committee to prepare such legislation, including submission of Constitutional amendments, as may be required to protect the interests of the State and its citizens in the event of a decision by the Supreme Court of the United States which destroys or impairs the principle of separation of the races in the public schools of this State.[9]

The committee reported to the Legislature at the next regular session in 1955 and proposed the repeal of section 256 of the Alabama Constitution, which ex-pressly prohibited the operation of desegregated schools, and the enactment of a panoply of legislation designed to replace the constitutional provision which so obviously would have acted as a lightning rod for Negro plaintiffs and the fed-eral courts. The Legislature responded enthusiastically. A pupil assignment law was enacted that session,[10] which included several ingenious provisions. Among them was a grandfather clause which required students to continue in their old schools unless their parents applied for a transfer. The assignment law provided for a system of administrative review and appeal to the state courts, which would effectively render any application moot by the time it could be reviewed by a fed-eral court because the school year would be over before a final determination would have been made. The 1955 Act did not make integration illegal, as had been done in several other states,[11] but it permitted any parent to keep his child out of any school "in which the races are co-mingled" and promised State assis-tance for children who withdrew from integrated schools.[12]

The next year, in special session, the Legislature passed a Resolution of Inter-position and Nullification which was more colorful than efficacious.[13] A three-judge district court declared that "[i]t amounted to no more than a protest, an es-cape valve through which the legislators blew off steam to relieve their tensions" and declined to dignify it with a declaration of its unconstitutionality.[14] In 1957, the Legislature repealed the compulsory school attendance laws and authorized school districts to close any of their schools if the local board determined that the continued operation of such school will be accompanied by "such tensions, fric-tion or potential disorder or ill will within the school as substantially to impair effective standards or objectives of education of its pupils, or by potential impairment of peace, order and good will in the community, school district, or county involved. . . ."[15]

The local boards were authorized to turn the closed physical plants over to "private" schools set up to avoid desegregation,[16] or to provide support for parents who sent their children to private schools.[17] Another statute declared the school boards to be "judicial" bodies and granted them "the immunities of all other judicial tribunals" of the State.[18] The Alabama Supreme Court ruled that a county personnel board could not be sued for refusing to allow a Negro to take a competitive examination to become a policeman because, acting as a judicial body, it was immune from suit.[19]

The ultimate weapon in the State's arsenal was the threat to close the public schools rather than desegregate. This potential bomb was not defused until 1965 when the Supreme Court held, in *Griffin v. County School Board of Prince Edward County*,[20] that Negro students' constitutional right to the equal protection of the laws had been denied when the Prince Edward County, Virginia, public schools were closed to avoid desegregation and the State gave tuition grants and tax concessions to assist white students to attend private segregated schools.

Today the threat is that white students will flee to private segregated schools leaving an all-black public school system. Desegregation will have been defeated and, once the white students have left the system, the local white government, it is argued, will refuse to support the public schools which will then deteriorate. The Supreme Court has held that the district courts may not yield to the threat that white students will abandon the public schools.[21] But the Court has not indicated what a district court faced with a now all-black public school system should do. *Griffin* may provide authority for keeping the public schools open and tax supported up to an acceptable standard, although there was a dissent by Justices Clark and Harlan on that question. To the extent that whites flee in those districts where they are a minority, the problem of adequate financial support for the public school system will solve itself if and when Negroes gain control of local governments in areas where they are in the majority. This process has begun and local school boards in Negro-controlled areas are attempting to maintain and upgrade their school systems. After the predominantly black National Democratic Party of Alabama won the local elections in Greene County, Alabama, last summer, the local school board with a black majority, began to submit remarkably different and more cooperative proposed plans for disestablishing the county dual school system. Foreseeing this possibility, whites in some predominantly black counties are encouraging the emigration of Negroes so that the Negroes' voting power will be reduced enough to prevent any change in local government.[22]

A second important factor in the long delay was the lack of clarity in the Supreme Court's *Brown II* decision. The decision was designed to make it clear that the Court was not encouraging or condoning unnecessary delay. Nevertheless, school boards and some judges were slow to respond. Much of the delay in the courts was due to disagreement with the *Brown I* decision on the part of almost everyone involved, including some Judges, except the plaintiffs.[23]

Real desegregation—beyond tokenism—was held up for a while when the Fifth Circuit was sidetracked and followed[24] the dictum in *Briggs v. Elliott*[25] to the effect that the Constitution forbade discrimination but did not require integration and left undisturbed the people's "freedom to choose the schools they attend."[26] No court now disputes that the correct statement of the law is that the school districts must take affirmative action to disestablish the former dual school systems and eliminate the effects of state imposed segregation.

These difficulties aside, there were other legal stumbling blocks. An entire new area of the law had been opened up in 1954 and many questions had to be answered before courts could order the relief sought. Questions of standing to sue took years to solve. For example, the Fifth Circuit quickly decided that it was not necessary that the plaintiffs exhaust their administrative remedies before they turn to the federal courts, at least in those cases where the school system had a policy of segregation,[27] but the Fourth Circuit denied standing to plaintiffs who had not done so.[28] Not until 1965 was it decided that Negro students and parents have standing to challenge faculty segregation.[29] The availability of class actions, one of the most effective devices used by plaintiffs, had to be thrashed out in each circuit.

Each of the state laws enacted to block desegregation had to be laboriously attacked. The long legal battle between civil rights attorneys and the attorneys for southern governors and legislatures is still not over. The freedom-of-choice laws passed in Alabama and Georgia this spring are only the most recent episodes in the contest.

Moreover, the plaintiffs often had to prove that the statutes were unconstitutional as applied, frequently a difficult task. For example, a three-judge district court held that the Alabama Pupil Placement Law was not unconstitutional on its face in 1958[30] and civil rights attorneys did not successfully demonstrate that it was being applied unconstitutionally until 1964.[31]

The second striking feature of southern school desegregation is the immense amount of litigation which has been necessary for the enforcement of the fundamental legal and moral right declared in *Brown I*. There are, and will continue to be, a tremendous number of cases before the courts. For example, more than 50,000 complaints of discrimination in employment have been filed under section 706 of the Civil Rights Act of 1964 during the past three years![32] From 1956, when the first school case after *Brown* reached the Fifth Circuit Court of Appeals, through 1966 the district courts in this Circuit considered 128 school cases while the Court of Appeals reviewed 42, many more than once.[33] The number has increased significantly since then. I have before my court 107 school districts which have either disestablished their dual school systems or will within the next 30 days be under a terminal order to do so effective September, 1970. You can imagine the time and effort required of the plaintiffs, the Justice Department as a plaintiff-intervenor, the school boards and their attorneys and the court to prepare, present, and decide all the issues which must be resolved in moving from dual to unitary systems. During the past 18 months these cases have occupied approximately 50 percent of my time. In addition to the desegregation suits, every district court is subjected to a steady stream of ancillary cases arising from the problems of transition to a unitary system. For example, school boards ask for injunctions to prevent mobs from blocking integration.[34] One of the disadvantages of a dual school system is the wasteful duplication of faculty and facilities. School districts which could scarcely afford one set of schools used to try to maintain two complete systems. Both white and black students suffered, but the black children inevitably suffered more. One of the unintended benefits of desegregation has been the elimination of this costly duplication. Consolidation of the school systems has meant the elimination of redundant faculty and staff. Although most desegregation orders require equal treatment of black and white personnel, there has been a considerable amount of litigation arising out of alleged discriminatory dismissals and demotions. When a white and a black school are consolidated, there is room for only one principal and vice-principal. Almost invariably it is the black principal who is demoted or dismissed. Teaching staffs face the same problem. When North Carolina began large scale consolidation in 1965, over five hundred Negro teachers were dismissed.[35] Many of the dismissed or demoted teachers come to court for protection. Not all the claims are justified because many of the faculties were not qualified and the school districts often use consolidation to upgrade their teaching staffs, but the courts must sort out the valid claims from the specious ones.

Black plaintiffs are no longer satisfied with access to formerly all-white schools. They often insist on a voice in the curriculum to be offered. The demand for black studies has moved south. When the school officials are unresponsive to requests for special programs, the plaintiffs often turn to the courts. For example, in one of the reversals of the district court in the *Stell* case, the Fifth Circuit ordered the Savannah, Georgia, schools to provide remedial education programs to overcome the past inadequacies in the education of the transferring Negro students.[36]

Segregation has been so thoroughly ingrained in the South that its effects touch almost everything. The courts have had to forbid segregated P.T.A.s, buses and bus routes, extracurricular activities, athletic associations, libraries, faculties and staffs.

The number of judges on the Court of Appeals was expanded in order to handle the increased case load; the Fifth Circuit now has more active appellate judges than any other circuit. Senate Bill 952[37] to increase the number of district judges in the country, includes several new judgeships in the Fifth Circuit.

The mass of litigation resulted in major disparities among court approved plans. In order to eliminate the variations, the Fifth Circuit prepared a model decree in 1966, which served as a minimum standard for the school boards and district courts.[38] I shall not go into the details of the decree because subsequent Supreme Court and Fifth Circuit decisions have made it obsolete, but basically it called for faculty desegregation and freedom-of-choice pupil placement combined with the closing of inferior Negro schools effective by the beginning of the 1967–68 school year. The decision was important because it emphasized the affirmative duty of the school districts not merely to end segregation but to eliminate discrimination and its effects. Tactically, it was important because it meant that the delay inherent in litigation and appellate review was cut to a minimum. The courts now had a standard against which to evaluate proposed plans. For example, shortly after the model decree was issued, two school cases reached the Court of Appeals.[39] The district courts had approved plans which lacked the safeguards provided in the model decree and waived the choice form mailing requirement. Within four days the court summarily reversed and remanded the cases with instructions to the district courts to enter decrees containing desegregation plans conforming to the *Jefferson* decree.[40] The district court on remand entered a decree almost identical to the model decree[41] within a month.

Of course, a model decree, although denominated a minimum, may soon come to be the maximum for all practical purposes. This danger did not materialize because the *Jefferson* decree went much further than the majority of district court judges had been willing to go theretofore.[42] When it became evident that freedom of choice was not going to work, the courts turned to other, more effective means. District courts are now attempting to follow the standards set in

Singleton v. Jackson Municipal Separate School District[43] although no model decree as such was made part of that decision. The Court of Appeals directed the
district courts to approve only those plans which provided for immediate and
complete desegregation of faculty and staff, transportation, facilities, athletics
and other extracurricular activities. Commencing in September 1970, the student bodies are to be merged into a unitary system. No more delay is to be toler-
ated by the courts.

All this has been very abstract and intellectual. In order more adequately to
understand some of the problems, let me describe in some detail one case, *Lee
v. Macon County Board of Education.*[44] It began as an ordinary school desegregation case when 13 Negro children brought a class action in the United States
District Court for the Middle District of Alabama seeking admission to the white
high school in Tuskegee. Tuskegee is located in Macon County just east of
Montgomery. The county is predominantly black but until recently the whites
controlled all the political offices, including the Board of Education. In July
1963, the Department of Justice entered the suit to represent the public interest,
and in August 1963, I entered an order requiring the school board and its superintendent to make an immediate start in the desegregation of the Macon County
public schools. The Board assigned the 13 Negro plaintiffs to the until then all-
white Tuskegee Public High School.

When the school opened Labor Day morning it was surrounded by over one
hundred State highway troopers dispatched during the night by Governor Wallace, who had ordered that the school opening be delayed one week because the
"forced and unwarranted integration" had produced a condition in Alabama
"calculated to result in a disruption of the peace and tranquillity of this state and
to occasion peril to the lives and property of the citizens thereof." Governor Wallace had also sent State troopers to block court-ordered desegregation in Birmingham and Mobile schools. All five federal district judges in Alabama joined
in issuing a temporary injunction restraining Governor Wallace and others from
enforcing the Governor's orders forbidding school desegregation.[45] Nevertheless,
the harm was done: The tensions and fears aroused by the Governor's inflammatory statements and actions undid the efforts of the Macon County school
board to prepare the community for desegregation. When the high school finally
opened, only 35 of the 250 white students appeared for classes. Within three days
public pressure forced all of them to withdraw. Some of the whites organized a
private school, called the Macon Academy, and applied for tuition grants from
the State under a statute enacted to cover such emergencies as the one in Tuskegee. The others transferred to all-white schools in neighboring towns, using

the public school buses. After the County Board was ordered to cease the transportation of white students to nearby Shorter and Notasulga High Schools, State highway patrol cars and a school bus previously used by a State public vocational school were pressed into service by the State. In January and February 1964, the State Board ordered the Macon County Board to close Tuskegee High and transfer the students to the nearest school—which meant the all-black Tuskegee Institute High School—and to provide grants-in-aid to the students who had enrolled in Macon Academy. The State Board of Education concluded by resolving that "the Board . . . deplores the order of Judge Johnson and pledges every resource at our command to defend the people of our State against every order of the Federal courts in attempting to integrate the public schools of this State and will use every legal means at our command to defeat said integration orders. . . ."[46]

Acting pursuant to a court order after Tuskegee High was closed, the Negro students attempted to enroll at Shorter and Notasulga High Schools on February 5. However, the Mayor of Notasulga prevented the entrance of six Negro students to the Notasulga School, claiming that their attendance would create a fire hazard in violation of a city ordinance enacted the night before. Mayor Rea yielded to an injunction; meanwhile, the State Department of Education expedited accreditation of Macon Academy.

The massive intervention by the Governor and other State officials provided the means to shortcut in Alabama the slow district-by-district litigation which was taking so much time and effort all over the South. The plaintiffs asked for the convening of a three-judge district court to declare the State grant-in-aid law unconstitutional and requested the court to find that the Governor as ex officio president of the State Board of Education had "asserted a general control and supervision over all public schools of the state." They prayed for a single desegregation order directing the State officials to carry out the desegregation of all the public school systems not then under court order.

The three-judge court held the grant-in-aid payments unconstitutional and forbade the State to close schools in some areas while maintaining them in others.[47] It found that the State of Alabama continued to have an official policy favoring racial segregation in public education and that the State Board of Education and Superintendent of Education enforced that policy through their control of funds, textbooks, transportation and school construction. The court ordered the Macon County Board to prepare a plan for the implementation of further desegregation in the county and enjoined the State officials from interfering with the local board, but the court refrained at that time from issuing a state-wide desegregation order on the representation of the defendant State officials that they would not interfere with local school systems in the future.

Early in 1965, several counties, which have such a low Negro population that the maintenance of a dual school system was very burdensome, had submitted compliance plans for all twelve grades even though the Office of Education Guidelines then only required four grades. The Governor sent telegrams urging the county boards of education to reconsider their action. Most of the boards yielded to the pressure from the Governor's office. The State Board of Education, using its power over school construction and transportation, required local boards to continue to maintain dual school systems.

In the fall of 1966, Governor Wallace mounted an attack on the 1966 Guidelines. A new tuition grant law was enacted[48] and a new interposition resolution, directed at the "Washington bureaucrats," was enacted,[49] over the opposition of a handful of State legislators and the white teachers' lobby.

The local boards of education throughout the State that were not under court order (102 of them) were now caught between HEW and the new State statutes. When the superintendent of the Tuscaloosa schools assigned two Negroes to teach white students, he received an indignant telephone call from the Governor's legal advisor who threatened that the Governor might use his "police power to enforce the law." When the superintendent refused to back down, the State Board of Education announced that it would allocate additional teacher units to any school which had an integrated faculty so that students could have choice of the race of their teacher.

In *Lee v. Macon County Board of Education*, plaintiffs returned to court, now able to demonstrate beyond peradventure that the State had usurped the power of the local school board and was likely to continue to do so in the interest of maintaining segregation unless enjoined by the court.

The three-judge court found that the State officials had used their "authority as a threat and as a means of punishment to prevent local school officials from fulfilling their constitutional obligation to desegregate the schools, and . . . they have performed their own functions in such a way as to maintain and preserve the racial characteristics of the system."[50]

The court brought under its injunction all 102 of the State's 120 school districts which were not already under court order, and placed upon the new State Superintendent of Education, Ernest Stone, the duty of carrying out the court's order. Each local district was required to begin desegregation upon pain of losing

State funds and to make periodic progress reports. The court specified the steps the local districts were to take in a *Jefferson*-type order. The tuition grant law was declared unconstitutional.

The vast majority of school districts complied with the order and continue to do so with significant results. In 1966 only 0.34 percent of the Negroes in Alabama attended integrated schools; for the 1967–68 school year the number increased to 6.3 percent. In this school year the percentage jumped to over 33 percent. With the commencement of the next school year in September 1970, it will reach over 90 percent.

Supervising 102 school systems is a tremendous task for three federal judges who have been obliged to become experts in desegregation and education almost overnight. There is a multiplicity of details to be taken into account. For example, in April 1968, the court ordered the merger of the two high school athletic associations, one black and one white.[51] Only recently have black athletic teams begun to play white teams.

The volume of litigation has become so great that the attorneys for the original Negro plaintiffs have been forced to rely, to a considerable degree, on the Justice Department to handle the bulk of the preparation and presentation of the cases. This problem was alleviated somewhat when the black teachers' organization, Alabama State Teachers Association (ASTA) was permitted to intervene as a plaintiff to protect the rights of the black teachers. ASTA had a litigation fund, and it engaged Fred Gray and the other civil rights lawyers who had been handling the desegregation suits. ASTA has now merged with the Alabama white teachers organization, but NEA, the national teachers organization, replaced ASTA as a plaintiff-intervenor.

Freedom of choice, the plan adopted by almost all of the school districts, really began to work only after the court began ordering the closing of substandard Negro schools, leaving the Negroes no place to go but the nearest white school. In 1968, the plaintiffs and the Justice Department asked the court to order the abandonment of freedom of choice in 76 of the 102 school systems. In August 1968, the court denied the motions, but permitted continued operation of freedom of choice only on condition that faculties be integrated on a one to six basis, certain Negro schools be closed, and minimum percentages of Negroes choose or be assigned to white schools.

In October 1968, the court entered an order finding that most of the school systems had complied with the faculty desegregation provision of the August order, but that some 19 systems had failed to comply. The Boards of Education and the superintendents for these systems were made parties-defendant and ordered to show cause why the court should not require the systems to adopt some plan other than freedom of choice. The remaining school systems then brought themselves into compliance.

Last summer, after motions for further relief were filed by the government and the plaintiffs, the court required all those systems which had not fully disestablished their dual school systems to submit a terminal plan no later than December 1, 1969, whereby complete disestablishment was to be accomplished by September 1970. The court has spent most of this winter and spring evaluating the plans and holding formal hearings and conferences on the merits of the plans and objections submitted by the plaintiffs, the Justice Department, and the school boards.

In 1969–70—the current school year—approximately 33 percent of Negro students in the 102 school districts in *Lee* attended desegregated schools and 32 school systems completely abolished their dual systems prior to this school year. Most of these districts had a relatively low percentage of black students and accomplished disestablishment by closing their Negro schools and assigning the black students to white schools. The black teachers and staff were absorbed into the now unitary school systems.

The terminal plans the court is approving usually provide for zoning and/or consolidation and pairing of black and white schools. It is difficult to predict what the reaction to the implementation of the plans next fall will be. No one expects anything like the ugly violence that has occurred in Lamar, South Carolina. Because the remaining questions before the court in the systems where unitary plans have been formulated and ordered are local in nature and the State officials have stopped resisting, the three-judge court just two weeks ago transferred approximately 50 of these systems to the Northern and Southern Districts of Alabama, pursuant to title 28, section 1404a, United States Code. This decentralization will make the school boards' task of reporting to the court easier and relieve the three-judge court of much of the administrative detail with which it has been dealing heretofore.

Perhaps it is possible to extrapolate from the experience of the school districts which were ordered to disestablish their school systems this January and February by the Supreme Court and the Fifth Circuit. Of course, it must be remembered that some of the problems those systems incurred may have been due to the disruption caused by the speed and unexpectedness with which they were required to complete the desegregation process. The general pattern has been that in those schools where the whites are a majority of 60 percent or more, the desegregation has been accomplished without serious incident. Where the whites are in a minority, they have withdrawn from the public schools and established private schools. The cost of tuition is a staggering burden for many parents. Some of the states are resurrecting grant-in-aid laws and contemplating tax relief for parents and donors.[52] State tuition aid laws have been held unconstitutional by the courts many times on the ground that they are merely a device for perpetuating segregated schools. In effect the state aid was available only to white children because the statutes or school board policy limited the aid to whites who refused to attend integrated schools or because only white private schools had been established.

Many private schools have managed to maintain successful operations in Alabama so far, but it is not clear whether they will be able to continue to do so when every county has its own academy or academies. Many people all over the State contribute on principle to the private schools already in existence. When these contributions have to be spread over many more schools, each school will be much less well off. Macon and Lowndes Academies, for example, have been receiving support from all over Alabama. When that support is diverted to nearer schools, the academies will suffer. If the Internal Revenue Service denies the charitable deduction benefit to contributors to segregated schools, the amount of support the schools can expect will decrease further. There will be a large number of private academies in Alabama next year, in any case. There are several counties in Alabama where the whites are in the minority. Even in a county like Montgomery, where the whites constitute 62 percent of the population, there are plans for four new private schools to open next fall, supplementing the existing six private schools.

The South is beginning to confront the problem of de facto segregation. Although there is less residential segregation than in large Northern cities and their suburbs, the amount in the South is increasing and court-ordered desegregation is speeding up the process as whites whose children have been assigned by zoning to majority black schools move to neighborhoods where the schools are majority white.

Neither the Supreme Court nor the Fifth Circuit has ruled on the constitutionality of de facto segregation. In *Jefferson* the Court of Appeals left "the problems of *de facto* segregation in a unitary system to solution in appropriate cases by the appropriate courts."[53] It is ironic and tragic that as the end of State imposed segregation in the South comes into view, the perhaps more intractable problem of de facto segregation looms ahead.

The Role of the Organized Bar
in Providing Legal Services

36 Alabama Lawyer 12 (1975)

This was an address to a Regional Conference of Bar Presidents.

This speech addresses the problem of the lack of availability of minimum legal services to the poor. It begins by lamenting the absence of organized legal aid. Then the judge argues that the bar is uniquely qualified, above all others, to devise solutions to these problems. Johnson notes the passage of the Legal Services Corporation Act of 1974, which provides for a federal corporation to fund and regulate state legal services programs. As a result, bar associations needed to develop long- and short-range plans for the provision of services to the poor. Additionally, the bar associations should take other steps to ensure that the poor have access to legal services. Included among these are an expansion and revitalization of the small claims court system; a more efficient use of paraprofessional employees who are capable of performing extralegal work not requiring the expertise of a lawyer; a closer working relationship with law schools to provide clinical instruction to students; and finally the writing and distribution of intelligible manuals explaining the laws and legal problems that most often affect the poor so that they can understand their rights and obligations under the law.

Johnson noted at least two additional considerations underlying his concern that the poor receive effective legal assistance. First, he referred to the impact that high inflation was having on Americans of all economic classes. Even so, the steadily mounting inflation, which increasingly dominated the American economy of the 1970s, did not merely undercut consumers' purchasing power: above all, it threatened social order by heightening social conflict between property holders and those with little or no property. Providing adequate legal services to the poor reduced such tensions and thereby fostered faith in the inherent justice and fairness of the nation's government and economic system. Second, Johnson wanted the legal profession itself to retain primary control over legal aid to the poor. Johnson hoped to avoid the sort of bureaucratization that had overtaken the medical profession as a result of Congress enacting federal Medicare and Medicaid programs. Inferentially, keeping legal aid in the hands of lawyers also gave courts and judges greater influence in its uses, particularly in the administration of fee structures and the bearing that had on encouraging public interest litigation. Accordingly, Johnson's concluding reference to the issue of client representation in race cases suggested that he perceived a connection between legal aid and the conservative defense of civil disobedience he had made six years earlier.

[*This address was delivered by Johnson before the Regional Conference of Bar Presidents at Point Clear, Alabama, October 11, 1974. Judge Johnson has been United States District Judge for the Middle District of Alabama since November 1955. He is recognized as one of the great trial judges of the nation. Addresses of Johnson previously published in the* Alabama Lawyer *are "Supremacy of the Law," 30:237, July 1969, and "Responsibility for Integrity in Government," 3–3:12, January 1974.*]

Mrs. Johnson and I are pleased to be here with you in Point Clear tonight, and I consider it a real privilege to be invited to address this distinguished gathering of the Regional Conference of Bar Presidents. More importantly, perhaps, I see this invitation as an opportunity to speak about a subject which has been of concern to me for quite some time — and to speak about it to a group of persons uniquely situated to help find the solutions to the problems that I want to discuss with you this evening.

As your program indicates, I am interested in examining the role of the organized bar in the delivery of legal services. More specifically, I am interested in the critical problem which our profession is now facing in attempting to provide quality legal services to those unable to pay for the help they need. You will notice that I am not addressing myself to the whole area of providing legal services to people of middle incomes able to pay something for legal assistance, but unable to pay the full price for the services they require. I do not intend to suggest that the problems of middle income people are not acute, and growing more so daily as inflation destroys the purchasing power we organize our lives around. I do not mean to imply that the number of people with moderate incomes and only a very limited amount of discretionary income is not great; about 70 percent of our population have incomes between $5,000 and $15,000 per year. But I have a particular reason for not focusing my attention and yours tonight on the problems of economically average Americans. Great progress is being made right now, and new ideas are being implemented, to ensure that persons of moderate means will have sufficient access to the legal resources they need for the ordinary legal crises inevitably associated with life in our complex society. Organized labor has made significant contributions to this quest for available legal resources, as exemplified by Congress's recognition of group legal services as a permissible subject of collective bargaining and by the number and variety of prepaid legal services programs currently in the planning, experimental, and operative stages. The American Bar Association may be involved somewhat in the open panel–closed panel controversy, lingering antitrust doubts, and advertising and solicitation prohibitions, but these difficulties are certainly temporary hurdles rather than enduring obstacles to workable, successful prepaid legal services programs. Consumer power is now a fact of life, and on no front are consumers more actively productive than on the legal services front. One further consideration leads me to the conclusion that legal help is on the way to middle America: The legal profession and, perhaps, the growing legal insurance industry will profit by a more efficient delivery system supplying legal skills where they are demanded at reduced prices, reflecting the benefits of risk sharing. In short, since both the public and the legal profession will benefit from the improved distribution of legal services to those of moderate incomes, I am confident that meaningful strides will soon be made in this area.

But I am not nearly so hopeful that progress will be forthcoming in regard to the availability of minimum legal services for those too poor to pay anything at all for the assistance they sometimes desperately need. Twenty percent of our population in this country has an annual income of less than $5,000. More than 25 percent of our citizens here in Alabama have annual incomes below the poverty level of approximately $4,000, and — perhaps most tragically of all — over 45 percent of Alabama citizens over the age of 65 have incomes below the poverty line. Quite obviously, these groups of people are in no position to buy the legal skills they need — at whatever cost. I submit to you that comparable percentages exist in a large number of the other states represented here at this conference.

There is more to the problem, however, than simply recognizing that poor people are less able to afford legal help than are their wealthier fellow citizens. There is every reason to believe that the poor have a great many more legal problems than do typical middle-class clients, who ordinarily approach an attorney with one or possibly two discrete problems. The poor client, on the other hand, is likely to have a multitude of legal or quasi-legal problems at any given time: past-due rent, public assistance, employment discrimination, domestic relations, debts. And in addition to the number of legal problems he has, the poor client is likely to have problems of an entirely different sort from his wealthier counterpart. We are becoming increasingly aware of the fact that the substantive rules of law in many respects affect the disadvantaged in an unfair way: rules governing private relationships — for instance, between landlord and tenant — do not take adequate account of the disparate bargaining power of the parties; the rules governing eligibility for public benefits do not, in many instances, recognize the real measure of need; and our laws do not take into account the fact that the poor ordinarily lack the ability and resources to enforce those rights which the law does confer.

How insufficient the supply of legal services to the poor actually is is a matter about which we can only guess. The former Director of the Office of Economic Opportunity, Frank Carlucci, recently estimated that available legal services in this country met only 28 percent of poor people's need for counsel in civil matters. Another way of looking at the magnitude of the problem is to consider the availability of legal services programs in a single state. In our home state of Alabama, for instance, 62 out of our 67 counties have no organized legal aid whatsoever! Of the more than two million persons living in these 62 counties, at least half a million have incomes below the poverty level.

It is, of course, true that some indigent persons receive free legal assistance even though there is no formal legal services organization in operation locally. Most private attorneys do a certain amount of free work or work at a reduced fee for indigent clients who come to them with problems. This is certainly a commendable practice, and one that I hope continues — regardless of the future of legal services programs. But this case-by-case *pro bono* practice is clearly not sufficient. It depends upon the good will of individual practitioners, their ability to take on additional work for which they will not be compensated, and — most of all — the perseverance and resourcefulness of indigent persons in locating and requesting help from attorneys willing and able to handle their problems.

The American Bar Association, in its Code of Professional Responsibility, has indicated that donating his services to a disadvantaged client "can be one of the most rewarding experiences in the life of a lawyer." Indeed, the Code states that "[t]he rendition of legal services to those unable to pay reasonable fees continues to be an *obligation* of each lawyer. . . ." However, the ABA has also recognized that the uncompensated efforts of individual lawyers are often not enough to meet the need and that organized programs must be instituted to provide legal services. The Code expressly advises that "[e]very lawyer should support all proper efforts to meet this need for legal services."

Although we occasionally discuss the need for legal assistance to the poor and examine ways in which the bar can fulfill this need, we rarely consider why it is that the bar should take the initiative in seeing that these services are provided. On one level, we might say that it is our duty to support and participate in legal services programs because many of us took oaths upon admission to the bar that we would not delay justice for want of money. On another level, we might feel that the organized bar should take the initiative and bear the primary responsibility for legal services in order to ensure that the administration of justice remains a predominantly local matter — one of the factors that has contributed to the success of our system through the years. We cannot fail to perceive the significance of the trend now evolving in the delivery of medical services in this country: where the profession has priced its services beyond the means of necessitous recipients, the federal government has interceded to make such services available — first through FELA, then Medicare, next Medicaid, and soon through national health insurance. It will be only a matter of time before the federal government enters the legal services business if we fail in our responsibility. But there is a more profound reason why it is our duty as members of the legal profession to devise solutions to this problem ourselves and not to rely upon others to initiate and administer, as well as to fund, workable programs. No group understands the legal system and lawyers, their strengths and weaknesses, like the organized bar; no one knows better than we ourselves how to marshal our resources and fit our capabilities to the demands legitimately made of us. In short, this is our business, and until it is demonstrated that we are unwilling or unable to manage it, we remain responsible for it.

What is required is an effective, adequately staffed, adequately funded legal aid office within the reach of every poor citizen of the United States. We now have the opportunity to begin taking the critical steps which make this a reality. On July 25, 1974, the Legal Services Corporation Act became law. This Act provides for the establishment of a nonpolitical, bipartisan independent federal corporation to fund and regulate state legal services programs. Money is available now for the establishment or continuation of locally organized legal services programs meeting certain minimum requirements. Now is the time for every bar association represented here — indeed, for every bar association in this country — to critically examine and evaluate the legal services situation in its state. In conjunction with local legal services organizations, where they exist — or on its own — each bar association should formulate both long and short-range plans for providing needed services to the community, and timely application should be made to the Legal Services Corporation for the funding that has been made available to local programs through the Corporation.

It has been demonstrated repeatedly that the support of the organized bar is one of the crucial factors in assuring the professional quality, political acceptability, and financial capability of legal aid operations. Nowhere has this been more vividly pointed out than in the case of the remarkably successful Georgia Services Programs established by the State Bar of Georgia and the Younger Lawyers Section of that bar.

President Fellers has recently pledged his efforts and those of the American Bar Association in support of the Legal Services Corporation. As he so appropriately noted, "Our concern with Justice is not academic or frivolous. We have a solemn obligation to seek justice actively and passionately. That is our reason for existing." As important as I believe that the Legal Services Corporation Act is, I also believe that the organized bar will be remiss in its responsibility if it confines its efforts in promoting legal assistance for the poor to the successful implementation of the Act. What is urgently called for is a wide variety of solutions, an assortment of techniques designed to solve this multi-faceted problem.

I shall not discuss these additional measures in detail, but I would like to call your attention to some of the more important steps which can — and must, in my opinion — be taken. I urge each bar association represented here this evening to work actively in bringing about an expansion and revitalization of the small claims court system introduced at the beginning of this century with such high hopes that justice might be available to every citizen swiftly, simply, and inexpensively. I encourage you to make wise and efficient use of para-professional employees trained to perform many of the extra-legal duties which do not require the skill of attorney or warrant the cost of his services. I urge you to work closely with the law schools which you accredit to formulate programs which provide quality clinical instruction to students and at the same time enable them to work under the supervision of practicing attorneys in the research and preparation of actual cases. And, finally, I hope that those bar associations which have not already done so will undertake immediately the simple, but critically important, task of drafting, printing, and distributing intelligible manuals or brochures explaining the most-often encountered laws affecting the poor so that these citizens will have an opportunity to know and understand the basic rights and obligations which they have.

Let us make no mistake about what it is that we must do. In order for any legal services program to be truly successful, that program must reach the "hard-core poor" — not only those whose poverty is economic, but also those afflicted with the more insidious type of poverty manifested by inadequate awareness, lack of knowledge about the available resources, fear of attorneys and courts, and failure to perceive the existence of legal problems and to articulate them.

I should like to close this evening by recalling some remarks I had occasion to make over a decade ago, at the height of the intensity in the struggle for the basic principle of equal justice under law for persons of all races:

> Many lay citizens cannot understand jurisdictional problems or legal procedures; the principles of jurisprudence are not for their comprehension. Nevertheless, they repose with confident security—with the knowledge that there is a limit which oppression cannot transgress; that no agency or power can go upon them but by judgment of a duly constituted court applying the law of the land; that for any wrong there is a remedy under the Constitution of this country to be guaranteed by the judges who sit upon the courts of the United States.

Ladies and gentlemen, however true those words may be in describing our own view of the legal system we know and respect, they are woefully inaccurate in describing the system of justice known to and feared by the disadvantaged in our midst. It is the solemn responsibility of each of us as members of an honorable and humanitarian profession to see to it that justice is made available to the rich and poor alike.

Observation: The Constitution and the Federal District Judge

54 Texas Law Review 903 (1976)

This article is a defense of federal judicial intervention when a state abdicates its role and fails to meet minimum constitutional standards. Federal judicial intervention is also compelled by the denial of constitutional rights to citizens. Johnson illustrates this pattern by describing some of his more important cases. Among these are Newman v. Alabama *(constitutional sufficiency of medical care available to prisoners);* Wyatt v. Stickney *(minimum constitutional standards of care in a state mental hospital); and* James v. Wallace *(minimum constitutional conditions in state penal system). Johnson then calls on state governments to reassume their obligation and bring an end to the days of the "Alabama Federal Judicial Intervention Syndrome."*

Johnson's examination of the uses of federal judicial authority in the institutional cases and the ensuing controversy occurred amid increased national recognition of the judge's decision making, ongoing political criticism from Wallace, and a family tragedy.

In the April 26, 1976, issue of New York, *commentator Steve Brill published an article devoted to Johnson entitled "The Real Governor of Alabama." Brill presented the story of Johnson's historic role over the previous twenty years, focusing on the many points at which the federal courts had intervened in Alabama's public life as a result of the state government's default or intransigence.*

On October 12, 1975, the Johnsons' only child, James Curtis, shot himself to death in the family home. The twenty-seven-year-old adopted son had recently graduated from the University of Alabama and was preparing to enter law school there. At the time, Wallace publicly attempted to use the death for political gain.

This combination of developments added new levels of tension to the political and legal confrontations Johnson addressed from the bench. Most especially, his assertions made in the public lectures rang true that federal judges like himself did not relish the wider interventionist role thrust upon them because political leaders denied citizens their legitimate constitutional rights.

[*Throughout our history judges and commentators have actively debated the propriety of federal judicial intervention into state affairs to protect national and individual interests. The recent expansion of state services and institutions, coupled with growing federal power, has intensified the need to determine a proper equilibrium between the states and the federal courts. Johnson contends that state laws, policies, and procedures that systematically deny the substantial constitutional rights of citizens require federal courts to vindicate those rights and to compel obedience to the Constitution. Johnson dramatically illustrates the argument with examples drawn from his long and diverse experience as a federal district judge for the Middle District of Alabama.*]

Modern American society depends upon our judicial system to play a critical role in maintaining the balance between governmental powers and individual rights. The increasing concern paid by our courts toward the functioning of government and its agencies has received much comment[1] and some criticism[2] recently. As governmental institutions at all levels have assumed a greater role in providing public services, courts increasingly have been confronted with the unavoidable duty of determining whether those services meet basic constitutional requirements. Time and again citizens have brought to the federal courts, and those courts reluctantly have decided, such basic questions as how and when to make available equal quality public education to all our children; how to guarantee all citizens an opportunity to serve on juries, to vote, and to have their votes counted equally; under what minimal living conditions criminal offenders may be incarcerated; and what minimum standards of care and treatment state institutions must provide the mentally ill and mentally retarded who have been involuntarily committed to the custody of the state.

The reluctance with which courts and judges have undertaken the complex task of deciding such questions has at least three important sources. First, one of the founding principles of our Government,[3] a principle derived from the French philosophers of the eighteenth century, is that the powers of government should be separate and distinct, lest all the awesome power of government unite as one force unchecked in its exercise. The drafters of our Constitution formulated the doctrine of separation of powers to promote the independence of each branch of government in its sphere of operation. To the extent that courts respond to requests to look to the future and to change existing conditions by making new rules, however, they become subject to the charge of usurping authority from the legislative or executive branch.

Second, our Constitution and laws have strictly limited the power of the federal judiciary to participate in what are essentially political affairs. The tenth amendment[4] reserves any power not delegated to the United States to the individual states or to the people. Reflecting the distrust of centralized government expressed by this amendment, courts and citizens alike since the Nation's beginning have regarded certain governmental functions as primarily, if not exclusively, state responsibilities. Among these are public education;[5] maintenance of state and local penal institutions;[6] domestic relations;[7] and provision for the poor, homeless, aged, and infirm.[8] A further limitation on the role of federal courts with respect to other governmental bodies lies in the creation and maintenance of these courts as courts of limited jurisdiction.

Last, federal judges properly hesitate to make decisions either that require the exercise of political judgment[9] or that necessitate expertise they lack.[10] Judges are professionally trained in the law—not in sociology, education, medicine, penology, or public administration. In an ideal society, elected officials would make all decisions relating to the allocation of resources; experts trained in corrections would make all penological decisions; physicians would make all medical decisions; scientists would make all technological decisions; and educators would make all educational decisions. Too often, however, we have failed to achieve this ideal system. Many times, those persons to whom we have entrusted these responsibilities have acted or failed to act in ways that do not fall within the bounds of discretion permitted by the Constitution and the laws. When such transgressions are properly and formally brought before a court—and increasingly before federal courts—it becomes the responsibility of the judiciary to ensure that the Constitution and laws of the United States remain, in fact as well as in theory, the supreme law of the land.

On far too many occasions the intransigent and unremitting opposition of state officials who have neglected or refused to correct unconstitutional or unlawful state policies and practices has necessitated federal intervention to enforce the law. Courts in all sections of the Nation have expended and continue to expend untold resources in repeated litigation brought to compel local school officials to follow a rule of law first announced by the Supreme Court almost twenty-two years ago.[11] In addition to deciding scores of school cases, federal courts in Alabama alone have ordered the desegregation of mental institutions,[12] penal facilities,[13] public parks,[14] city buses,[15] interstate and intrastate buses and bus terminals,[16] airport terminals,[17] and public libraries and museums.[18] Although I refer to Alabama and specific cases litigated in the federal courts of Alabama, I do not intend to suggest that similar problems do not exist in many of our other states.

The history of public school desegregation has been a story of repeated intervention by the courts to overcome not only the threats and violence of extremists
attempting to block school desegregation[19] but also the numerous attempts by
local and state officials to thwart the orderly, efficient, and lawful resolution of
this complicated social problem.[20] Desegregation is not the only area of state responsibility in which Alabama officials have forfeited their decision making
powers by such a dereliction of duty as to require judicial intervention. Having
found Alabama's legislative apportionment plan unconstitutional,[21] the District
Court for the Middle District of Alabama waited ten years for State officials to
carry out the duty properly imposed upon them by the Constitution and expressly set out in the court's order. The continued refusal of those officials to
comply left the court no choice but to assume that duty itself and to impose its
own reapportionment plan.[22] State officers by their inaction have also handed
over to the courts property tax assessment plans;[23] standards for the care and
treatment of mentally ill and mentally retarded persons committed to the State's
custody;[24] and the procedures by which such persons are committed.[25]

Some of these cases are extremely troublesome and time consuming for all
concerned. I speak in particular of those lawsuits challenging the operation of
state institutions for the custody and control of citizens who cannot or will not
function at a safe and self-sustaining capacity in a free society. Ordinarily these
cases proceed as class actions seeking to determine the rights of large numbers of
people. As a result, the courts' decisions necessarily have wide-ranging effect and
momentous importance, whether they grant or deny the relief sought.

A shocking example of a failure of state officials to discharge their duty was
forcefully presented in a lawsuit tried before me in 1972, *Newman v. Alabama*,[26]
which challenged the constitutional sufficiency of medical care available to prisoners in the Alabama penal system. The evidence in that case convincingly demonstrated that correctional officers on occasion intentionally denied inmates the
right to examination by a physician or to treatment by trained medical personnel, and that they routinely withheld medicine and other treatments prescribed
by physicians. Further evidence showed that untrained inmates served as ward
attendants and x-ray, laboratory, and dental technicians; rags were used as bandages; ambulance oxygen tanks remained empty for long periods of time; and unsupervised inmates without formal training pulled teeth, gave injections, su-
tured, and performed minor surgery. In fact, death resulting from gross neglect
and totally inadequate treatment was not unusual.

A nineteen-year-old with an extremely high fever who was diagnosed as having acute pneumonia was left unsupervised and allowed to take cold showers at
will for two days before his death. A quadriplegic with bedsores infested with

maggots was bathed and had his bandages changed only once in the month before his death. An inmate who could not eat received no nourishment for the three days prior to his death even though intravenous feeding had been ordered by a doctor. A geriatric inmate who had suffered a stroke was made to sit each day on a wooden bench so that he would not soil his bed; he frequently fell onto the floor; his legs became swollen from a lack of circulation, necessitating the amputation of a leg the day before his death.[27]

Based on the virtually uncontradicted evidence presented at trial, the district court entered a comprehensive order designed to remedy each specific abuse proved at trial and to establish additional safeguards so that the medical program in Alabama prisons would never again regress to its past level of inadequacy.[28] The State was ordered to bring the general hospital at the Medical and Diagnostic Center (now Kilby Corrections Facility) up to the minimum standards required of hospitals by the United States Department of Health, Education, and Welfare for participation in the Medicare program.[29] The court also directed the Alabama State Board of Health to inspect regularly for general sanitation all the medical and food processing facilities in the prison system.[30] Finally, the court decreed that all inmates receive physical examinations by physicians at regular intervals of not more than two years.[31]

One of the most comprehensive orders that I have entered concerning the operation and management of state institutions relates to the facilities maintained by the Alabama Department of Mental Health for the mentally ill and mentally retarded. Plaintiffs in *Wyatt v. Stickney*[32] brought a class action on behalf of all patients involuntarily confined at Bryce Hospital, the State's largest mental hospital, to establish the minimum standards of care and treatment to which the civilly committed are entitled under the Constitution. Patients at Searcy Hospital in southern Alabama and residents at the Partlow State School and Hospital in Tuscaloosa joined the action as plaintiffs, thereby compelling a comprehensive inquiry into the entire Alabama mental health and retardation treatment and habilitation program.

At trial plaintiffs produced evidence showing that Bryce Hospital, built in the 1850's, was grossly overcrowded, housing more than 5000 patients.[33] Of these 5000 people ostensibly committed to Bryce for treatment of mental illness, about 1600—almost one-third—were geriatrics neither needing nor receiving any treatment for mental illness. Another 1000 or more of the patients at Bryce were mentally retarded rather than mentally ill. A totally inadequate staff, only a small percentage professionally trained, served these 5000 patients. The hospital employed only six staff members qualified to deal with mental patients—three medical doctors with psychiatric training, one Ph.D. psychologist, and two social workers with master's degrees in social work. The evidence indicated that the general living conditions and lack of individualized treatment programs were as intolerable and deplorable as Alabama's rank of fiftieth among the states in per patient expenditures would suggest.[34] For example, the hospital spent less than fifty cents per patient each day for food.[35]

The evidence concerning Partlow State School and Hospital for the retarded proved even more shocking than the evidence relating to the mental hospitals. The extremely dangerous conditions compelled the court to issue an interim emergency order[36] requiring Partlow officials to take immediate steps to protect the lives and safety of the residents. The Associate Commissioner for Mental Retardation for the Alabama Department of Mental Health testified that Partlow was 60 percent overcrowded; that the school, although it had not, could immediately discharge at least 300 residents; *and that 70 percent of the residents should never have been committed at all.*[37] The conclusion that there was no opportunity for habilitation for its residents was inescapable. Indeed, the evidence reflected that one resident was scalded to death when a fellow resident hosed water from one of the bath facilities on him; another died as a result of the insertion of a running water hose into his rectum by a working resident who was cleaning him; one died when soapy water was forced into his mouth; another died of a self-administered overdose of inadequately stored drugs; and authorities restrained another resident in a straitjacket for nine years to prevent him from sucking his hands and fingers. Witnesses described the Partlow facilities as barbaric and primitive;[38] some residents had no place to sit to eat meals, and coffee cans served as toilets in some areas of the institution.

With the exception of the interim emergency order designed to eliminate hazardous conditions at Partlow, the court at first declined to devise specific steps to improve existing conditions in Alabama's mental health and retardation facilities. Instead, it directed the Department of Mental Health to design its own plan for upgrading the system to meet constitutional standards.[39] Only after two deadlines had passed without any signs of acceptable progress did the court itself, relying upon the proposals of counsel for all parties and amici curiae, define the minimal constitutional standards of care, treatment, and habilitation[40] for which the case of *Wyatt v. Stickney* has become generally known.

During the past several years conditions at the Partlow State School for the retarded have improved markedly. It was pleasing to read in a Montgomery newspaper that members of the State Mental Health Board (the *Wyatt* defendants) recently met at Partlow and agreed that "what they saw was a different world" compared to four years ago; that "things are now unbelievably better," with most students "out in the sunshine on playground swings or tossing softballs[,] . . . responding to a kind word or touch with smiles and squeals of delight"; and that "enrollment has been nearly cut in half, down from 2,300 to just under 1,300 while the staff has tripled from 600 to 1,800."[41]

Persons incarcerated in state and local prison and jail facilities around the Nation increasingly have attacked the conditions of their confinement as unconstitutional. In recent years, federal courts in Alabama,[42] Arkansas,[43] Florida,[44] Maryland,[45] Massachusetts,[46] and Mississippi,[47] among others, have been forced to declare that the constitutional rights of inmates are denied by the mere fact of their confinement in institutions that inflict intolerable and inhuman living conditions. In Texas a federal judge has held unconstitutional the detention of juveniles in certain facilities maintained by the Texas Youth Council because of the extreme brutality and indifference experienced in these institutions.[48] In fashioning appropriate remedies in these cases, the courts have exhibited sensitivity to the real but not the imagined limitations imposed on correctional officials forced to operate penal facilities with the meager sums appropriated by legislators who see few or no political rewards in supporting constitutional treatment of prisoners. Some courts have ordered that entire institutions be closed and abandoned;[49] others have required substantial improvements in facilities and services as a precondition to their continued operation.[50]

Knowing firsthand the considerable time, energy, and thought that must precede any decision affecting mental hospital or prison conditions, I seriously doubt that any judge relishes his involvement in such a controversy or enters a decree unless the law clearly makes it his duty to do so. The Fifth Circuit adheres to the well-settled rule that federal courts do not sit to supervise state prisons or to interfere with their internal operation and administration.[51] The American system of justice, however, equally acknowledges that inmates do not lose all constitutional rights and privileges when they are confined following conviction of criminal offenses.[52]

James v. Wallace,[53] a recent class action tried before me objecting to conditions in Alabama's state penal facilities, presents another graphic example of how a state's irresponsibility in carrying out an essential governmental function necessitated federal judicial intervention to restore constitutional rights to citizens whose rights were systematically disregarded and denied. Preserving prisoners' rights is no less vital than safeguarding the liberties of school children, black citizens, women, and others who have found it necessary to resort to the courts to secure their constitutional rights.[54] The *James* trial began last August following extensive pretrial discovery, which included more than 1000 facts stipulated to by all parties and filed with the court. At the close of the defendants' case, the lead counsel for the Governor and the State Board of Corrections acknowledged in open court that "the overwhelming majority of the evidence . . . shows that an Eighth Amendment violation has and is now occurring to inmates in the Alabama prison system."[55]

Plaintiffs in *James* demonstrated the intolerability of life in Alabama's prisons by proof of both general living conditions and commonplace incidents. Fighting, assault, extortion, theft, and homosexual rape are everyday occurrences in all four main institutions. A mentally retarded twenty-year-old inmate, after testifying that doctors had told him he had the mind of a five-year-old, told in open court how four inmates raped him on his first night in an Alabama prison.[56]

The evidence showed that most prisoners found it necessary to carry some form of homemade or contraband weapon merely for self-protection. One prisoner testified that he would rather be caught with a weapon by a prison guard than be caught without one by another prisoner.[57] Seriously dilapidated physical facilities have created generally unsanitary and hazardous living conditions in Alabama's prisons. Roaches, flies, mosquitoes, and other vermin overrun the institutions. One living area in Draper prison housing over 200 men contained one functioning toilet.

A United States public health officer, testifying as an expert witness after having inspected the four major prisons, pronounced the facilities wholly unfit for human habitation according to virtually every criterion used for evaluation by public health inspectors. He testified that as a public health officer, he would recommend the closing of any similar facilities under his jurisdiction because they presented an imminent danger to the health of the exposed individuals.[58] Moreover, all the parties to the lawsuit agreed that severe overcrowding and understaffing aggravated all these other difficulties. At the time of trial over 3500 prisoners resided in facilities designed for no more than 2300. The Commissioner of the Alabama Board of Corrections testified that although the prison system required a minimum staff of 692 correctional officers, it then employed 383.[59] Correctional experts testified that such an overflow of prisoners, coupled with the shortage of supervisory personnel, precludes any meaningful control over the institutions by the responsible officials. The facts bore out that conclusion. Prison guards simply refused to enter some dormitories at night,[60] and one warden testified that he would not enter a certain dormitory at his institution without at least four guards by his side.

Understaffing and lack of funds have deprived nearly all the inmates who are confined twenty-four hours a day of meaningful activity; usually they lie around idle. Most live in dormitories or barracks that afford them neither privacy nor security for their personal possessions. The defendants stipulated that over half of the prison population possessed no skills, and that in the first quarter of 1975 the average entering inmate could not read at the sixth-grade level. The few vocational training and basic education programs offered can accommodate only a tiny fraction of the inmates, and the entry requirements for the programs are highly restrictive. Alabama prisons do not have a working classification system, an essential ingredient of any properly operated penal system. A functioning classification system enables officials to segregate for treatment and for the protection of other prisoners not able or willing to function in any social setting. Currently, mentally disturbed inmates receive no special care or therapy, and are housed and treated like the general prison population. Consequently, violent and aggressive prisoners live together with those who are weak, passive, or otherwise easily victimized. For example, when the twenty-year-old inmate I spoke of earlier reported the rape to prison officials, the warden of the institution told him that he, the warden, could do nothing about it.

Since the final order in *James*, news reports have revealed other instances of what at best constitute questionable management practices. A committee of the Alabama Legislature investigating prison operations disclosed that financial records reflect the use of prison funds to purchase cases of caviar, evidently consumed in the course of entertaining legislators.[61] The committee also questioned a recent transaction in which the Alabama Board of Corrections approved the bartering of fifty-two head of beef cattle owned by the Board in exchange for three Tennessee walking horses. The Commissioner of Corrections publicly explained that the horses were acquired for breeding purposes.[62] It later developed that the horses obtained for breeding purposes were geldings.[63]

Based on the overwhelming and generally undisputed evidence presented at trial, the court granted immediate partial relief to plaintiffs in the form of two interim orders,[64] which remain in effect. One order enjoined the State from accepting additional prisoners, except escapees and parole violators, until each State prison facility decreases its population to its design capacity. The second ruling banned the use of isolation and segregation cells that fail to meet minimum standards. Before this order, as many as six inmates were confined in four-by-eight foot cells with no beds, no lighting, no running water, and a hole in the floor for a toilet that only a guard outside could flush.

The final opinion and order entered in *James* in January 1976 established a broad range of minimum standards[65] designed to remedy the broad range of constitutional deprivations proven at trial and conceded to exist by the State's lawyers. The standards govern staffing; classification of prisoners; mental and physical health care; physical facilities; protection of inmates; and educational, vocational, recreational, and work programs.

The fourteenth amendment,[66] which generates much of the litigation discussed above, forbids a state to "deprive any person of life, liberty or property, without due process of law" or to "deny to any person within its jurisdiction the equal protection of the laws."[67] The Supreme Court has interpreted the due process clause to require that the states fulfill most of the obligations toward citizens that the Bill of Rights imposes on the federal government.[68] Each state in all its dealings with its people must recognize and preserve their guaranteed freedoms. Nevertheless, state officials have frequently raised the tenth amendment's reservation of powers to the states as a defense to the exercise of federal jurisdiction over actions alleging state violations of constitutional rights. While the tenth amendment clearly preserves for the states a wide and important sphere of power, it does not permit any state to frustrate or to ignore the mandates of the Constitution. *The tenth amendment does not relieve the states of a single obligation imposed upon them by the Constitution of the United States.* Surely the concept of states' rights has never purported to allow states to abdicate their responsibility to protect their citizens from criminal acts and inhumane conditions. I find it sad and ironic that citizens of Alabama held in "protective custody" by Alabama had to obtain federal court orders to protect themselves from violent crimes and barbaric conditions.

The cornerstone of our American legal system rests on recognition of the Constitution as the supreme law of the land,[69] and the paramount duty of the federal judiciary is to uphold that law.[70] Thus, when a state fails to meet constitutionally mandated requirements, it is the solemn duty of the courts to assure compliance with the Constitution. One writer has termed the habit adopted by some states of neglecting their responsibilities until faced with a federal court order "the Alabama Federal Intervention Syndrome," characterizing it as

the tendency of many state officials to punt their problems with constituencies to the federal courts. Many federal judges have grown accustomed to allowing state officials to make political speeches as a prelude to receiving the order of the district court. This role requires the federal courts to serve as a buffer between the state officials and their constituencies, raising the familiar criticism that state officials rely upon the federal courts to impose needed reforms rather than accomplishing them themselves.[71]

As long as those state officials entrusted with the responsibility for fair and equitable governance completely disregard that responsibility, the judiciary must and will stand ready to intervene on behalf of the deprived. Judge Richard T. Rives of the Court of Appeals for the Fifth Circuit, in joining a three-judge panel that struck down attempts by state officials to frustrate the registration of black voters, eloquently expressed the reluctance with which the vast majority of federal judges approach intervention in state affairs:

> I look forward to the day when the State and its political subdivisions will again take up their mantle of responsibility, treating all of their citizens equally, and thereby relieve the federal Government of the necessity of intervening in their affairs. Until that day arrives, the responsibility for this intervention must rest with those who through their ineptitude and public disservice have forced it.[72]

We in the judiciary await the day when the Alabama Federal Intervention Syndrome, in that State and elsewhere, will become a relic of the past. To reclaim responsibilities passed by default to the judiciary—most often the federal judiciary—and to find solutions for ever-changing challenges, the states must preserve their ability to respond flexibly, creatively, and with due regard for the rights of all. State officials must confront their governmental responsibilities with the diligence and honesty that their constituencies deserve. When lawful rights are being denied, only the exercise of conscientious, responsible leadership, which is usually long on work and short on complimentary news headlines, can avoid judicial intervention. The most fitting Bicentennial observance I can conceive would be for all government officials to take up the constitutional mantle and diligently strive to protect the basic human rights recognized by the founders of our Republic two hundred years ago.

The Role of the Judiciary with Respect to the Other Branches of Government

II Georgia Law Review 455 (1977)

The first part of this article is a historical description of the early attacks on and defenses of federal judicial power. Judge Johnson then reiterates that it is the duty of the federal courts to intervene in order to uphold and vindicate the constitutional rights of citizens when those rights are threatened by state action. There are restraints on the federal judicial power generally, however, such as the doctrine of separation of powers and the doctrine of "Our Federalism" which is incorporated into the Tenth Amendment. Johnson asserts his own notion of the Constitution as "dynamic and living, requiring constant reexamination and reevaluation." He rejects any doctrinal approach to interpreting the Constitution, preferring instead to decide cases solely on their particular facts. Once federal courts are called on to decide constitutional issues, they must then fashion relief that approximately remedies the constitutional violations shown. Johnson illustrates this process by discussing the case of Wyatt v. Stickney. *He concludes by asserting that what is often criticized as judicial activism is not really activism at all but the exercise of a fundamental duty of federal courts to decide constitutional issues properly before them (often because of state inaction).*

Johnson's commentary on the clash between Chief Justice John Marshall and the Virginia Supreme Court's Spencer Roane during the early nineteenth century showed that criticism of the federal judiciary in the 1960s and 1970s was not unprecedented. Moreover, Marshall's defense of the federal courts appealed to the same tradition of judicial independence that Johnson said also guided him. Thus Johnson's use of history helped the legal profession and the public to grasp that the federal judiciary's duty to defend constitutional rights was fundamental to the Constitution's very structure. The nature of rights claims may have changed over time, but the right to assert such claims in the federal courts was inherent in the system of checks and balances. Still, the unremitting assaults continued to have personal consequences for Johnson. In August 1977 President Jimmy Carter's U.S. attorney general, Griffin Bell, announced Johnson's nomination as FBI director.

Bell said that Johnson's reputation for integrity would improve the negative public image the organization had acquired in recent years. Accentuating the problem was the enormous popular distrust of their institutions the American public shared as a result of the Watergate crisis, President Richard Nixon's resignation, and the final defeat in the Vietnam War. But after the nomination, a routine physical examination revealed a swelling blood vessel in Johnson's abdomen. While the corrective surgical procedure was standard, the fact that the problem had implications for the heart heightened concern. The operation was a success, and within a month Johnson returned to work on the court; within the same period he withdrew his name from consideration for the FBI position. All this occurred beginning just six months after Johnson gave the John A. Sibley Lecture at the University of Georgia in February 1977. Within two years Johnson accepted when Carter nominated him to the U.S. Fifth Circuit Court of Appeals.

[*As some readers may not be familiar with Judge Johnson's background and the breadth of his decided opinions, the* Georgia Law Review *is pleased to reprint the remarks made by one of the Judge's former law clerks, now Assistant Professor at the University of Georgia School of Law, Charles R. McManis, in introducing Judge Johnson to the Sibley Lecture audience.*]

Introduction by Professor McManis

Frank M. Johnson Jr. is a native of Winston County, Alabama. That by itself explains a great deal about the man. To this day that hill country county is known as the "Free State of Winston" — commemorating its legendary decision to secede from Alabama when Alabama seceded from the union. Since that time the county has remained staunchly Republican in its voting habits.

Judge Johnson's own Republican antecedents were instrumental in his eventual appointment to the federal bench. After working his way through law school at the University of Alabama and serving as an infantry lieutenant in Patton's Army, where he won a Bronze Star in the Normandy invasion and was twice wounded, Judge Johnson returned home to private practice. He served as a campaign manager for General Eisenhower in 1952 and was appointed, at age 34, U.S. Attorney for the Northern District of Alabama. Two years later, in 1955, President Eisenhower appointed Frank M. Johnson to the United States District Court for the Middle District of Alabama — the youngest judge to have been appointed to the federal bench. Thus began what has become one of the most distinguished careers in the federal judiciary.

Hardly had the Judge assumed his new duties in Montgomery when he joined the three-judge court opinion in *Browder v. Gayle*,[1] which, at the height of the Montgomery bus boycott, ordered the city buses desegregated. This case was one of the first to extend the Supreme Court's decision in *Brown v. Board of Education*[2] beyond the desegregation of schools. Sensing what lay ahead, the Judge told his first law clerk, "Well, we got up on this horse, now we got to ride him." Ride him the Judge did.

With the *Browder* decision began a stream of cases applying the constitutional principle enunciated in *Brown v. Board of Education* to public parks, bus terminals, airports, public libraries and museums, penal institutions and mental health facilities. The Judge's desegregation opinions culminated in the sweeping decision in *Lee v. Macon County Board of Education*[3] in 1968. The court, in the face of repeated efforts by the Governor of Alabama to thwart the court's desegregation orders, found that the state itself controlled the public schools in Alabama, and it ordered immediate state-wide desegregation of the schools. Thereafter, the Judge presided over the desegregation of over 100 school systems in Alabama.

Closely linked with the decisions desegregating public schools and public accommodations were the decisions assuring equal access to the ballot box. In one of his earliest confrontations with a former law school classmate, Judge Johnson ordered then circuit judge Wallace to hand over to the United States Civil Rights Commission certain voting records which Wallace had sequestered to thwart an investigation of discriminatory voter registration.[4] There began a long series of voter registration cases which ultimately required boards of registrars to register any black whose qualification equaled those of the least qualified white.[5] Called the "freeze doctrine," it became the Fifth Circuit's standard formula in voting cases[6] and was substantially incorporated into the Voting Rights Act of 1965.[7]

Perhaps the most dramatic example of the Judge's protection of the right to vote and its associated political freedoms came in 1965 when the Judge enjoined Governor Wallace from interfering in the famous Selma-to-Montgomery march,[8] the political demonstration which ultimately provided the impetus for the passage of the Voting Rights Act of 1965. He also presided over the trial of three Klansmen who in the aftermath of his order gunned down Viola Liuzzo as she returned to Selma from Montgomery. Notwithstanding the highly charged racial climate which resulted in an earlier acquittal on murder charges in state court and despite eyewitness testimony, the Judge so inspired the jury with a sense of responsibility that after twenty-seven hours of deliberation they returned a verdict of guilty against three defendants for having violated Viola Liuzzo's civil rights.

In addition to assuring equal access to the ballot box, the Judge was instrumental in ensuring that the vote of each individual carries equal weight. He participated in the famous three-judge court decision,[9] affirmed by the Supreme Court in 1964 under the name of *Reynolds v. Sims*,[10] that resulted in the first court-ordered reapportionment of a state legislature in U.S. history.

Indeed, the second decade of his judgeship has been marked by an increasing number of decisions vindicating a wide variety of constitutional rights by innovative use of the remedial authority of the federal court. In 1966, for example, the Judge enjoined the exclusion of women from juries in Alabama state courts.[11] In 1971, he dissented in a three-judge court case which found no sex discrimination in the disparate treatment accorded to dependents of female members of the armed services.[12] Reversing the majority by an 8-to-1 vote, the Supreme Court, in *Frontiero v. Richardson*,[13] followed closely the reasoning in Judge Johnson's original dissent.

In *NAACP v. Allen*[14] the Judge found a blatant and continuing pattern and practice of discrimination in the hiring of Alabama State Troopers and ordered that Troopers hire one qualified black for every white recruit until the force was approximately 25 percent black. Two years later it was.

In *Wyatt v. Stickney*,[15] the Judge took what the *Harvard Law Review* described as the most extensive action to date in defining and enforcing the constitutional right of civilly committed mental patients to receive adequate treatment.[16] To enforce his order, the Judge appointed a Human Rights Committee of Alabama citizens to monitor compliance.

In *Newman v. Alabama*,[17] the Judge held that state prisoners throughout the Alabama penal system had been deprived of their right to adequate medical treatment and entered a detailed order requiring that specific deficiencies be corrected. Just last year, in *James v. Wallace*,[18] the Judge extended his decree to the entire operation of the Alabama penal system, finding that the gross over-crowding and other inhumane conditions, revealed in undisputed evidence, constituted cruel and unusual punishment in violation of the eighth amendment. Again he appointed a Human Rights Committee.

While the Judge is best known for his decisions in civil rights cases, they are only a small percentage of his total caseload. Indeed, one aspect of his judicial career is that over the years the Middle District of Alabama has served as a model of efficient judicial administration. The year I clerked for the Judge, for example, the Middle District of Alabama ranked first in the nation in the speed with which it disposed of civil cases. The median elapsed time from filing of the complaint to final disposition of a civil case that year was four months, and in criminal cases the time was less than three months. This was accomplished even though the weighted workload per judge was over forty cases greater than the national average. As Chief Judge, Judge Johnson takes seriously the maxim that justice delayed is justice denied. As one lawyer remarked, "When you appear in Judge Johnson's court, you'd better be wearing your track shorts."

Efficiency, however, is not achieved at the expense of justice. In Judge Johnson's court, day-in and day-out, the law is applied in the small, routine cases with the same care and fairness as in the landmark cases. Whatever the subject matter of the litigation, he displays an uncanny ability to cut through to the heart of the issue. His intolerance of sloppy lawyering in the courtroom is exceeded only by the patience and dignity he accords jurors, witnesses, and litigants. Indeed, one senses that he views the courtroom as his principal forum for instilling in all those who enter there a renewed respect for the law.

And so I welcome him to this forum and commend him to you with the words of the late Dr. King, who said of Judge Johnson, "He gives true meaning to the word Justice."

The Sibley Lecture

I. INTRODUCTION

"Of all the tyrannies that afflict mankind, that of the Judiciary is the most insidious, the most intolerable, the most dangerous."[19] That statement was not made by the President of the John Birch Society or by the Grand Dragon of the K.K.K., but was the New York Tribune's editorial response to the decision of Chief Justice Taney of the Supreme Court of the United States, sitting as a Circuit Judge, in 1861 that affirmed the right to habeas corpus.

This 1861 criticism of the federal judiciary was nothing new. It had erupted from time to time since shortly after the adoption of the Constitution when the Supreme Court rendered the decision of Marbury v. Madison,[20] in which Chief Justice Marshall announced the court's power to pass on the constitutionality of congressional enactments. The Marbury decision was severely criticized by

President Jefferson, other prominent politicians, and the press.[21] But these attacks upon the judicial branch were mild when compared with the furor that arose after the decision of *McCulloch v. Maryland*[22] in 1819.

The first attacks on the *McCulloch* decision were made in a series of newspaper essays signed by "Amphictyon." The Amphictyon Essays have traditionally been ascribed to Spencer Roane, Chief Justice of Virginia's highest appellate court.[23] These essays attacked the United States Supreme Court, claiming the Court was usurping control over certain areas of American life. Amphictyon felt control of those areas of life should remain the sole responsibility of the state legislatures, stating that if the *McCulloch* decision were allowed to stand,

> the powers of the federal government would be enlarged so much by the force of implication as to sweep off every vestige of power from the state governments. . . . To counteract that irresistible tendency in the federal government to enlarge their own dominion, the vigilance of the people and state governments should constantly be exerted.[24]

Amphictyon then asked why the federal government should

> grasp at powers not necessary for carrying into effect their acknowledged powers? why should they trench upon those interior measures which are reserved by the states for their own regulation and control? why should they so eagerly, year after year, and session after session, encroach on state rights, and make one encroachment a precedent for another? or why should they assume even doubtful powers, when they are vested with so many undoubted powers perfectly adequate for all their legitimate purposes?[25]

Chief Justice John Marshall worried about Amphictyon's attack on the Court's decision and expressed his concern to Associate Justice Bushrod Washington: "The storm which has been for some time threatening the Judges has at length burst on their heads and a most furious hurricane it is . . . I believe the design to be to injure judges and impair the constitution. I have, therefore, thoughts of answering these essays. . . ."[26]

Chief Justice Marshall answered in a series of essays under the pen name "A Friend to the Union," and refuted the charges made by Amphictyon. Additionally, Marshall asserted that the judiciary was subject to vicious attacks because

> the Judges . . . [are] separated from the people by the tenure of office, by age, and by the nature of their duties. . . . They have no sops to give; and every coffeehouse furnishes a Cerberus, hoping some reward for that watchfulness

which his bark proclaims; and restrained by no apprehension that any can be stimulated by personal considerations to expose the injustice of his attacks.[27]

As a result of the "Friend to the Union" essay, Spencer Roane felt forced to personally lead the attack against the federal judiciary. Roane, in his "Hampden" essays, bitterly attacked the Supreme Court and the principles enunciated in *McCulloch*. Roane contended that judicial power historically has

> only invaded the constitution in the worst of times, and then, always, on the side of arbitrary power. . . .
>   . . . [T]his opinion of the court, in so far as it outgoes the actual case depending before it, and so far as it established a *general* and *abstract* doctrine, was entirely extrajudicial, and without authority. . . .
>   . . . The crisis [which this case created] is one which portends destruction to the liberties of the American people.[28]

Roane then concluded:

> It is not denied but that the judiciary of this country is in the daily habit of far outgoing that of any other. It often puts its veto upon the acts of the immediate representatives of the people. It in fact assumes legislative powers, by repealing laws which a legislature have enacted. . . . It claims the right, in effect, to change the government. . . .
>
>   . . . [T]he Supreme Court has, without authority, and in the teeth of great principles, created itself the *exclusive* judge in this controversy.[29]

The *Richmond Enquirer* joined "Hampden's" expression of fear, stating, "We solemnly believe the opinion of the Supreme Court in the case of the bank to be fraught with alarming consequences, the federal constitution to be misinterpreted, and the rights of the states and the people to be threatened with danger."[30]

During the past two decades federal judges have again come under attack by politicians and various special interest groups. Members of Congress have attempted to limit federal court jurisdiction in the civil and human rights areas. State legislatures have called for a constitutional convention to nullify the results reached in *Baker v. Carr*.[31]

I submit to you that the attacks now being made are not based upon any new concepts or theories, but are in substance the same as those that have been made since the adoption of the Constitution. Furthermore, I would suggest that in many instances the individuals and groups making the most vocal attacks against the courts are those who have forced the courts to take positive action in the first place.

The renewal of criticism is prompted by the fact that the past several decades have been extremely active and dynamic ones for the federal judiciary in the area of constitutional law. The general citizenry, demonstrating a new awareness of rights or increasingly affected by government controls and dependent upon government programs and services, has looked more and more to the federal courts for the guarantee of rights or for protection against unconstitutional conduct on the part of the states and federal executive and legislative branches. The organized Bar has, in the finest tradition of the legal profession, repeatedly called upon the federal courts to extend and expand to all groups and persons in our society the freedoms and protections afforded by the Constitution. True to its constitutional imperative, the federal judiciary has responded cautiously but unwaveringly, adjudicating and upholding the rights of, among many others, black persons and women to equal educational and employment opportunities;[32] the involuntarily committed mentally ill to minimum care and treatment;[33] and incarcerated offenders to a safe and decent environment.[34]

Involving, as they do, judicial review of legislative and executive action and resolution of oft-times complex and controversial issues, it is not surprising that these constitutional adjudications have generated much discussion and debate among both lawyers and laymen. While the discussion among lay persons, especially among members of the executive and legislative branches of government, has been more graphic and glandular and perhaps, therefore, more entertaining, it is a more serious and scholarly debate, recently rekindled among lawyers and legal commentators, which I have selected as the subject of my lecture here today. This debate, both sides of which have merit, centers on the proper role and function of the federal judiciary with respect to the other branches of government.

II. RESOLVING THE CONSTITUTIONAL ISSUES

The power of the federal judiciary to review and to decide matters involving the legislative and executive branches of government is circumscribed by two basic constitutional doctrines. The first, the doctrine of separation of powers, reflects the deeply held belief of our founding fathers that the powers of government should be separate and distinct, with the executive, the legislative, and the judicial departments being independent and coordinate branches of government. It is this doctrine which is responsible, in great part, for the creation and maintenance of the federal courts as courts of only limited jurisdiction.

The second doctrine, which also reflects the founding fathers' distrust of centralized government, is commonly referred to as "Our Federalism." This doctrine, incorporated in the tenth amendment to the Constitution, restricts the power of the federal courts to intercede in the functions and affairs of the states and their political subdivisions.

In deference to these constitutional doctrines, the federal courts have traditionally been reluctant to intervene in the affairs and activities of the other branches of government. Such self-imposed restraints as the "case and controversy" doctrine, the "political question" doctrine, and the abstention doctrine attest to the judiciary's recognition of and respect for these venerable principles.

Yet, these doctrines serve only to restrain, not to interdict, the exercise of judicial power. The authors of the Constitution never intended for these or any other doctrines to render impotent the power of the federal judiciary to restrain unconstitutional action on the part of governmental institutions. Had they, in fact, desired to insulate governmental conduct from judicial scrutiny, the founding fathers would have adopted a constitution modeled after the Articles of Confederation, which document vested all judicial authority in the legislative branch of government.[35]

Instead, the founding fathers prudently and discerningly perceived that the survival of our republican form of government depended on the supremacy of the Constitution and that maintaining the supremacy of the Constitution depended, in turn, on a strong and independent judiciary, possessing the power and the authority to resolve disputes of a constitutional nature between the states, between the states and the national government, and, most importantly, between individuals and governmental institutions. These crucial features of our form of government are embraced in Article VI, Section 2, of the Constitution, which establishes the Constitution as the supreme law of the land; and in Article III, Section 2, of the Constitution, which extends to the federal courts jurisdiction over all cases arising under our Constitution and laws.

In granting to the federal judiciary the power to decide cases arising under our Constitution and laws, the framers of the Constitution fully recognized that the exercise of such power would inevitably thrust the courts into the political arena. In fact, as the writings of the founding fathers illustrate, this grant of power was, in effect, a mandate to the federal courts to check and to restrain any infringement by the legislative and executive branches on the supremacy of the Constitution. James Madison, in cautioning his colleagues that the protections afforded by the Bill of Rights would be hollow without a judiciary to uphold them, referred to the federal judiciary as "an impenetrable bulwark against every assumption of power in the legislative or executive; [the courts] will be naturally led to resist every encroachment upon [the Bill of] rights. . . ."[36]

Thus, the judiciary's role as defender of the Bill of Rights and its occasional intrusion in the affairs of the legislative and executive branches of government result not from an arrogation of power but from compliance with a constitutional mandate. Those who criticize the federal courts for this occasional intrusion fail to recognize that, in the words of the French historian Alexis de Tocqueville:

> [T]he American Judge is brought into the political arena independently of his own will. He judges the law only because he is obliged to judge a case. The political question that he is called upon to resolve is connected with the interests of the parties, and he cannot refuse to decide it without a denial of justice.[37]

Nor did the founding fathers fail to recognize that the exercise of this power by the judiciary would, at times, create strains and tensions between the federal courts and the executive and legislative branches at the national level and between these courts and the various governmental institutions at the state and local levels. It was their sound and reasoned judgment, however, that the need to maintain the supremacy and integrity of the Constitution far outweighed any disadvantages resulting from this grant of power. The wisdom and correctness of this decision, attested to by the ability of our nation to survive each constitutional crisis which has arisen and by the strength and stability of our form of government over the past 200 years, is reflected in this observation by de Tocqueville:

> The peace, the prosperity and the very existence of the Union are vested in the hands of the seven Federal judges. Without them the Constitution would be a dead letter: the executive appeals to them for assistance against the encroachments of the legislative powers; the legislature demands their protection against the assaults of the executive; they defend the Union from the disobedience of the states, the states from the exaggerated claims of the Union, the public interest against private interests. . . .[38]

And, it should be added, the interests of private citizens against government.

With the framers of the Constitution thus having clearly bestowed upon the federal courts the power to review and to decide cases arising under our Constitution and laws, the issue arises "how and under what circumstances should this power be exercised?"

The function of the judiciary is "to find the law and pronounce it." This now classic statement by Blackstone is often quoted by those who perceive the role of the judge as primarily a passive one. Easier to quote, however, than apply, Blackstone's model has provided little guidance to the federal courts with respect to adjudicating cases arising under the Constitution.

Blackstone's model necessarily assumes that the law which the judge is to "find and pronounce" is clear and well defined. Yet, the rights and freedoms enumerated in the Constitution are expressed in only the most broad and general terms. Speaking about the role of the judge in deciding constitutional questions, Judge Learned Hand observed that "[t]he words [the judge] must construe are empty vessels into which he can pour nearly anything at will."[39] Is the sixth amendment right to public trial absolute? Or may the government impose limitations on this right? And, if so, when and to what degree?[40] Does a prohibition of the use of birth control devices violate the first amendment, or the fifth amendment, or the ninth amendment?[41] While each person is entitled to due process of law, exactly how much process is each person due? These examples suffice to show that the Constitution, consisting of just 5,000 words, only roughly defines the contours of the rights and powers contained therein.

Nor is Blackstone's prototype of the totally objective and passive judge a realistic or necessarily desirable one. While no judge should ignore binding precedent or decide a case on personal whim or predilection, there is both a propriety and inevitability of a personal element present in the decision of disputed constitutional issues. As Justice Cardozo acknowledged, "[w]e may try to see things as objectively as we please. Nonetheless, we can never see them with any eyes except our own."[42]

That Blackstone's model is neither a satisfactory nor a viable one, that it has, in fact, been more honored in its breach than in its observance, is tellingly shown by the inability of even its most vocal and ardent judicial supporters to apply the doctrine with any consistency. Justice Brandeis, while expressing doubt whether the due process clause should have been extended to the protection of civil liberties, fathered the "right to privacy."[43] Justice Black, while criticizing his associates in *Griswold v. Connecticut*[44] for establishing a right not expressly provided for in the Constitution, could and did author an opinion requiring the states to appoint free counsel to indigents though at the time of the adoption of the Constitution there was no such requirement.[45]

In his dissent in *Baker v. Carr*,[46] Justice Frankfurter presented this eloquent defense of the doctrine of judicial restraint:

[T]here is not under our Constitution a judicial remedy for every political mischief, for every undesirable exercise of legislative power. . . . In a democratic society like ours, relief must come through an aroused popular conscience that sears the conscience of the people's representatives.[47]

Yet, just several years before, Justice Frankfurter had authored an opinion invalidating the conviction of a narcotics dealer because the conduct of the police, in pumping morphine capsules from the man's stomach, was, in his opinion, "conduct that shocks the conscience" of the court.[48] This ruling evoked from Justice Black the statement that Justice Frankfurter was more likely to rule on his notion of right and wrong than he was, for he [Justice Frankfurter] claims "the right to knock down anything under the due process clause that, 'shocks the judicial conscience.'"[49] Nor can Justice Frankfurter's strong effort to bring about a unanimous decision in *Brown v. Board of Education,*[50] a decision which has had the most profound impact on our society of any court ruling this century, be squared with a philosophy of judicial restraint. The following excerpt written by Justice Frankfurter during the Court's deliberations in *Brown v. Board of Education* is, in fact, a compelling endorsement for the judicial activist position:

> But the equality of laws enshrined in a constitution which was "made for an undefined and expanding future, and for a people gathered and to be gathered from many nations and many tongues," . . . is not a fixed formula defined with finality at a particular time. It does not reflect, as a congealed summary, the social arrangements and beliefs of a particular epoch. Law must respond to transformation of views. . . . The effect of changes in men's feelings for what is right and just is equally relevant in determining whether a discrimination denies the equal protection of the laws.[51]

These tests and models are, therefore, somewhat illusory. They are premised on a number of faulty and unwarranted assumptions about the Constitution, about judges, and about the judicial process itself. The Constitution is not an inert and lifeless body of law from which legal consequences automatically flow. To the contrary, it is dynamic and living, requiring constant reexamination and reevaluation. As the Supreme Court's decisions in *Dred Scott,*[52] *Plessy v. Ferguson,*[53] and *Brown v. Board of Education*[54] make clear, the doctrine of stare decisis may be totally inappropriate with regard to decisions based upon constitutional questions. The true strength of the Constitution lies in its flexibility, its ability to change, to grow and to respond to the special needs and demands of our society at a particular time.

Thus, any doctrinal approach to interpreting the Constitution, at whichever extreme, is both inappropriate and unworkable. Adjudication of constitutional issues requires an openness of mind and a willingness to decide the issues solely on the particular facts and circumstances involved, not with any preconceived notion or philosophy regarding the outcome of the case. While a refusal to show proper deference to and respect for the acts and decisions of the coordinate branches of government is judicial intrusion and is, therefore, improper, a blind and unyielding deference to legislative and executive action is judicial abdication and is equally to be condemned.

The role of the federal courts in deciding constitutional questions is and always has been an activist one. It is not a role which has been usurped by the judiciary, however, but is one which is inextricably intertwined with its duty to interpret the Constitution. The federal courts have never acted directly on the states or assumed jurisdiction of mere political issues, but in cases involving individual rights and liberties, these courts are compelled to construe the law in order to determine such rights and liabilities. As Chief Justice Marshall so eloquently expressed in responding to congressional attempts to take away the Supreme Court's power to review state supreme court decisions involving constitutional issues, "As this Court has never grasped at ungranted jurisdiction, so will it never, we trust, shrink from the exercise of that which is conferred upon it."[55]

In describing the role of the federal judiciary in deciding constitutional issues, I ascribe no particular political or social philosophy to the word "activist." Justice Sutherland, a staunch conservative on the Court, was no more nor no less "activist" in striking down social legislation and upholding governmental regulation of first amendment rights than Justice Black was in upholding social legislation and invalidating state regulation of first amendment rights. The "activism" I refer to is measured not only by the end result but by how and under what circumstances the result is achieved.

III. FASHIONING APPROPRIATE RELIEF

Once having decided the issues, the court must concern itself with the second and final phase of the adjudicatory process — the formulation and entry of an appropriate decree. If the evidence fails to disclose a constitutional violation, or if the evidence discloses a constitutional violation which can effectively be remedied by an award of damages or the issuance of a prohibitory injunction, the court's role is a limited one terminating upon entry of the decree. If the constitutional or statutory violation is one, however, which can be adequately remedied only by the issuance of a decree providing for affirmative, ongoing relief, the court's involvement is necessarily enlarged and prolonged. The federal judiciary finds itself today increasingly called upon to fashion and to render this latter type of decree. This trend, I assure you, results not from the judiciary's masochistic yearning for hard work, but from several relatively recent developments in the law.

The most significant procedural change has been the adoption and promulgation by Congress and the courts of liberalized standing and joinder requirements. Under code pleading, for example, litigation involved but two individuals or at least two competing interests, diametrically opposed, with the winner taking all. Today, however, there are often competing, if not conflicting, interests among members of the same class, among different classes, and among parties and intervenors. This has made the task of formulating appropriate relief an increasingly complex and difficult one.

A significant development in the substantive area has been the shift in subject matter from business and economic issues to social issues. During the latter part of the nineteenth century and the first half of this century, the major focus in the area of constitutional law was on the power of Congress and the states to enact statutes regulating and restricting private businesses and property. The constitutional theory most frequently advanced was substantive due process. Since only property rights were at stake, an award of damages to compensate the litigant for any economic loss and the issuance of a prohibitory injunction to restrain the operation of the statute provided the litigant with all the relief to which he was entitled.

During the past several decades, however, there have been in our society a growing awareness of and concern for the rights and freedoms of the individual. This awareness and this concern are reflected in the steady shift in emphasis in constitutional litigation from property rights to individual rights. Congress has enacted social welfare statutes in such areas as education, voting, consumer protection, and environmental protection. Speaking through enactments, Congress has made clear its desire that freedom, justice, and equality become a reality to and for all Americans. In many instances the responsibility for seeing that this salutary goal is accomplished lies with the federal judiciary.

The traditional forms of relief—an award of damages and the issuance of a prohibitory injunction—while adequate to remedy most constitutional violations of a business or economic nature, are but ingredients in remedying constitutional statutory violations of a personal and social nature. The prisoner, who lives in constant fear for his life and safety because of inadequate staffing and overcrowded conditions, will not have his rights protected merely by an award of damages for the past injury sustained by him. If we, as judges, have learned anything from *Brown v. Board of Education* and its progeny, it is that prohibitory relief alone affords but a hollow protection to the basic and fundamental rights of citizens to equal protection of the law.

Once a constitutional deprivation has been shown, it becomes the duty of the court to render a decree which will as far as possible eliminate the effects of the past deprivations as well as bar like deprivations in the future. Because of the complexity and nature of the constitutional rights and issues involved, the traditional forms of relief have proven totally inadequate and the courts have been left with two alternatives. They could throw up their hands in frustration and claim that, although the litigants have established a violation of constitutional or statutory rights, the courts have no satisfactory relief to grant them. This would, in addition to constituting judicial abdication, make a mockery of the Bill of Rights. Utilizing their equitable powers, the federal courts have pursued the only reasonable and constitutionally acceptable alternative — fashioning relief to fit the necessities of the particular case.

With the acknowledgment that they are professionally trained in the law, not in penology, medicine, or education, the federal courts have approached these areas cautiously and hesitatingly. Further recognizing that many of the issues they are being asked to decide call for sensitive social and political policy judgments, the courts have shown great deference to those charged with making these judgments and have intervened only when a constitutional or statutory violation has clearly and convincingly been established.

Nor have the courts attempted to enter these often murky and uncharted waters without navigational aids. In addition to evidence from experts, the parties, intervenors, and amici are invited to submit their recommendations and suggestions, usually in the form of proposed plans. This process, in addition to minimizing the need for judicial resolution of many of the remedial issues, increases the likelihood of voluntary compliance by the parties with the decree eventually adopted and entered by the court. The courts have also turned to outside sources for advice and assistance. Biracial committees are, for example, now routinely required in school desegregation decisions in the Fifth Circuit.[56] In addition to putting forward their own remedial suggestions, these outside groups can and do play an invaluable role in implementing and, if necessary, monitoring the decree.

So that I might hopefully illustrate why these comprehensive remedial decrees are often necessary and how they are shaped and fashioned, I would like briefly to go over with you the case of *Wyatt v. Stickney*,[57] decided by me several years ago. Let me caution that this case is not used as a perfect model, but it has been reviewed and approved by the United States Circuit Court of Appeals for the Fifth Circuit.

Wyatt v. Stickney was a class action lawsuit filed on behalf of all patients involuntarily confined at Bryce Hospital, Alabama's largest mental hospital, to determine whether and to what extent they were constitutionally entitled to minimum standards of care and treatment. Patients at Searcy Hospital in South Alabama and residents at the Partlow State School and Hospital for the retarded were subsequently added as plaintiffs.

Resolution of these important constitutional issues necessitated a detailed and thorough examination of the state's entire mental health and retardation treatment and habilitation program. Because of the nature and scope of this inquiry and my little expertise in mental health and mental retardation areas, I solicited and was given assistance and advice from a number of outside sources. The United States of America (acting through the Department of Justice), the American Civil Liberties Union, and the National Mental Health Law Project were each allowed to intervene with full rights of a party. The leading experts in the country were called by the parties to testify and make recommendations.

The evidence presented at trial showed that Bryce Hospital, built in the 1850's, was grossly overcrowded, housing over 5,000 patients. Of these persons ostensibly committed to Bryce Hospital for treatment of mental illness, about 1,600 — or approximately one-third — were geriatrics neither in need of nor receiving any treatment for mental illness. Another 1,000 or more of those confined at Bryce Hospital were mentally retarded rather than mentally ill. To serve these 5,000 patients, there was a totally inadequate staff, only a small percentage of whom were professionally trained. There were only three medical doctors with psychiatric training, one Ph.D. psychologist, and two social workers having masters degrees in social work. The evidence indicated that the general living conditions and lack of individualized treatment programs were as intolerable and deplorable as the state's ranking of 50th among the states in annual per patient expenditures would suggest. For example, less than fifty cents was spent per patient each day for food.

The evidence concerning Partlow State School and Hospital for the retarded was, if anything, even more dramatic than the evidence relating to the mental hospitals. According to the testimony of the Associate Commissioner for Mental Retardation for the Alabama Department of Mental Health, Partlow was 60 percent overcrowded; he also testified that at least 300 residents could be discharged immediately, although the school had not undertaken to do so, *and that 70 percent of the residents should never have been committed at all.* The conclusion that there was no opportunity for habilitation for its residents was inescapable.

As I have previously emphasized here today, courts should not intervene in the affairs and activities of the coordinate branches of government without a clear showing of a constitutional violation. I submit to each of you that in *Wyatt* such a showing was made. As I held at that time:

> There can be no legal (or moral) justification for the State of Alabama's failing to afford treatment — and adequate treatment from a medical standpoint — to the several thousand patients who have been civilly committed to

Bryce's for treatment purposes. To deprive any citizen of his or her liberty upon the altruistic theory that the confinement is for humane therapeutic reasons and then fail to provide adequate treatment violates the very fundamentals of due process.[58]

Having found a constitutional violation, it then became necessary for me to formulate and render an appropriate decree. Clearly, monetary relief was not an appropriate remedy, nor would the mere issuance of an injunctive order restraining future constitutional violations suffice. The only constitutionally acceptable way to remedy the conditions existing in the state's mental health and mental retardation facilities was to issue a comprehensive remedial order.

The first stage was the submission by the parties and amici of proposed plans for bringing the system up to constitutional standards. It was only after two deadlines had passed during which acceptable progress had not been forthcoming that the court itself, relying upon the proposals submitted, set forth the minimal constitutional standards of care, treatment, and habilitation for which the case of *Wyatt v. Stickney* is generally known.

Since the decree was one of an ongoing nature, human rights panels, comprised of individuals from all walks of life, were created to assist in implementing and monitoring the decree at each of the institutions. These panels, acting solely in an advisory capacity, have been of immeasurable assistance to both the various institutions and myself.

I should like to state that the conditions, while still not perfect, have improved dramatically in each of the institutions. The population at each facility has been reduced by approximately 50 percent, while staff has at least doubled at most institutions. A not altogether unexpected benefit resulting from the public exposure given the problem has been a substantial increase in legislative appropriations for the state's mental health system.

IV. CONCLUSION

I would again observe that, in an ideal society, all of these judgments and decisions should be made, in the first instance, by those to whom we have entrusted these responsibilities. It must be emphasized, however, that when governmental institutions fail to make these judgments and decisions in a manner which comports with the Constitution, the federal courts have a duty to remedy the violation.

In summary, it is my firm belief that the judicial activism which has generated so much criticism is, in most instances, not activism at all. Courts do not relish making such hard decisions and certainly do not encourage litigation on social or political problems. But, I repeat, the federal judiciary in this country has the paramount and the continuing duty to uphold the law. When a "case or controversy" is properly presented, the court may not shirk its sworn responsibility to uphold the Constitution and laws of the United States. The courts are bound to take jurisdiction and decide the issues — even though those decisions result in criticism. The basic strength of the federal judiciary has been — and continues to be — its independence from political or social pressures, its ability to rise above the influence of popular clamor. And, finally, I submit that history has shown, with few exceptions, that decisions of the federal judiciary over a period of time have become accepted and revered as monuments memorializing the strength and stability of this nation.

Equal Access to Justice

41 Alabama Law Review 1 (1989)

Johnson explains that constitutional guarantees of individual rights have little value without the means to enforce them. Accordingly, rights are real only if people truly have access to the legislative process and the courts. Equal access then makes law the primary alternative to force; it also prevents law from becoming a source of alienation for those who otherwise would have no voice. Johnson contrasts this American constitutional order with totalitarian regimes whose constitutions possess the forms but not the substance of rights. In Alabama confrontations from the 1950s to the 1970s suggested, however, that African Americans and women did not achieve equal access without protracted struggle and the intervention of the federal courts. These conflicts, in turn, established procedural remedies fostering a still wider vindication of rights claims throughout the state's mental health and prison systems. Meanwhile, the federal judiciary and Congress instituted fee-shifting principles that gave lawyers incentives to represent indigent, minority, small claim, and female clients. Finally, Johnson warns that expanded access cannot be maintained without a continuing commitment from the American people and government.

When Johnson delivered this address on March 31, 1989, his affirmation of constitutional ideals repeated during decades of struggle seemed vindicated. Wallace left the governor's office for the last time at the end of 1987. By then, he publicly acknowledged that he had erred in defying the rights claims that had driven so many individuals and groups to seek redress before federal judges like Johnson. Wallace and other political leaders, either publicly or privately, apologized to Johnson for their conduct. Meanwhile, wherever the federal judiciary had intervened throughout Alabama society, conditions were qualitatively better than they had been before judicial action. Nevertheless, while the state's leaders no longer formally resisted constitutional rights and the improved social conditions that resulted from judicial sanction, they declined to take political responsibility for public school desegregation, maintaining more humane conditions in mental health institutions and prisons, defending racial justice, or even correcting on an ongoing basis evils arising from legislative malapportionment. In every case, rather than subject themselves to the risks of democratic accountability,

Alabama's political leaders found it easier to shift the constitutional obligation and blame to unelected federal judges. Thus it was clear that without continuing federal judicial intervention in these areas, Alabama's democratically chosen representatives had no incentive to act. This reality gave increased credibility to Johnson's assertion that judicial access was essential to the preservation of social order because it provided an outlet to those whose legitimate needs and interests were otherwise ignored by the majority's popularly elected leaders.

I thank you for inviting me here to speak as part of this year's Law Day celebration. The President has declared the theme of this year's Law Day to be "Equal Access to Justice." The substance of this theme is carved in the granite over the great steps at the entrance to the beautiful building in Washington that houses the United States Supreme Court—"Equal Justice Under Law." Legend has it that when the building was near completion the architect chose the words because the length of the phrase fit the space available on the front of the building. However, research has revealed that Chief Justice Hughes was responsible for the inscription. I will endeavor to stay within the thematic boundaries posed by this text.

Specifically, I would like to concentrate on the concept of *access.* The more abstract notions of equality and justice make fine subjects for speechmaking, but these high-minded words may provide little comfort to those denied a practical means for the implementation of those ideals. Without access to the legal process, our most important rights become unenforceable and positive social change becomes practically impossible. Access is the byword for the possibility of translating public expression into legal action.

I. Introduction

One introduction I would like to give to the concept of equal access is illustrated by a conversation I had with one of my law clerks several months ago. We were discussing the aftermath of the decision in the Montgomery bus desegregation case, and I mentioned to him that I had found it necessary to assign one of my law clerks at that time to do nothing but answer the telephone. That clerk spent more than a week dealing with calls from irate, frustrated, and sometimes abusive citizens. On occasion, he would try to explain the law, but mostly he listened and provided an outlet for their anger. My present clerk's reaction was to bemoan the waste of precious time which could have been spent on legal work. My own reaction was quite different. That clerk was providing a crucial service. Although

I did not share the legal views of the angry citizens who called, they experienced a need. It was for that phone to be answered! I certainly do not encourage people to ring up the courthouse and rail at the judiciary. But how much better an angry phone call than violence in the streets?

This is a story about access in its crudest form. We usually conceive of more noble forms of invoking justice — for example, the lengthy and well-orchestrated class action which forces a government into compliance with the Constitution. But at its most basic level, access is about providing a mechanism for popular expression. The mechanism may be as simple as an answered telephone; the expression may be as distasteful as a segregationist slogan.

I think the story is also appropriate to illustrate the point that equality of access to justice does not mean an equal right to impose a particular view on society. Although the Constitution guarantees that all groups have a voice, it is obvious that not all groups can or should be able to see their will translated into law. This country is simply too diverse. The concept of majoritarian rule by its nature includes a minority which disagrees to a greater or lesser extent with the way things are done by the majority. However, in our system all groups have an equal right to have their grievances heard and an equal opportunity to have the law enforced. This is crucial because in a constitutional scheme the will of the majority is not always the law. The views expressed to my beleaguered law clerk did not carry the day. But they were heard — not only over the phone, but in court. The same access to the legal process which worked such change in the social fabric of the South also permitted the forceful expression against that change.

Both faces of access work the orderly sort of social evolution contemplated by the Constitution. Although I am not a particularly great admirer of members of the so-called critical legal studies movement, they have made at least one contribution to our understanding of law. That is, law can become a vehicle for alienation if the people directly affected by its dictates do not have a voice.[1] Procedural due process assures this voice, and participation maintains the dignity of the affected parties. The value of the participatory function served by procedural due process is suggested in Justice Marshall's dissent in *Arnett v. Kennedy.*[2] In *Arnett* he wrote that all government employees should have a right to a pretermination hearing if they lose their jobs, even in the absence of a statutory entitlement to such a hearing.[3] Although the dissent speaks of the practical benefits of pretermination hearings, it implicitly recognizes the notion that confrontation, explanation, and access to power are important values in and of themselves.[4] For Justice Marshall, it is not necessary for all, or even a substantial portion, of those affected by a government decision to obtain substantive relief. Where a procedure provides affirmative access to a decision maker, the public usually benefits. Without endorsing Justice Marshall's legal position, I think the answer has to be that the opportunity to complain, the opportunity to seek explanation, and access to power are important values in and of themselves.

In a sense, the public's access to opportunities to be heard (of course, this does not guarantee a substantive right to get what you want) is the steam whistle on society's teapot. Dissatisfaction, anger, and frustration will seldom boil over into violence or civil unrest when such an outlet exists. As Justice Moody wrote in *Chambers v. Baltimore & Ohio R.R.*, "[t]he right to sue and defend in the courts is the alternative of force. In an organized society it is the right conservative of all other rights, and lies at the foundation of orderly government."[5] The promise of access which underlies the American legal system is just as important as the substantive rights which our Constitution guarantees. We are all familiar with totalitarian regimes which have startlingly similar constitutions to ours. The difference between the United States and such countries lies not in the words in their organizational charters, but in our commitment to access — our commitment to preserving the right of citizens to implement those charters. And, because the words themselves assure us of nothing, we must remain committed to maintaining that access and extending it to those who may still be disenfranchised. I think the need to rededicate ourselves to this principle should be a major focus of this year's Law Day celebration.

II. Alabama

In a more concrete vein, it might be useful to reexamine the form the struggle for equal access to justice has taken in our own state of Alabama. I think analytically we can identify two different spheres of concern: participation in the legal process and vindication of rights through the legal process. By participation in the legal process I mean direct access to the legislative process via the ballot and direct access to the judicial process via jury service.

A. VOTING

Until the 1960s and '70s, numerous unconstitutional practices effectively prevented the equal participation of minorities in the electoral process. The decisions in *United States v. Alabama*[6] signaled the beginning of the long process of voting rights reform. The reenfranchisement of the minority voter made possible the reality of minority participation in state and local government. This may constitute equal access to justice in its truest sense: the ability to play a role in the making and implementation of the law itself. I do not mean to invite complacency or suggest that no problems remain. We still see plenty of Voting Rights Act cases in the Eleventh Circuit, but the broadening of the electoral process in the last twenty-five years has surely evidenced the working of a greater equal access to justice. In fact, I ran across an article in *The Montgomery Advertiser* earlier this year entitled "Dallas Makes History." The piece documented how after more than one hundred years Dallas County, Alabama, with 55% of its population black citizens, once again will have a black county commissioner working in Selma, the county seat.[7]

B. THE COURTROOM

Moving from a legislative to a judicial vein, I should note another door which has opened in the last twenty-five years. Some of you may not remember that until 1966 women in Alabama were excluded by law from sitting on juries. A clearer denial of access to equal participation in the legal process cannot be imagined. In 1966, in *White v. Crook*,[8] the express prohibition against women serving on juries and the prohibition in practice against blacks serving on juries were held unconstitutional. Commenting on the inclusion of women on juries, Louis Nizer wrote:

> The jury system is a microcosm of this democratic process. We leave to twelve ordinary citizens the decision as to right or wrong. Contemptuous comments have been made about the jury representing average ignorance, or deciding merely which side has the better lawyer. The fact is that the jury represents the crystallization of common sense, which is the source of our laws. The jury system is the extension of mass judgment as applied in the courts. In the last analysis, this is the best reason for the participation of women in the jury system. Democracy functions best when it is permitted to synthesize the variegated view of the greatest number.[9]

Minority and female representation in the jury box has become so commonplace now as to be taken for granted. It should not be. A society speaks through its juries. Equal representation assures access to the chance to serve the community and to be adjudged by a true cross-section of one's peers. I should also note that not all the progress in this area occurred twenty-five years ago. Earlier this year an Eleventh Circuit panel (of which I was not a member) held for the first time that the Supreme Court's decision in *Batson v. Kentucky*[10] applies to civil cases. In *Batson*, the Supreme Court held that a defendant in a criminal prosecution may object to a prosecutor's use of peremptory strikes to exclude from the jury members of the defendant's race.[11] The Eleventh Circuit in

Fludd v. Dykes[12] extended this principle to the process of selecting the civil jury, stating:

> As the Court observed in *Batson*, there are times when a party has enough peremptory challenges to remove all of his adversary's racial peers from the venire and indeed exercises them for the purpose of obtaining a petit jury that may have a greater sympathy for him than for his adversary. This situation obviously arises in the civil context as well. Nor can we perceive any distinction in the harm to the individual's constitutional rights. Finally, we see no reason why a civil litigant would be unduly prejudiced by explaining the purpose of a strike where the circumstantial evidence indicates that he made it for a discriminatory purpose.[13]

Both the Supreme Court in *Batson* and our Court in *Fludd* were concerned about the denial of a litigant's right to be judged by a fair cross-section of his or her peers. But I think another rationale lurks in the background. If *Batson* and *Fludd* are decided differently, it in effect becomes permissible for a lawyer to tell a juror she may not serve on a particular jury because of her sex or race — that she may not participate in an essential part of a legal system because of her sex or race. *Batson* and *Fludd* work to prevent this purposeful and outrageous denial of access to participation in the justice system.

C. ENFORCEMENT OF RIGHTS

The concept of equal access to justice encompasses more than equal participation in our law-making process and justice system; it necessarily must include access to the vindication of legal rights. Rights are meaningless if those possessing them are unable to obtain relief from the executive or the judiciary. Certainly, the most visible vehicles providing such access are direct actions to enforce constitutionally guaranteed rights, actions brought pursuant to 42 U.S.C. § 1983, and the writ of habeas corpus.

In 1970 and 1972 class action suits were brought on behalf of the patients of Alabama's mental health system,[14] and inmates of the State's prison system,[15] respectively, in an attempt to obtain minimally adequate living conditions. After trial and upon appeal by the state officials, the Fifth Circuit described the conditions in two Alabama mental health facilities:

> Bryce Hospital was built in the 1850's; it had 5000 inmates of whom 1500 to 1600 were geriatrics. . . . There were severe health and safety problems: patients with open wounds and inadequately treated skin diseases were in

imminent danger of infection because of the unsanitary conditions existing in the wards. . . . Malnutrition was a problem: the United States described the food as "com[ing] closer to 'punishment' by starvation" than nutrition. [T]he food distribution and preparation systems were unsanitary, and less than 50 cents per day per patient was spent on food. . . . Partlow [hospital] was a "stepchild" in the State of Alabama; . . . the physical environment was inadequate for treating inmates. . . . [A]bout 70 percent of the inmates should never have been committed; yet it was 60 percent over-crowded. Patients at Partlow were forced to perform uncompensated labor. . . . [N]ine working residents would feed 54 young boys ground food from one very large bowl with nine plates and nine spoons. . . . Seclusion rooms were large enough for one bed and a coffee can, which served as a toilet. The patients suffered brutality, both at the hands of the aides and at the hands of their fellow patients.[16]

Conditions in Alabama prisons were no better:

[I]t is necessary that unsupervised inmate assistants administer treatment and medication, take x-rays, give injections, and perform suturing and minor surgery on patients. . . .

Beyond staff deficiencies, the institutions suffer from unsanitary conditions. For example, although Mt. Meigs contains separate wards for tuberculosis and hepatitis patients, soiled linens and dishware from these wards are cleaned in the same area as the linens and dishware of the general ward population. . . .

. . . [A]pproximately one-third of the inmate population suffer[ed] from mental retardation, and [although] an assessment by Dr. Alderete [indicated] that 60 percent of the inmates [were] disturbed enough to require treatment, the APS provide[d] only nominal assistance. . . . [T]he Board of Corrections employed one clinical psychologist who devoted one afternoon per week to disturbed inmates at Mt. Meigs and spent an equally limited amount of time at Draper and Tutwiler. No psychiatrists, social workers or counsellors were employed in the system.[17]

Conditions in these state-operated facilities were eventually improved, but only through protracted litigation which still continues. *Wyatt* and *Newman* provide a valuable reminder of the need for access to the equal implementation of the rights guaranteed by the Constitution.

In the same vein as these cases, actions under section 1983 illustrate how equal access makes the promise of rights and entitlements a reality. Passed by the Reconstruction Congress, section 1983 long lay dormant and unused. Although it grants no new substantive rights, it does provide a remedy for the violation of rights guaranteed by the United States Constitution and federal law. Section 1983 provides a key to the federal courthouse and has allowed substantial reform to take place. The writ of habeas corpus provides another means of access to the vindication of constitutional rights. The writ has been attacked of late.[18] Its critics claim most petitions are frivolous; they say the petitions are costly to litigate and generally constitute the expressions of people with too much time on their hands. Champions of the state judiciary resent the federal courts' reevaluation of legal issues. Finally, members of the general public are concerned by what they perceive as a federal judiciary which coddles criminals. These citizens do not think that frivolousness is a problem — they wish the courts would consider all petitions frivolous!

These attacks must be resisted if we are to accept the notion of *equality* of access. As Chief Justice Hughes said in *Bowen v. Johnston*, "[I]t must never be forgotten that the writ of *habeas corpus* is the precious safeguard of personal liberty and there is no higher duty than to maintain it unimpaired."[19] Whether we acknowledge it or not, courts do, on occasion, incarcerate a defendant in violation of his or her constitutional rights. Most state judges throughout our nation are elected; they often feel intense reelection pressures, especially in areas where the slightest perception of being "soft on crime" is fatal to a career in public service. The non-frivolousness of some habeas claims is illustrated by a study conducted of habeas petitions arising out of capital cases adjudicated by the Eleventh Circuit over a thirty-month period from 1979 to 1982. Over that period, in twenty-eight of fifty-six cases the Eleventh Circuit either affirmed the relief granted by the federal district court or reversed the denial of relief by the district court.[20] Now, this study may not be of scientific accuracy because the sample number of cases is quite small and the cases were not tracked to the United States Supreme Court. I would be surprised if an updated study revealed a current relief rate as high as 50%, but the study does much to dispel the notion that habeas petitions are merely an enjoyable hobby engaged in by bored prison inmates.

A much more comprehensive study published by the Federal Justice Research Program about ten years ago presents some other relevant statistics.[21] In all cases surveyed (not just death cases) the rate of relief granted habeas petitioners was about 3%.[22] However, of petitioners represented by court-appointed counsel, relief was granted in 18% of the cases.[23] Of course, that statistic is skewed somewhat by the typical practice of appointing counsel only for arguably meritorious claims. Even so, in cases where petitioners were represented by non-court-appointed counsel, the relief rate was over 8%, more than ten times the rate of habeas petitioners proceeding pro se.[24] Obviously, the role of counsel is crucial and is one area calling out for increased participation from the bar. Safeguarding prisoner access to justice may be one of the less popular mandates of this year's Law Day theme; it nevertheless remains one of the most important.

D. IMPARTIAL JUDICIARY

Another important safeguard was established in the case of *Hulett v. Julian*,[25] which struck down the former practice in Alabama which allowed justices of the peace to retain a monetary interest in convictions rendered in their courtrooms. If a justice of the peace did not convict, he often would not be paid. As might be imagined, the practice resulted in arbitrary and unpredictable results. It violated core values of due process. I mention the case as a reminder that impartiality is an essential part of equal access to justice. No one has access to justice when monetary or political considerations play any role in adjudication. Impartiality is easily taken for granted, and yet it provides the most fundamental justification for the judicial process.

III. Practical Mechanisms

I have mentioned previously the expanding access afforded in recent years to several disenfranchised groups. No less remarkable have been the improved opportunities afforded those who lack financial resources. Most visible has been the Supreme Court's extension of the right to counsel for felony defendants at trial and on appeal.[26] However, I think more recently the door to the courtroom has been opened in a dramatic way in the context of civil actions.

The enforcement of rights and entitlements becomes a reality only when economic incentives exist for lawyers to bring suit. Long gone are the days described in Arthur Hays' *City Lawyer*:

> The barristers and King's counsel were robed in black flowing garments with white surplices around the necks. A little hood hung in back, the original of which was said to be derived from the time when litigants would drop the fee into the hood because dignified law pleaders would not deign to appear interested in such mundane matters as compensation for services.[27]

Today the attorney's fee has become an important part of civil rights litigation. Praiseworthy and important pro bono work has been done in the past and must continue to be done in the future. But in my mind, the two most important cornerstones which make equal access to justice a reality are 42 U.S.C. § 1988 and 28 U.S.C. § 2432 (appropriately named "The Equal Access to Justice Act"). They, combined with the class action provisions of rule 23,[28] provide mechanisms for the realization of those rights and entitlements guaranteed by the Constitution and federal statutes.

How many Title VII suits would be brought in the absence of section 1988? How many violations of civil rights would go unredressed if no monetary incentive existed for a lawyer to litigate? Making civil rights litigation a business has been distasteful to some, but fee-shifting statutes have undeniably increased victims' access to the mechanisms of redress. I referred earlier to the return of minority representation on the Dallas County Commission. The same article reported that the cost of the litigation leading to that historic event has been estimated at two-hundred thousand to one million dollars.[29] I do not have the particulars of the disposition of the fees in that case, but it does provide a concrete example of the enormous cost of civil rights litigation — a cost which would be prohibitive were it to be wholly absorbed by the potential plaintiff.

Another important mechanism is the class action. I sometimes hear criticism of the class action procedure. I am told stories of greedy "class action lawyers" who are overly concerned about a quick settlement and a substantial attorney's fee. The potential for abuse does exist, but I would point critics in the direction of Judge Richard Posner's economic analysis of the class action. Judge Posner makes it clear that beyond any altruistic reasons for providing plaintiffs with the class action mechanism, economic common sense and efficiency concerns mandate its use.[30] I am no economist, but it does not take a computer to figure out that many times a meritorious suit will be brought only if many small claims can be aggregated in one suit. The class action has become an essential part of increasing access to justice.

IV. Conclusion

To conclude, I think the function of this year's Law Day observance should be to remind us of our role as lawyers in preserving and expanding the opportunities which we have seen presented in the last three decades. The avenues of access we have seen opened cannot be maintained through inertia. I have noted at various times today the existence of criticism of changes that have been worked in our justice system. That criticism underscores the need for clear thinking, vigilance, and a renewed commitment to the maintenance of the combination of rights, procedures, and practical mechanisms which make equality of access to justice a possibility.

Finally, if you do not remember anything else that I have said today, it is important that you remember there cannot be "Equal Justice Under Law," as promised by the inscription on the Supreme Court Building that I made reference to at the beginning of this talk, unless there is "Equal Access to Justice."

What Is Right with America

Address delivered by Honorable Frank M. Johnson Jr. at the Montgomery County Bar Association's 1990 Celebration of Law Day, May 2, 1990

This talk stated concisely Johnson's basic constitutional ideals and the conservative personal values underlying them. The introduction described the wider socioeconomic recession of the early 1990s. Within a context of wrenching social dislocation, however, Johnson chose to articulate and celebrate a distinctive rights consciousness which he believed was the source of enduring strength and renewal for the American people. The nation's constitutional institutions and laws established a foundation for attaining the individual's well-being, orderly social progress, and effective government. The meaningful realization of these societal goals nonetheless depended upon the guarantee and enforcement of four rights: to safety and security of the person, to citizenship and its privileges, to freedom of conscience and expression, and of equality of opportunity. Suggesting that the exercise of these rights had been contested throughout recent American history, Johnson drew upon his own decisions from the 1950s to the 1970s while serving as a federal district court judge in Montgomery. Even so, from these sources Johnson formulated the rights which by 1990, he asserted, all Americans could claim as fundamental. Yet true to the past struggles his opinions embodied, he concluded by urging all members of the legal profession that this "great tradition of freedom . . . is not a treasure to be hoarded and counted periodically. Those responsible for its conduct and stewardship — and that is all of us — must use it as a source of dynamic energy to assure that change and the solution of our social and legal problems are accomplished with integrity, with conscience, and with fidelity to that noble tradition." Johnson's audience on that day knew that he, at least, had always been true to the constitutional ideals he so forcefully declared.

I am pleased to have the opportunity to be with you members of the Montgomery County, Alabama, Bar Association and your guests this evening and to participate in our 1990 Law Day Celebration. As all of you are aware, we are now living in an exciting time in this world and many, if not all, of you will during your legal career face challenging and, I hope, rewarding experiences. However, we should keep in mind that to many American citizens this is not an exciting time, it is a gloomy period in the history of this nation. Our problems are legion. The solutions are far from evident. Our resources—both spiritual and physical—are under strain. Our national debt is scandalous. Full employment seems to have become only a dream. In our large metropolitan areas the streets are full of homeless people. Our commitment to clean up our environment has made little, if any, progress. Prices are so high as to be utterly impossible. There has, within the past few years, been an alarming increase in drug importation and crimes in general. The national and international political cauldron seethes and bubbles with uncertainty. Of our troubles, no person can see the end.

In such a setting and at this 1990 Law Day Celebration, when our nation is embarking on another hundred years, I have chosen to talk to you about not what is wrong but what is right with America. It is not too simplistic to begin at the beginning with the Constitution which our governmental forefathers formulated and which, with some critically necessary amendments,[1] has been the organic law of our country ever since. From this organic law we have received our basic American heritage: The promise of freedom and equality.

Contrary to many countries in this world, the central theme in our American heritage is the importance of the individual person. We believe that the welfare of the individual is the final goal of group life. Our American heritage further teaches that, to be secure in the rights one wishes for himself or herself, each person must be willing to respect the rights of other persons. This is the conscious recognition of a basic moral principle: all persons are created equal as well as free. Stemming from this principle was and is the obligation to build social institutions designed to guarantee equality of opportunity to all citizens. Without this equality, freedom becomes an illusion. Thus, the only aristocracy that is consistent with our way of life in America is an aristocracy of talent and achievement. The grounds on which our society accords respect, influence, or reward to its citizens are limited only to the quality of one's personal character and of his or her talents and contributions.

This concept of equality which is so vital a part of the American heritage knows no kinship with notions of human uniformity or regimentation. We abhor the totalitarian arrogance which makes one man say that he will respect another man as his equal only if he has "my race, my religion, my economic status, my political views, my social position." In our land, citizens are equal, but they are free to be different. From these very differences among our people has come the great human and national strength of America. Thus, our basic laws in America permanently denied the government power to abridge or interfere with certain personal rights and freedoms.

Freedom, however, as we now use the term, means even more than the traditional freedoms listed in our Bill of Rights—important as they are. Freedom in our country has come to mean the right of a person to manage his or her own affairs as he or she sees fit up to the point where what is done interferes with the equal rights of others in the community to manage their affairs—or up to the point where the exercise of that right begins to injure the welfare of the whole group.[2] It is clear that in our modern society a person's freedom in this broader sense is not and cannot be absolute—nor does it exist in a vacuum—but instead is hedged by the competing rights of others and the demands of the social welfare.[3] In this context it is government which must referee the clashes which arise among the freedoms of citizens, and protect each citizen in the enjoyment of the maximum freedom to which he or she is entitled.

There is no basic conflict in America between freedom and government. Bills of rights restrain government from abridging individual civil liberties, while government itself by sound legislative policies and judicial decisions protects citizens against the aggressions of others seeking to push their freedoms too far. Thus, in the words of our Declaration of Independence: "Man is endowed by his Creator with certain inalienable rights. Among these are life, liberty, and the pursuit of happiness. To secure these rights, governments are instituted among men."

The rights of the American citizen in our free society can be described in different words and in varying orders. However, I suggest that four very broad but still basic rights flow from our laws, and each is essential to the well-being of the individual, to the genius of our government, and to the orderly progress of our society.

1. The Right to Safety and Security of the Person

Our American government recognizes that freedom can exist only where the citizen is assured that his or her person is secure against bondage, lawless violence,[4] and arbitrary arrest and punishment.[5] Freedom from servitude in all its forms—sophisticated and unsophisticated—is clearly necessary if all persons are to have equal opportunity to use their talents and to lead worthwhile lives. Moreover, to be free, persons must be subject to discipline by society only for commission of offenses clearly defined by law and only after trial by due process of law. Some libertarians overlook the fact that the criminal laws must be enforced. Others, at another pole, view the need to solve crime as an open invitation to substitute government by gestapo for due process of law, with the concomitant loss of cherished constitutional liberties.[6]

Our system of laws assures that persons charged with crime will be promptly brought to trial, will be promptly tried in a fair and just manner with an adequate prosecution and defense guaranteed by our government.

Obviously, the criminal process does not end when the trial is over. Because a society based on law is inevitably weakened and endangered by violations of the law — particularly of the criminal laws — effective punishment of those who violate our criminal laws directly involves the safety and welfare of our society. However, it is important to recognize that punishment must be meted out in a civilized and uniform fashion.

We lawyers cannot subscribe to the theory that persons who commit crimes are somehow not responsible for their actions. When they commit and are duly tried and convicted for crimes, they should be punished. Punishment can involve, however, involuntary and forcible restraint in a prison and, when it does, the state and its officials must conduct themselves in a manner not prohibited by essential constitutional guaranties. Among the guaranties which restrict those who conduct the business of punishment is the prohibition against cruel and unusual punishment.[7]

This right to the security of the person includes in our nation the right not to be deprived, even in a civil proceeding, of liberty by the government — state or federal — without the guaranties of due process — both procedurally and substantively.[8]

It's right with America that our government stands for the principle that all be secure in their persons and their property and that human beings cannot be civilly or criminally imprisoned and deprived of their liberty under cruel and inhuman conditions or in the absence of due process of law.

2. The Right to Citizenship and Its Privileges

Since it is a purpose of our government to regulate the activity of each citizen in the interest of all citizens, it necessarily follows that every mature and responsible person must be able to enjoy full citizenship and have an equal voice in his or her government. Because the right to participate in the political processes is customarily limited to citizens, there can be no denial of access to this basic right based upon race, sex, creed, or national origin.[9] Our government in America through its Constitution and laws recognizes that a denial of citizenship for those reasons cheapens the personality of those who are confined to this inferior status and endangers the whole concept of a democratic society. To deny qualified citizens the right to vote or to sit on juries while others exercise that right is to do violence to the principle of freedom and equality.[10] Therefore, our citizens repose with confidence that in America all are entitled by law to the full rights of citizenship and thus the right to meaningfully participate in all political processes.[11]

3. The Right to Freedom of Conscience and Expression

In our society there is faith in the ability of the people to make sound, rational judgments. But such judgments are possible only where the people have access to all relevant facts and to all prevailing interpretations of the facts. How can such judgments be formed on a sound basis if arguments, viewpoints, or opinions are arbitrarily suppressed?[12] How can the concept of the marketplace of thought in which truth ultimately prevails retain its validity if the thought of certain individuals is denied the right of circulation?[13] Our government through its laws and its courts assiduously protects this tradition that freedom of expression may be curbed by law only where the danger to the well-being of society is clear and present.

One of our most basic and precious rights of conscience and expression is the right to worship according to the varied dictates of conscience without interference or coercion by the government—state or federal. Therefore, complete religious liberty has been accepted as an unquestioned personal freedom.[14] We have insisted only that religious freedom may not be advanced as an excuse for criminal or clearly anti-social conduct. It's right with America that our Constitution protects and guarantees freedom of conscience and expression.

4. The Right of Equality of Opportunity

It is not enough that full and equal membership in society entitles the individual to an equal voice in the control of government; our laws also give the citizen the right to enjoy the benefits of society and to contribute to its progress. The opportunity of each individual to obtain useful employment and to have access to services in the fields of education,[15] housing,[16] health,[17] recreation,[18] and transportation[19] is now provided in America for all citizens. We now recognize that to discriminate against a class of our citizens because of their race, religion or because of their sex violates the whole concept of our government.[20] Without this equality of opportunity, the individual will be deprived of the chance to develop his or her potentialities and to share the fruits of our society.

And so, our American heritage of freedom and equality gives us strength and prestige among the nations of the world and a strong feeling of national pride at home. What is right with America is that great gift bestowed upon us as citizens of this country, our birthright—that is, our right to share in the freedoms which our government was established to secure and protect.

In closing, let me emphasize on this 1990 Law Day Celebration, there is an enormous challenge to all citizens to maintain and preserve human rights and individual rights. While I have spoken as a judge and lawyer about values embodied in our Constitution and laws and safeguarded by our legal processes, I speak also as a joint heir with you lawyers of a great tradition of freedom. But this tradition is not a treasure to be hoarded and counted periodically. Those responsible for its conduct and stewardship—and that is all of us—must use it as a source of dynamic energy to assure that change and the solution of our social and legal problems are accomplished with integrity, with conscience, and with fidelity to that noble tradition.

Conclusion

The four sections that follow draw together insights from Moyers's PBS interview, the articles, and the introduction into a summary commentary on Johnson's jurisprudence and constitutional ideals. The first section examines Johnson's leading decisions in the field of racial justice, from the civil rights movement's struggle against the South's massive resistance during the 1950s and 1960s, to the controversies involving busing and affirmative action in the 1970s. The second section considers Johnson's contribution to the post–World War II broadening of constitutional rights claims beyond race to include women, criminal defendants, white urban and suburban voters, religious minorities, students and teachers, handicapped workers, and gays. The focus of the third section is Johnson's central role in creating new judicial forms of equity relief which extended claims of constitutional rights to benefit public protest demonstrators, prisoners, and mental health patients. The last section returns to Johnson's own words to summarize his jurisprudential thinking and constitutional faith.

Johnson and Racial Justice

A deep involvement with racial justice characterized Johnson's tenure as a trial judge. Indeed, Johnson's first year on the bench coincided with the Montgomery bus boycott of 1955–56. His pivotal role in settling that confrontation was a defining moment for Johnson's judicial consciousness and constitutional ideals and their future contribution to the civil rights struggle and the peaceful mass protest strategy that struggle increasingly followed, identified especially with Martin Luther King. Subsequent cases in the field of voting rights, school desegregation, and affirmative action, as well as individual decisions regarding the Freedom Riders, differing styles of peaceful demonstration, and the end to both gender and racial discrimination in jury selection revealed Johnson's capacity for adapting his judicial role and constitutional faith to new dimensions of conflict, particularly the protracted defiance Governor George Wallace perfected during the 1960s and 1970s.[1]

In 1956 Johnson confronted the case arising from the Montgomery bus boycott, *Browder v. Gayle*. Following Mrs. Rosa Parks's arrest for refusing to comply with the city's ordinance requiring racially segregated bus seating, Martin Luther

King Jr. led a boycott that significantly curtailed the operation of the city's transportation system. The NAACP challenged the ordinance before a federal panel of Rives, Lynne, and Johnson. The NAACP's lawyers argued that the ordinance's constitutional basis was *Plessy*'s separate-but-equal doctrine, but the Supreme Court had for all intents and purposes overturned that doctrine in *Brown I*. The city's counsel, which included the state's assistant attorney general, responded that *Brown* applied to public education, not public transportation; the three-judge court should not act, they said, until the Supreme Court decided that particular issue, therefore providing clear precedent. Montgomery's mayor testified that ending segregation would engender "violence and bloodshed." The prediction occurred against the background of a mob successfully preventing Autherine Lucy's desegregation of the University of Alabama and also of the announcement of the Southern Manifesto, in which the southern states' congressional delegations declared *Brown* unconstitutional and called upon state leaders to prevent its enforcement through "massive resistance."[2]

The federal court's approach to precedent in the case required discretion. In order for the three-judge court to adopt the NAACP's theory, it would have to hold that *Brown* applied analogously, since the Supreme Court had not yet directly decided the status of segregated public transportation facilities under the *Plessy* doctrine. Such analogical reasoning thus required a creative exercise of judicial authority. Following the state's wait-and-see argument, however, gave rise to no such creativity, thereby limiting the scope of discretionary judgment. Rives and Johnson formed a majority extending *Brown* to overturn Montgomery's segregation ordinance. "We cannot in good conscience perform our duty as judges," Rives wrote, "by blindly following the precedent of *Plessy v. Ferguson* when . . . we think that *Plessy v. Ferguson* has been impliedly, though not explicitly, overruled." Accordingly, the ordinance violated the due process and equal protection clauses of the Fourteenth Amendment. In his first ever dissent, however, Lynne took a contrary view of precedent. Although Lynne shared with Rives a heritage of active involvement with Alabama's National Democrats, he rejected the majority's use of analogical reasoning to extend the reach of *Brown*. It was his "simple belief that the laws which regulate the conduct, the affairs, and sometimes the emotions of our people should evidence not only the appearance but the spirit of stability." Lower courts therefore should not decide new issues on the basis of some perceived "new doctrinal trend" emerging from the Supreme Court but should wait until the Court "in a proper case" overturned "established precedent . . . explicitly."[3]

Various factors may have influenced Johnson's vote in the two-to-one decision.

On one level it followed logically from his negative view of the *Plessy* decision and the preference for Harlan's dissent that he had formed in law school. The state's formal imposition of race separation was, he believed, contrary to American traditions and institutions embodied in the Constitution, including the Fourteenth Amendment. Undoubtedly shaping this view were the family values he absorbed and the positive racial encounters he had growing up in Winston County. These experiences, in turn, fostered a conscious repudiation of racial discrimination after he was "nauseated" by the bullwhipping of black convicts. Such a reading suggests that Johnson's past experience and formal legal education instilled a belief in basic norms of justice such as equality before the law, which were distinctively American. Courts declared and legislatures enacted legally binding measures that were often contrary to such norms. When in due course the Supreme Court chose to return to fundamental principle and overrule one of these particular measures, however, it was appropriate for lower federal courts to strike down similar measures through analogous reasoning. The Court's reaffirmation of elemental constitutional principle was so important that lower federal judges were bound by their oath to extend it into related areas where justice was being denied.

A related but distinct factor determining Johnson's vote in *Browder* was his faith in courts. Johnson's upbringing established a basic conviction that courts were best equipped to treat minority and other weaker groups fairly. In the peonage case, U. S. Attorney Johnson won from an all-white jury a guilty verdict in the death of an African American. Reliance on the courts to attain racial justice was also consistent with the wartime defense of the enlisted men from the wrongdoing of superior officers in the Litchfield case. It was noteworthy, too, that the mountain Republicans of northwest Alabama were a political minority that sometimes encountered discrimination from the local Democratic establishment. As a lawyer, Johnson overcame such discrimination through the legal process. In addition, the evenhanded way Johnson's father dispensed justice as a probate judge reinforced the belief that courts could best protect vulnerable groups. Both Rives and Lynne appealed to conscience to justify their opposing approaches to precedent. The logic of Johnson's position also started from a conscientious conviction that any precedent that sanctioned racial segregation violated a core value of American constitutionalism. If through *Plessy* the Supreme Court had established a doctrine that was repugnant to the fundamental principle of equality before the law, the Court also possessed the power to correct its error. For his part, Lynne did not deny the Court's authority to overturn even the most established precedent. What he dissented from was an exercise of discretion by the lower federal courts which through analogical reasoning in effect did the same thing. For Lynne this violated the federal courts' dependence within the judicial system. By contrast, Johnson believed that once the Supreme Court acknowledged its error, the very fact of dependence imposed upon federal judges the obligation to employ discretion on a scale commensurate with the problem requiring correction.

Still, Johnson distinguished equality before the law from the moral principle that segregation was evil. He later told an interviewer that his vote for the plaintiffs in the boycott case "was not based on any personal feeling that segregation was wrong: it was based on the law, that the state imposing segregation violated my interpretation of the Constitution. . . . It wasn't for a judge to decide on the morality question, but rather the law."[4] In the Montgomery case, this meant extending the reach of *Brown* beyond education to include transportation facilities. Yet the court's creative assertion of authority in this instance left open the question of whether the judicial process was equipped to eradicate discrimination on the enormous scale that the system of segregation imposed.

Johnson's ability to treat controversial issues efficiently and fairly was also evident in school desegregation cases. In 1958, Birmingham civil rights activists challenged the city's Board of Education for failing to comply with *Brown*. The board argued that the state's pupil assignment law permitted administrative discretion in assigning students to schools. Without question, local officials could, if they wished, use the statute to maintain segregation, but Rives and Johnson refused to overturn it on that basis. Instead, they presumed that the statute would be administered in good faith so as to achieve desegregation. The court nonetheless asserted that it would grant appropriate relief to the African American plaintiffs if they could show that the board had used the statute to preserve segregation. The Supreme Court affirmed this moderate approach.[5]

The federal court's presumption that Alabama's officials would act on the basis of good faith proved to be misplaced. In 1962, George Wallace, Johnson's former law school classmate, campaigned on a strident segregationist platform and won the office of governor. The year following Wallace's election, Johnson found that the Macon County school board had used Alabama's pupil assignment law unconstitutionally to maintain segregation. Following the pattern established in Birmingham, Johnson declined to coerce the board immediately and gave it time to develop an appropriate desegregation plan. The school board responded with defiance; and state troopers, following Wallace's direction, kept blacks from the Macon County schools. Meanwhile, Wallace made state patrol cars available to transport white students to the all-white county schools and a new private school. At the same time, exercising authority as ex-officio State Board of Education president, Wallace convinced the board to close Tuskegee High School, the principal school affected by Johnson's desegregation decree. Wallace's intervention formally maintained racially segregated schools in defiance of Johnson's order. State and local authorities thus met the judge's patient moderation with intransigence.

Johnson responded in *U.S. v. Wallace* (1963) and a long series of detailed orders identified by the leading opinion, *Lee v. Macon County* (1967). The *Lee* decision was the most creative use of judicial authority yet. On questionable formal authority he ordered the Justice Department to enter the case as a party. Following the practice of Judge Ronald N. Davies in the Little Rock, Arkansas, desegregation case, Johnson employed the FBI to develop a strong factual record documenting Wallace's and the school board's unconstitutional actions. He then used this evidence and the federal court's discretionary authority to fashion injunctive relief reaching all of the state's public schools. Wallace used state power to intervene and block desegregation; Johnson now relied on that same statewide authority to justify implementation of a comprehensive remedial order, not just for Macon County but for all of Alabama. The order enjoined Wallace and state board members from preventing desegregation and employing state funds to maintain racially segregated schools. Also, it compelled one hundred school systems throughout Alabama to fashion "realistic" desegregation plans.[6]

Johnson's approach to injunctive relief in the Macon County schools desegregation case was pioneering. Johnson nonetheless administered the reparative injunction with moderation. Once the federal court issued the injunction, the reliance on facts continued as Johnson retained jurisdiction and required school authorities to provide ongoing progress reports. As a result, the injunction legitimated a continuous give and take between the court and all the parties guaranteeing that change would proceed gradually. All interested groups had access and contributed to the decision-making process as long as they acted in good faith. By capably handling this process, Johnson solidified a deserved reputation for fairness. In this process, moreover, he opposed the controversial remedy of busing in *Carr v. Montgomery Bd. of Education* (1974). During an earlier phase of that case, Supreme Court justice Hugo L. Black said that the judge's "patience and wisdom" were "written for all to see and read on the pages of the five year record." Ultimately, Johnson's combination of activism and restraint gave school officials someone to blame for desegregation.[7] According to Johnson, school authorities would come in with their lawyers and say, "'Now judge, we know we are going to have to desegregate our school, but we have to have a court order to do it. We can't live in the community without a court order.' We'd give them a court order—get cussed for it. They would go back and implement it. I consistently through the years required reports to keep me advised."[8]

Voting rights issues further defined the contours of the legalistic limitations within which Johnson innovated. An initial clash with Wallace, who in 1958 was a local judge in Barbour County, set the tone for Johnson's handling of voting rights confrontations. When the U.S. Commission on Civil Rights ordered local voting records released, Wallace took a public stance of defiance. Johnson threatened Wallace with a contempt citation, whereupon Wallace transferred the records to the grand jury, which gave them to the commission. The incident convinced Johnson that patience combined with the threat of contempt could engender public officials' compliance with constitutional rights. At the same time, Johnson doubted whether use of the contempt power would actually achieve the desired results because it could easily heighten popular support for the public official. Johnson was determined to compel state authorities to comply with constitutional principles, and for him, the central question was merely, "How fast are we going to do it?"[9]

The clash with Wallace preceded years of voter registration litigation in which Johnson developed the "freeze doctrine." It required voter registration boards to use the least qualified white voter to determine the qualification of any black applicant. The freeze doctrine became the Fifth and, subsequently, the Eleventh Circuit's basic standard in voter registration cases. Congress incorporated essentially the same standard into the Voting Rights Act of 1965. Before developing the freeze doctrine, however, Johnson had dissented from the claim that federal judges should intervene in voting rights issues. In Tuskegee, Alabama, African American litigants argued that white local leaders were gerrymandering voting districts to exclude the great majority of black voters. Supreme Court precedent held that voting was a "political thicket" from which federal courts were excluded, but none had raised a claim of racial discrimination. When the Tuskegee case came before Johnson in *Gomillion v. Lightfoot* (1958), he followed precedent; he simply suggested that the racial dimension of the case provided a basis for revising the established rule. Consistent with Johnson's intimation, the Supreme Court reversed and established a new doctrine permitting extensive federal judicial protection of African American voting rights. Johnson vigorously applied the doctrine in *U.S. v. Alabama* (1961).[10]

In other cases involving race and equal rights Johnson demonstrated remarkable skill in establishing a constitutional boundary line. He compelled both state and local officials and the Freedom Riders to comply with court orders regulating the course of protests in *U.S. v. KKK* (1961).[11] During the Selma voting rights clash of 1965, he refused in *Forman v. City of Montgomery* to support SNCC demonstrations that were not consistent with the sort of legal forms he was employing in the expansive remedial decree governing the Selma-to-Montgomery march.[12] In the highly charged racial climate surrounding the march, Johnson also inspired an all-white jury to return guilty verdicts against three Klansmen for violating Viola Liuzzo's civil rights by killing her while she drove marchers back to Selma. Despite eyewitness testimony, white juries had acquitted the Klansmen in state court on murder charges. John Doar, the federal prosecutor in the case, emphasized Johnson's commitment to fairness: "Throughout the trial, from the time of the jury selection to the return of the verdict, Judge Johnson was the finest trial judge I have ever seen. He left no doubt that he was in charge; that his duty was to see that federal law was upheld; and that he expected the trial attorneys and the jurors to do likewise."[13] He also ended discrimination in admission to juries for reasons of both race and gender in *White v. Crook* (1966).[14]

A former Alabama governor explained the "blame shifting" strategy state officials employed in light of Johnson's decisions. John Patterson said of Johnson that "he had a distasteful job that had to be done and he had the courage to do it. . . . We in Alabama have had a federal judge who was willing and capable of grasping the situation and resolving it." Patterson stated frankly that without the constitutional accountability imposed by Johnson, Alabama's leaders lacked political will to challenge the status quo. The judge, he said, "brought about a desirable result which could not be done politically." Accordingly, Alabama's officials asserted: "'Look, I stood up here and fought this thing to the bitter end. I stood in the door, and that doggone judge down there, you gotta blame [him], not me.'" Thus Johnson "was about the best valve for bringing about change that couldn't be done politically I've ever seen. . . . If I'd said that we couldn't win [the clash between civil rights and states' rights], I'd have been dead as a doornail politically. . . . Judge Johnson just happened to be in the right place to do the job, and he did it without hesitation, fearlessly, courageously."[15]

Johnson's enforcement of constitutional rights against leaders like Patterson also aided the civil rights movement. Julian Bond wrote that the Constitution "provided the framework within which people could act to change the nation for the better. The story of the civil rights movement is a great testament to the Constitution's strength." For decades the South's segregation system and the Supreme Court's sanction of it "bent and twisted [the document] to deny black Americans their rights." But *Brown* symbolized a change, underway in the Court since the 1930s, which during the fifties and sixties "provided the basic tool used by the [civil rights] movement to win justice. Even when movement activists broke local laws, they remained conscious of their adherence to the Constitution's provisions [including their affirmation by federal judges such as Johnson]. They knew that segregation was wrong on the basis of the nation's highest law. People were willing . . . to fight through the legal system for change, because the Constitution was their ultimate shield."[16]

Martin Luther King agreed. In "Letter from the Birmingham Jail (1963)" and elsewhere he recognized the importance of the federal courts to the strategy of nonviolence.[17] The historian George M. Fredrickson noted the political advantage the Constitution and federal courts gave King and American civil rights protesters, compared to those fighting South Africa's apartheid system during the same period. Unlike the unified South African white minority, the "American protesters faced a divided, fragmented, and uncertain governmental opposition. The most important division among whites that the movement was able to exploit was between northerners who lacked a regional commitment to legalized segregation and southerners who believed that Jim Crow was central to their way of life." Implicitly acknowledging that federal courts such as Johnson's treated civil rights demonstrators fairly, King, Fredrickson said, "proclaimed that 'civil disobedience to local laws is civil obedience to national laws'; [in so doing] he exploited a tactical advantage the South African resisters did not possess." Like Bond, Fredrickson concluded that the "success of the movement stemmed ultimately from its ability to get the federal government [including the federal courts] on its side and to utilize the U.S. Constitution against the outmoded states' rights philosophy of the southern segregationists."[18]

Johnson's treatment of affirmative action policy involving employment discrimination raised similar issues. The 1964 Civil Rights Act's Title VII prohibited racial and gender discrimination in employment practices. During the 1970s, in such pathbreaking cases as *NAACP v. Allen* (1972) and *Paradise v. Shoemaker* (1979), where Johnson again confronted resistance from public officials, the federal government and Johnson applied Title VII vigorously. Even so, throughout these years Republican and Democratic presidential administrations and Supreme Court decisions construed the law's original purpose to mean that affirmative action and Title VII indirectly permitted limited quota remedies. This policy and judicial doctrine may be contrasted with the Reagan-Bush administration's campaign during the 1980s to prohibit quotas entirely. Nevertheless, moderate Republicans, liberal Democrats, and the civil rights lobby in Congress defeated this campaign in the Civil Rights Act of 1991, which sanctioned temporary quota remedies such as Johnson had employed years earlier to overcome intentional discrimination in the *Paradise* and *Allen* cases.[19]

Thus in affirmative action decisions, as in other cases, resistance from Alabama's public officials influenced but did not determine the boundaries Johnson established for judicial discretion. Wallace and other officials exploited the federal courts for political gain, shifting from state authorities to unelected federal judges the responsibility for remedying profound social problems. Resistance increased rather than diminished the federal court's involvement in Alabamians' lives. Yet Johnson's creative uses of injunctive relief and remedial decrees—imposing temporary quotas and other devices—mobilized a wide range of popular interests and values which gained new force when legitimated and protected by the federal judiciary's institutional autonomy. The balance struck between this autonomy and governmental authority confined remedial outcomes to relatively moderate limits. Both the means and ends Johnson pursued were consistent with a faith in fundamental fairness enforced by lawyers and judges conditioned by an understanding of human nature rooted in his past.

Johnson and the Rights Revolution Beyond Race

The Supreme Court's race decisions were part of a wider transformation in individual rights. During the 1930s and 1940s, partly as a reaction against growing popular fears that wartime authoritarianism and ideological totalitarianism threatened American democracy as never before, the Court rejected its old defense of economic liberty and established a constitutional presumption favoring civil rights and liberties. Accordingly, it applied the Bill of Rights selectively to the states through the Fourteenth Amendment's due process clause.[20] A second principle was articulated in the *Carolene Products* decision of 1938, where the Court suggested that it would employ a standard of strict scrutiny in civil rights and liberty cases.[21] From 1953 to 1969 the Warren Court used these and related principles to bring about the greatest expansion of individual rights in the nation's history. Throughout the period, Judge Johnson contributed significantly to the constitutional rights revolution. During the 1970s and 1980s, Johnson was also in the forefront of adapting this revolution to changing times, as rights claims were to some extent restricted but in other ways extended.[22]

Johnson's criminal procedure decisions gave substance to the Warren Court's due process revolution. In the *Wilson* and *Germany* cases of 1957 and 1963, respectively, Johnson sought to balance the rights of bootlegger defendants against effective federal prosecution under the U.S. tax code. Even so, the facts of race or poor social class of the defendants were typical of the tension between crime control and Americans' abiding commitment to fairness. Thus in the first case Willie Wilson and Morris Griffin claimed that federal alcohol and tobacco agents had violated the Fourth Amendment's prohibition against unreasonable searches. The federal authorities stopped them without a warrant on a rural Alabama road because their car was riding "extremely low" to the ground and the "Negro male" in the front seat "had a reputation for being in the non tax whiskey business." The "contraband" the agents found in the car trunk was used at the trial to prosecute the bootleggers. Defense lawyers asked Johnson to exclude the evidence because a warrantless search was unreasonable. The issue was whether, under the circumstances, the agents had probable cause to stop the vehicle. While Johnson was "more than fair to the defendants," he applied the doctrine of "probable cause" to decide in favor of the government. In the *Germany* case, Johnson's commitment to fairness expanded the due process rights of destitute defendants. Ned Germany was known in the rural community of Dozier, Alabama, as an indigent; his involvement with moonshine liquor brought "alleged offense(s) against the laws of the United States." To prepare Germany's defense, his court-appointed counsel incurred travel expenses in order to depose an informer who was the government's chief witness. The issue was whether the Warren Court's precedents expanding the Sixth Amendment's guarantee of counsel to indigent criminal defendants imposed on the government an obligation to reimburse the full costs arising from the need to prepare an effective defense. In a notable enlargement of precedent, Johnson held that Germany's right to fair representation included expenses attending his lawyer's deposition of witnesses.[23]

Johnson's capacity to institute fairer criminal procedures was further demonstrated in *Washington v. Holman* (1965).[24] The *Wilson* and *Germany* decisions struck a balance between government authority and criminal defendants' rights in federal litigation. The *Washington* case raised the question whether the Sixth Amendment's guarantee of right to counsel, which the Court extended to include indigents in *Gideon v. Wainwright* (1963),[25] applied to state criminal proceedings through the Fourteenth Amendment's due process clause. Johnson's *Washington* decision adhered to the Warren Court's nationwide expansion of criminal due process protections. Caliph Washington, a seventeen-year-old African American, was arrested, tried, and convicted for murdering an Alabama policeman. While in the custody of a state law enforcement officer, Washington admitted to having committed the crime and while in jail he signed a written confession. At no point before making either statement, however, did Washington have access to a lawyer. The Warren Court had recently declared in the *Escobedo* decision (1964)[26] that such confessions were unconstitutional. Noting that the facts and issues of the *Washington* case paralleled closely those in *Escobedo*—including the defendant being a member of a racial minority—Johnson extended the new doctrine to Alabama and ordered Washington released from death row. Johnson nonetheless declared that Alabama might "reprosecute" and "if appropriate, punish . . . Washington in such a manner that complies with the constitutional requirements."

These three decisions reflected public perceptions of fairness that favored the Warren Court's criminal due process revolution. Since the 1930s, the Supreme Court had steadily formulated uniform criminal procedures that converged with and sustained Americans' growing support for federal, state, and local efforts to upgrade law enforcement professionalism. Particularly during the decades immediately following World War II, the public embraced improved professional standards in part because of a feeling of common interest among middle-class people traveling the new interstate highways; these people felt vulnerable to the corrupt practices of local authorities, a sentiment reinforced by lingering memories of lax local enforcement during Prohibition. They also shared a broad-based concern about the humanitarian abuses and racial discrimination associated with fascist and communist totalitarianism. By the late 1950s these popular emotions promoted a popular reaction against McCarthyism's worst abuses. In addition, the NAACP and the civil rights movement appealed to this common antitotalitarian interest in their equal rights struggle, which included overcoming southern law enforcement officials' brutal treatment of African Americans.

Like members of the Warren Court, Johnson had experienced public concerns regarding fairer criminal procedures. Responding to enormous criticism from law-and-order advocates, Chief Justice Earl Warren and Justice Hugo Black pointed out that the Court's due process revolution was consistent with what they had learned as local and state prosecutors about both the public's desire for procedural fairness and law enforcement officials' potential for abuse. Similarly, Johnson's career as a trial lawyer in the wartime military prepared him for a law practice in Alabama's Winston County area that brought him into direct contact with this divergence between public sentiment and local police officials' discriminatory conduct. Democrats and Republicans alike elected Johnson's father as a probate judge and the lone Republican member of the state legislature largely because he maintained the Johnson family's reputation for being absolutely fair. As a young lawyer Frank Johnson Jr. continued this tradition, winning the release of moonshiner Republican Party members who had been unfairly prosecuted in criminal proceedings by a Democratic sheriff. Appointed United States attorney for north Alabama, he further demonstrated a rigorous attachment to fairness in the successful prosecution of a powerful planter whose illegal practice of peonage had resulted in an African American man's brutal death.

Many white Alabamians criticized Johnson, but others lauded his defense of equal justice.

Several other considerations suggested why Johnson believed that a truly even-handed judicial process would engender fair outcomes. Serving with Rives on the Fifth Circuit's federal courts over a quarter-century and facing Wallace's intractable defiance during the same period gave Johnson ample opportunity to reflect on the personal sources of fairness in the judicial process. As a socially prominent lawyer and well-connected Democratic operative in Alabama's black belt, Richard Rives, before his appointment to the U.S. Fifth Circuit Court of Appeals in 1951, maintained a profitable law practice that included successful representation of African Americans in criminal as well as civil cases in the local courts. Also, during the 1950s, George Wallace, a young elected circuit court judge in Barbour County, had earned a reputation for treating African Americans fairly, at least within bounds that white supremacy permitted. Southern politicians' reaction against the civil rights movement however, undercut public respect for due process and, ultimately, social order. In the Moyers PBS interview Johnson admired Judge Rives's willingness to defend equal justice and due process amid the social ostracism he suffered as a result of judicial independence. Johnson expressed consternation about Wallace's abandonment of procedural fairness toward African Americans in order to further his political ambitions.

Even so, an image of potential malleability inherent in "southern" popular opinion was central to these assessments. The receptivity to fairness Johnson and his father encountered among their Winston County neighbors was not unique; the early parallel experience of Rives and Wallace in south Alabama demonstrated that. But the selfish demagoguery of southern politicians—Wallace foremost among them—overwhelmed the public's instinct for fairness. The institutional independence of the federal courts, combined with a more liberal national public opinion articulated during the Warren Court era, both neutralized this resistance and fostered among Alabamians and southerners generally a return to the popular respect for due process that since the 1930s had increasingly characterized the nation. Johnson's opinions in the *Wilson, Germany,* and *Washington* cases thus reflected a confidence that Alabama and the South's law enforcement officials, like their counterparts across the nation, could rise to the higher standards of procedural fairness and professionalism that the Warren Court was establishing.

Johnson's trust in judicially enforced fairness fostered a convergence of interests benefiting Alabama's white voters. Following World War II the difference in population distribution between rural and urban voting districts across the nation was more pronounced than at any time since the turn of the century. As a result, cities and their surrounding suburbs were significantly underrepresented in state legislatures and Congress. Middle-class voters and business groups organized active resistance to this legislative malapportionment. In *Colgrove v. Green* (1946) the Supreme Court nonetheless refused to enter what the four-to-three majority called the "political thicket." Justice Hugo Black, however, led the dissenters in stating: "What is involved here is the right to vote guaranteed by the Federal Constitution. It has always been the rule that where a federally protected right has been invaded the federal courts will provide the remedy to rectify the wrong done."[27] Johnson's background enabled him to readily understand Alabama's version of the national problem. His origins and public career in Winston County taught the judge that Alabama's black belt maintained its dominance over the state's more populous northern section partially because of legislative malapportionment. African American disfranchisement and the underrepresentation of white voters in places such as Birmingham were linked.

Justice William J. Brennan's controversial decision of *Baker v. Carr*[28] in 1962 favored those advocating reapportionment. Following the logic of Black's 1946 dissent, Brennan held for the Warren Court's majority that federal courts had jurisdiction to review the denial of white voters' rights. Brennan pointed out that the Court had employed the Fifteenth Amendment to strike down state impairment of African Americans' voting rights in the Alabama case of *Gomillion v. Lighfoot* (1960).[29] Although the constitutional basis for each decision differed, the fundamental principle underlying both was that federal courts were empowered to enforce all the rights the Constitution guaranteed. The *Baker* case itself arose in Tennessee; as the litigation moved forward, however, Alabama's malapportionment opponents initiated their own suit in Johnson's court. The black-belt county interests and their allies attempted to defeat the challenge by initiating in the legislature a reapportionment compromise patterned on the U.S. Constitution's grant in the Senate of equal representation to each state regardless of size. The Alabama proposal gave counties equal representation in the state senate. At the same time, the proponents of compromise assaulted the federal court's intervention as unwarranted judicial activism.

The Alabama case, styled *Sims v. Frink* (1962), was the first test of implementing the *Baker* principles. On a special three-judge panel Johnson joined Rives and Daniel H. Thomas to consider the meaning of legislative reapportionment. The plaintiffs were described simply "as U.S. and Alabama citizens, and as taxpayers and registered voters." Nothing suggested that they were part of a nationwide struggle. The defendants were state officials charged with conducting legislative elections, including leaders of the Democratic and Republican Parties, which selected their candidates through primary elections. The issue was whether the state's failure to reapportion its electoral districts in keeping with population shifts — as required by the Alabama constitution — violated the Fourteenth Amendment's equal protection clause. The court's opinion included much factual evidence revealing the unfairness of legislative malapportionment. One example the court noted, which the legislature's compromise proposal merely perpetuated, was that a citizen's vote "in the six smallest senatorial districts would be worth fifteen or more times that of a citizen in the Jefferson [Birmingham] senatorial district." Overall, 27.6 percent of the state's voters controlled the Alabama Senate. Following the principles laid down in *Baker*, the court decided against the state authorities, justifying its intervention in the political process by emphasizing that the "duty to reapportion rests on the Legislature. This Court acts in the matter reluctantly because of the long-continued default and total inability of the Legislature to reapportion itself." Moreover, if the Court's "moderate steps . . . should prove insufficient to break the stranglehold, the Court remains under the solemn duty to relieve the . . . citizens . . . from farther denial of the equal protection of the laws." The Warren Court upheld the "reapportionment revolution" in *Reynolds v. Sims* (1964).[30]

During two decades after the Warren Court ended, Johnson's individual rights decisions reflected continuing public conflict. President Richard Nixon selected Warren Burger as chief justice following Warren's retirement in 1969. Burger knew Johnson and urged Nixon to nominate him for one of several subsequent positions on the Supreme Court. Ironically, it was Alabama's Republican Party stalwarts who convinced Nixon not to make the appointment.[31] The incident suggested the Warren Court's ambivalent legacy. To a certain extent, Johnson's affirmation of the Warren Court's rights revolution was consistent with Americans' enduring commitment to postwar liberal democracy and antitotalitarianism. From the late 1960s on, however, blue-collar and middle-class Americans were increasingly receptive to conservatives' assertions that the expansion of individual rights not only threatened law and order but also had undermined popular support for the Vietnam War, leading to the nation's defeat. Chief Justice Burger's endorsement of Johnson's Supreme Court nomination was thus symptomatic of a respect for a persistent liberal strain in the nation's public consciousness; the opposition Johnson received from fellow Alabama Republicans indicated, by contrast, a powerful conservative reaction against liberalism that was taking hold throughout America. Ronald Reagan's elevation of William H.

Rehnquist to be chief justice in 1986 symbolized the conservative ascendancy. Johnson's decisions throughout the same period involving the First Amendment, gender and employment discrimination, the death penalty, and the right of privacy thus reflected a tension lasting into the 1990s and beyond.[32]

Johnson's First Amendment decisions were consistent with the most enduring liberal constitutional legacy. Since the 1930s, with the pronounced exception of the McCarthy era, Americans supported expanding the free speech, press, petition, and assembly guarantees of the First Amendment. As the Court wrestled with recurring demands to enlarge the official space in which to conduct what Justice Oliver Wendell Holmes Jr. called the "free trade in ideas," it sanctioned increased forms of expression that individuals or groups used to convince others that their cause was just. Conforming to this pattern were the mounting protests against the Vietnam War. A prominent protest leader was the Reverend William Sloan Coffin. Early in 1969 an officially chartered student organization and members of the faculty at Alabama's Auburn University invited Rev. Coffin to speak on campus. University president Harry M. Philpott instituted policies aimed expressly at preventing Coffin's visit. Students and faculty challenged the policies before Johnson's court; following a long line of precedents, he held in *Brooks v. Auburn University* that the president's actions were a blatant example of censorship, which violated the First Amendment. Johnson's reasoning related directly to the wider social benefits gained from preserving broad guarantees of free expression. He acknowledged that "many forces . . . tended to foster fear that the First Amendment is 'folly'. The paranoia of living under a nuclear balance of terror, the divisiveness of an unpopular war, the racial tensions existing throughout the country, the economic and social deterioration of our inner cities, and the insecurity of unprecedented technological change are but a few of the forces which continue to threaten our constitutional form of government." He concluded, "If our First Amendment's freedom to speak and freedom to listen are unduly infringed, our plan of self-government is seriously weakened." The Fifth Circuit affirmed Johnson and there was no further appeal.[33]

Johnson's leading religious freedom opinion concerned still more contested First Amendment issues. In 1947 Justice Black's *Everson* decision established the basic constitutional framework for interpreting the amendment's establishment and free exercise of religion clauses.[34] As various authorities have observed, the Court's subsequent development of precedent suggested a logical contradiction: "On the one hand, the Court read the establishment clause as saying that if a law's purpose is to aid religion, it is unconstitutional. On the other hand, the Court has read the free exercise clause as saying that, under certain circumstances, the state must aid religion."[35] The most successful reconciliation of this tension was the Burger Court's three-pronged *Lemon* test: "First, the [state] statute must have a secular legislative purpose; second, its principle or primary effect must be one that neither advances nor inhibits religion; finally, the statute must not foster an excessive government entanglement with religion."[36] By the 1980s, "culture wars" and "identity politics" associated with Reagan conservatism seriously challenged the *Lemon* test; but the Court adhered to its basic principles. Johnson's *Jager* decision in 1989 successfully applied these principles. At a public high school in Douglas County, Georgia, officials delivered a Christian invocation before every football game. A Native American student objected, asserting that the state-compelled sanction of Protestant Christian prayers impinged on his religious faith. The trial court declared unconstitutional the original invocations but upheld efforts to accommodate the Native American's beliefs through an "equal access" plan. Johnson's opinion for the circuit court applying two prongs of the *Lemon* test however, held that the whole program had a religious purpose and advanced a religion, contrary to the First Amendment.[37]

Johnson's decisions extending gender equality and the rights of disabled persons revealed the Warren Court's ambivalent legacy. The Burger Court began applying the strict scrutiny principle in favor of greater constitutional equality for women. Title VII of the Civil Rights Act of 1964 prohibited employment discrimination for reasons of sex as well as race. Johnson's Fifth Circuit court decision in *Weeks v. Southern Bell Telephone Co.* (1969)[38] established the direction the Supreme Court subsequently followed affirming women's workplace equality under the law. Shortly thereafter, Johnson declared another significant extension of gender justice. In *Frontiero v. Laird* (1972), a special three-judge panel held that military regulations granting male military personnel greater benefits than their female counterparts were lawful. Johnson dissented, arguing that gender no less than racial discrimination violated the Constitution's equal protection and due process guarantees. Reversing the lower court upon appeal, the Supreme Court adopted Johnson's theory in what became one of the Constitution's most important guarantees of gender equality.[39] A decade later, Johnson employed the same innovative analytical skills to establish for handicapped persons increased legal grounds for alleging employment discrimination. A lower federal court held that a worker lacked legal standing to argue that a state agency had unlawfully denied employment for reasons of his handicap. Johnson's circuit court decision reversed, holding on the basis of an original statutory construction that federal law established broad procedural protections for handicapped workers that state agencies must follow.[40]

Johnson's efforts to broaden the right of privacy, by contrast, had a more ambiguous outcome. In 1965 the Warren Court declared for the first time that various provisions of the Bill of Rights created a zone of privacy that through the
Fourteenth Amendment's due process clause protected a married couples' use of
contraceptives from state interference.[41] Eight years later in *Roe v. Wade* the
Burger Court dramatically enlarged the guarantee of privacy to include a
women's right to an abortion during the first trimester of pregnancy.[42] Although
the Court subsequently narrowed the right's scope, the fundamental principle as
it applied to abortions was repeatedly affirmed, despite enormous public criticism. Amid the abortion controversy, Johnson held in *Hardwick v. Bowers* (1985)
for the federal circuit court that police officials' efforts to enforce Georgia's
sodomy law against homosexuals violated the right of privacy. Upon appeal the
Supreme Court, by a five-to-four vote, reversed the decision.[43] Reportedly, Johnson personally disapproved of the conduct and hoped that society would "find a
cure"; but he did not believe that the state could prohibit it between consenting
adults in the privacy of the home.[44] Johnson's refusal to infuse public law with a
stricter moral standard in this case paralleled Americans increased toleration of
homosexuality in the face of continuing opposition. Ironically, thirteen years
later, Georgia's highest court applied a 1905 state precedent defending privacy in
civil actions and overturned the state's sodomy law as a violation of a right of privacy guaranteed by the Georgia constitution.[45]

Johnson's death penalty opinions had a similarly mixed result. In 1972 the
Burger Court declared for the first time that discrimination in the administration
of the death penalty constituted cruel and unusual punishment under the
Eighth Amendment, which applied to the states through the Fourteenth Amendment's due process clause. The states responded by attempting to eliminate discriminatory practices from capital punishment procedures; the Court held that
in principle these new measures were constitutional.[46] Meanwhile, over many
years, Justices William J. Brennan and Thurgood Marshall failed to win a majority on the Court for the principle that the Eighth Amendment made the death
penalty per se unconstitutional.[47] Within these limits the Court's precedents
sanctioned numerous procedural claims that death row inmates might raise
challenging the fairness of the state's process. The complexity of these rules was
such that delays in administering capital punishment were common. Nevertheless, at the end of the appeals there was usually death. Johnson was on the de-
fensive in the struggle over the death penalty. In *Hance v. Zant* (1983)[48] his circuit court decision held that a prosecutor's inflammatory statements about the
need for the death penalty during the trial's sentencing phase was a fundamen-

tally unfair violation of the Constitution. Briefly, the decision established a basis for ordering the state to impose a sentence less than death in capital cases; two years later, however, the circuit court overruled *Hance*. Even so, in 1985 Johnson's circuit opinion in *Dix v. Kemp*[49] shifted from the defendant to the state the burden of proving what constituted "mitigating circumstances" that might lead to a lower sentence than the death penalty. Thus the death penalty cases were typical of Johnson's proactive stance in the uneven transformation of American constitutional rights from the 1950s to the end of the century.

Johnson and the Revolution in Remedies

During the 1970s Robert F. Kennedy Jr. went to Alabama to study George Wallace but instead ended up writing about Johnson. Kennedy switched subjects because he found that the federal judge's authority had replaced the governor's in guiding the operation of large institutions responsible for such important social services as mental health and prisons.[50] Judicial policy making seemed to have taken over the duties of democratically elected officials. Another incisive observer was more explicit: the "real Governor" of Alabama was Johnson.[51] While the clash between Wallace and Johnson made the Alabama story especially dramatic, federal judges increasingly displaced elected politicians in the allocation of institutional resources. Throughout America a relative contraction of postwar economic growth compelled a new prioritization of spending for public services. Without judicial coercion, elected officials had little or no political reason to be responsive to such marginal groups as mental health patients and prisoners. Thus, "In institutional cases the courts have found in constitution and statute heretofore undreamed-of entitlements . . . representing fundamental choices respecting the distribution of social power."[52] In these institutional cases judges like Johnson applied the law of equity. "Above all," according to Peter C. Hoffer, the goal of equity was "fairness," pursued by "peering behind the formalities to seek the real extent of harm." The equitable power included a wide range of remedies imposed through injunction. This injunctive relief, Hoffer continued, enabled the judge "to induce parties to settle their differences, intruding himself and his appointees into the process, if necessary on continuing basis, to oversee the settlement. His decree brings the parties back before him, and he retains jurisdiction over the suit until its resolution satisfies him."[53]

Historically, courts employed injunctions to remedy past grievances by providing prohibitory relief. The injunction Johnson ultimately fashioned for Alabama's public schools was reparative in nature, intended to go beyond immediate prohibition to correct and prevent future wrongs through continuing judicial intervention. Johnson wrote,

> If we, as judges, have learned anything from *Brown v. Board of Education* and
> its progeny, it is that prohibitory relief alone affords but a hollow protection to
> the basic and fundamental rights of citizens to equal protection of the law.
> Once a constitutional deprivation has been shown, it becomes the duty of the
> court to render a decree which will as far as possible eliminate the effects of
> the past deprivations as well as bar like deprivations in the future. Because of
> the complexity and nature of the constitutional rights and issues involved the
> traditional forms of relief have proven totally inadequate.[54]

Johnson's faith in reparative judicial remedies engendered critics and defenders alike. Dismayed that numerous other courts had adopted Johnson's remedial innovations, one critic observed that "moral hubris and intellectual confusion has permitted judges to believe that 'the constitution' requires a more pervasive set of social policies." The same commentator suggested that judges such as Johnson were "psychically" attracted to the "role of moralist and the job of social reformer." As a result, the activist judicial intrusion Johnson represented sapped the "vitality of self government at the local level," which depended on "maintaining strong incentives for popular participation" that had "characterized the American political system since de Tocqueville's time."[55] By contrast, supporters of the policy-making role Johnson symbolized have argued that within the democratic order itself were "passionate and vested commitments to uphold . . . the apparatus of the state that is supporting and buttressing . . . [an] illegal, unconstitutional order, and the question is, how do you transform . . . [and] reconstruct it." To meet this challenge took courage, his defenders agreed, but the essence of Johnson's "legacy" had most "to do with the administration of law and how you make law real in practical affairs," which is the "paradigmatic job of a [federal] District judge."[56]

These contradictory policy presumptions shaped Johnson's handling of the most dramatic episode of the voting rights struggle. As noted above, in conjunction with brutal attacks by local law enforcement officials, Wallace interfered with the famous Selma-to-Montgomery march, the protest that brought about passage of the Voting Rights Act of 1965. In this explosive environment Johnson ordered that Martin Luther King Jr. could proceed only after he agreed in a hearing to comply with a court order regulating the course of the march. The court's order undercut Wallace's resistance and the march itself progressed peacefully. King's march pitted the "right to petition one's government for the redress of grievances" against the "rights by other citizens to use the sidewalks, streets, and highways." Johnson conceded that "where, as here, minorities have been harassed, coerced and intimidated, group association may be the only realistic way of exercising such rights." He emphasized, however, that these rights were not "unrestricted" and it was the court's duty to determine the "constitutional boundary line." To draw that boundary line, Johnson employed the principle of proportionality. In civil and criminal law the principle was used to provide "a larger award for a more serious personal injury, or a harsher penalty for a more serious crime." Essentially, Johnson held that proportional remedies were also permissible in constitutional conflicts. His order stated that it "seems basic to our constitutional principles that the extent of the right to assemble, demonstrate and march peaceably along the highways and streets in an orderly manner should be commensurate with the enormity of the wrongs that are being protested and petitioned against, in this case the wrongs are enormous. The extent of the right to demonstrate against these wrongs should be determined accordingly."[57]

Johnson's facility for adapting established principle to new purposes was indeed controversial. His order not only put the authority of a federal court behind a peaceful demonstration, it also resulted in President Lyndon Johnson federalizing the National Guard to protect the marchers at a cost of $500,000. In addition, the order blocked off miles of a public highway so that the march could proceed according to the "highest standards of dignity and decorum."[58] Even those who recognized the wisdom, innovation, and necessity of Johnson's remedy said that formal sanction of a protest march through court order and federal government action was "troublesome." Some of Johnson's keenest admirers, moreover, found the scope of the decree disturbing, particularly because it "didn't have any justification in the law whatsoever." Nevertheless, these and other observers conceded that, given the massive resistance from Wallace and other public officials, anything less than Johnson's order would have failed.[59]

Psychological motivations undoubtedly influenced Johnson's actions, but these were essentially neither moralistic nor reformist. In the Selma protest march Johnson rejected white supremacy primarily because of an overriding faith in fundamental fairness. He acquired this faith from his family, though clearly, powerful personal encounters with African Americans reinforced it. Moreover, he shared with only a small number of white southern lawyers such as Rives the atypical experience of successfully defending African Americans in court. As a result of the linkage between conviction and career, both men had reason to believe that through the lawyer's adversarial process and judicial independence, fairness could prevail over prejudice. Yet outside the court system public officials seeking political advantage through democratic appeals prevented the triumph of fundamental fairness, and inadequate access and representation by lawyers or a judge's self-restraint impeded achieving it from within the judicial process. Even so, it was apparent that what drove judges such as Johnson and Rives was not a "psychically" inspired reformist zeal and attachment to large moral philosophies but the narrower pursuit of basic fairness.

While Johnson's pioneering uses of injunctive relief aroused enormous criticism, it also encouraged extended application. Once lawyers realized the potential reach of Johnson's remedial principles, they brought cases seeking to have state mental health facilities provide patients with adequate care and treatment. Initially, some of these suits involved racial discrimination in the administration of treatment. When Wallace resisted the litigation, Johnson, again on technically questionable authority, brought in the federal government. Using its investigative resources, the government helped to establish a factual record of profoundly deplorable and often tragic conditions affecting all patients. Relying on this record and other factual data, Johnson attacked the problem with a broad range of administrative approaches based on the principle that handicapped and mental patients possessed fundamental constitutional rights under the Fourteenth Amendment. In the leading decision of *Wyatt v. Stickney* (1971) and its companion case *Wyatt v. Aderholt* (1972),[60] Johnson employed the reparative injunction at a new level of sophistication: to monitor compliance with the order he appointed a Human Rights Committee of Alabama citizens, which then reported to the court. According to an assessment appearing in the *Harvard Law Review* in 1980, the case "deserves paradigmatic status, for it has all the elements of a dramatic set piece: wretched mental patients, a steely-eyed judge of national prominence, a recalcitrant state bureaucracy, and a new constitutional right."[61]

During the 1970s, Johnson extended similarly complex injunctive relief to a case concerning Alabama's prison system. In *Newman v. Alabama* (1972), the court heard conclusive evidence that state officials had not provided prisoners with adequate medical care. Johnson employed a detailed order designed to enforce a prisoner's right to satisfactory medical treatment. Some years later, in *Pugh v. Locke* (1976), litigation produced undisputed evidence that overcrowding and other inhumane conditions were so extensive throughout the state's prison system as to constitute violation of the Eighth Amendment's prohibition against cruel and unusual punishment. Johnson extended the earlier decree to encompass the whole penal system despite opposition from Governor Wallace. To implement and monitor compliance with this order, Johnson again appointed a Human Rights Committee.[62]

The pioneering character of these large, institutional remedial decrees, while significant, obscured their restrained administration and outcome. Of course, Johnson initially had the opportunity to act only because lawyers brought suits involving significant violations of individual rights, often conditioned by resistance from Wallace and other public officials. Clearly, he reacted to this challenge with marked creativity and innovation. Yet his remedies always followed a process that accepted the "delicate" character of the "balance of power" between state and federal government. Accordingly, he formulated decrees to keep to a "minimum the disruption of state institutions and the intrusion into state inflictions." He readily conceded that his orders curtailed state officials' "autonomy and flexibility," but he entered those orders only after those officials failed to respond effectively once the court held that a problem existed.[63] And even if state and local officials failed to act, Johnson maintained all parties' involvement in order to legitimate remedial enforcement through what amounted to an ongoing process of negotiation.

As a result of Johnson's approach, change not only proceeded at a gradual pace, but it was relatively moderate in scope. In both the desegregated public schools and the large mental health or prison institutions, according to Larry Yackle, conditions were not "affirmatively good" under the reparative injunctions; they were "merely better," but this did not diminish the significance of the results. The wrongs were sufficiently great that Johnson's orders achieved a noteworthy degree of improvement. Nevertheless, the scale of the change could not exceed the limits of judicial action, as opposed to legislative or executive enforcement. As Yackle observed, the "issuance of an injunction only initiated a long-term relationship in which Johnson intervened again and again with supplemental orders, relaxing deadlines and establishing new ones, in the course of shaping an institution's operations into satisfactory order."[64] More profound change would have required a degree of community support that did not exist in Alabama. Put another way, judicial remedies were necessary because the state had defaulted on its policy-making role; yet the impact of judicial administration could only partially match the scale of that default.

Indeed, Johnson perceived his role within distinctly legal limits. Regarding the broad range of individual rights cases, he said, "I don't find them complex social issues. I don't regard them as societal issues. I regard them as legal issues."[65] Echoing Johnson's own explanation, a leading study of prison reform adopts the "premise that judicial decisions [decreeing extensive remedial justice] are de-termined by two sets of ideas—the judges' personal attitudes and existing legal doctrine."[66] Another keen observer of the judge's reparative remedial decrees emphasized that "Johnson didn't begin where he wound up. I think it was a kind of education that he got sitting on the bench trying to do his job, being con-fronted with outright and open defiance time and time again." He did not start with a large social theory; rather, he was "creative under the force of circum-stance—he was understanding, he was responding to the necessities of the situ-ation, and improvised and innovated. He didn't have a map of what he was do-ing." His creativity was "a creativity that comes from a man of great integrity, of great courage, determined to do a difficult job. Just going back and doing the job sometimes forces you to sort of shatter old forms of law and create new ones. Every step that Johnson took was pushed by historic circumstances."[67]

Ultimately the remedial justice of Johnson and other federal judges reflected a fundamental irony in American democracy. Profound social inequities and de-plorable conditions were addressed through judicial action in the Selma-to-Montgomery march and the mental health and prison cases because the elected officials most directly responsible lacked political incentives to develop remedies without coercion. It was not that majoritarian democracy fostered inaction but, rather, that it encouraged the politics of blame. Thus in Alabama leaders such as Wallace aggressively resisted progressive social policies in order to force upon others the political accountability for change. A defender of Alabama's segrega-tion system grasped how Wallace's defiance in the Selma march actually fur-thered the wider democratic outcome that he purportedly opposed: "George [Wallace] did more to bring about what he professed to oppose than any other three people I can name. Standing in the school house door—well, that gave him nationwide attention. But it sure did integrate our schools faster than any other state in the South. And this adamant, defiant attitude on the Selma march thing—whatever point they were trying to make, George just made it for 'em."[68]

In the Selma march Martin Luther King also appreciated that judicial action could facilitate greater democracy. King's "Tuesday turn-about" at Pettus Bridge engendered angry criticism from SNCC and other activists who, according to Garrow, "were outraged that a deal to terminate the march had been cut with-out their knowledge." King and fellow SCLC leaders were "caught in a strange crossfire between movement workers seeking his assurance that he had not made a secret deal and newsmen asking if he had agreed to the turnaround so as not to violate . . . [Johnson's] court order."[69] Yet this embrace of a protest strategy, in which Johnson's decree embodied the main points of the "march plan" black lawyers themselves had presented to the court, was consistent with King's reported observation that Johnson was "a man of great honor . . . [who] gave true meaning to the word 'justice.'"[70] Moreover, since the Montgomery bus boycott, civil rights activists, including SNCC's leaders, had looked upon the federal courts as allies necessary for compelling southern state authorities to comply with federal law and the Constitution. King condoned Johnson's expansive remedial decree because, "as federal courts have consistently affirmed . . . it is immoral to urge an individual to withdraw his efforts to gain his basic constitutional rights because the quest precipitates violence. Society must protect the robbed and punish the robber."[71] Thus a protest strategy centered upon remedial justice precipitated one of American democracy's most important laws, the Voting Rights Act of 1965.

Similarly, Johnson's remedial orders in the mental health and prison litigation were ironic affirmations of democracy achieved through judicial action. As a practical matter, the same democratic process that encouraged elected officials to exploit the politics of blame before and during the formulation of the judge's remedial order also aroused at least some public support for compliance. The enormous extent of harm demanding correction in these institutional cases required ongoing allocation of public resources. Clearly, judicial coercion was necessary; but it also facilitated a democratic mobilization of resources within political parties, legislatures, and executive administrations and between federal and state governments. Peter C. Hoffer's insightful study recognized the complexity: "Without political support, if not directly from the other branches of government, then indirectly through the assistance of political parties, interest groups, and local elites, court orders . . . may be reduced to nullities." Thus "effective" remedial justice often "owed as much to . . . the sometimes grudging acquiescence of local leaders, as to the persistence and authority of the federal courts."[72]

The goal of achieving fairness conditioned the impact of Johnson's remedial decrees on democratic institutions. From the 1930s to the Warren Court, Americans' reaction against diverse totalitarian threats fostered the emergence of a majoritarian consciousness which favored rights guarantees in the abstract. The Court's constitutional legitimation of these guarantees broadly sustained the emerging democratic consensus, but Johnson's and other federal judges' actual enforcement of particular rights claims spawned resistance from, or aggravated the default of, public officials, who in turn justified their opposition by appealing to democratic values. Thus, as the rights revolution proceeded, democracy was at war with itself. Johnson's analogical use of precedent, applications of the proportionality principle, and reparative injunctions generally represented the employment of the wide discretion judicial independence sanctioned to reconcile the tensions within the growing majoritarian consensus. Given the enormity of the challenge posed by George Wallace and other leaders following the *Brown* decision, Johnson's pursuit of fundamental fairness was an attainable goal, one consistent with the moderate results his remedial justice actually achieved. While the stand Johnson and other federal judges took was certainly courageous, the true life it gave to individual rights transcended personal accomplishment, strengthening rather than weakening American democracy.

Quoting Johnson's Constitutional Ideals

In an address delivered to the Montgomery County Bar Association in 1990, Johnson stated some fundamental beliefs. He was sure that despite innumerable problems and injustices, a distinctive commitment to basic rights characterized America. This singular regard for rights recognized that the "welfare of the individual is the final goal of group life," embodying "a basic moral principle: all persons are created equal as well as free." This established the "obligation to build social institutions designed to guarantee equality of opportunity to all citizens. Without this equality, freedom becomes an illusion. Thus, the only aristocracy that is consistent with our way of life in America is an aristocracy of talent and achievement." The "American heritage" of equality rejected the "totalitarian arrogance" which imposed "human uniformity or regimentation." Thus, Johnson said: "In our land, citizens are equal, but they are free to be different. From these very differences . . . has come the great human and national strength of America." Consistent with the Declaration of Independence, the Constitution, and the Bill of Rights, government was "denied . . . power to abridge or interfere with certain personal rights and freedom." This same government nonetheless "must referee the clashes which arise among the freedoms of citizens and protect each citizen in the enjoyment of the maximum freedom to which he or she is entitled." From the nation's heritage, institutions, and formal pronouncements of rights flowed the fundamental right to safety and security of the person, right to citizenship and its privileges, right to freedom of conscience and expression, and right of equality of opportunity. The persistent gap between the articulation and fulfillment of these rights did not diminish Johnson's conviction that they were what was "right with America."[73]

These convictions were consistent with other ideas articulated during thirty-six years of judicial service. As early as 1962, in an address on juvenile delinquency given before federal probation authorities, Johnson revealed a keen awareness of the multidimensional nature of individual character, responsibility, culpability, and accountability. Starting with a "knowledge of human nature," which was informed by advances in psychiatry, psychology, sociology, and social work, it was possible to formulate "basic concepts and philosophies" with which to analyze a given problem. There were "no ready-made answers, no simple formula, no firm rules." Instead, the combination of intuition and acquired formal knowledge that shaped conceptual approaches gave public officials the means to "analyze our procedures, analyze our authority for adequacy or inadequacy . . . in practical application of these concepts of philosophy." The goal of this process was an objective comprehension of the facts of each individual's "story." Sentencing was "above all else an individual problem." Once the facts gleaned from the professionals in the field were clear, the judge could fashion a "fair and appropriate sentence." Johnson emphasized that he could not achieve a fair result without the institutional support of experienced professionals. There should be "uniformity in objectives, yes; uniformity in philosophy, yes; uniformity in sentencing, no."[74] Staff work provided the factual content that enabled the judge to fashion a remedy that took into account the influence of extenuating circumstances such as the emotional state and social background of defendants. Defined in these terms, fairness helped to diffuse the defendant's resentment and to foster the public's faith in both the law and the judicial system.

Johnson's core beliefs and sensitivity to the complexities underlying human conduct shaped his view of judicial authority. Throughout his career Johnson confronted the criticism that he and other federal judges were "activists," violating William Blackstone's prescription that judges should merely "find" and "declare" law. Such total objectivity was, Johnson believed, neither possible nor desirable. The constitutional and legal questions that came before courts demanded of judges "an openness of mind and a willingness to decide the issues solely on the particular facts and circumstances involved, not with any preconceived notion or philosophy regarding the outcome of the case." In constitutional cases especially, federal courts trod a middle course: "While a refusal to show proper deference to and respect for the acts and decisions of the coordinate branches of government is judicial intrusion and is, therefore, improper," he wrote, "a blind and unyielding deference to legislative and executive action is judicial abdication and is equally to be condemned."[75]

A court's obligation to decide cases that lawfully came before it made a degree of activism inevitable. The "duty" to uphold law meant that a court was not free to "shirk its sworn responsibility to uphold the Constitution and laws of the

United States. The courts are bound to take jurisdiction and decide the issues — even though those decisions result in criticism." This role was not "usurped by the judiciary" but was "one . . . inextricably intertwined with its duty to interpret the Constitution" and laws generally. According to Johnson, moreover, the federal courts "have never acted directly on the states or assumed jurisdiction of mere political issues, but in cases involving individual rights and liberties, these courts are compelled to construe the law in order to determine such rights and liabilities."[76]

The judge's decisional obligations resulting from linking jurisdiction to rights was essentially "not activism at all." Given his own profound struggles with Wallace (which included labeling the judge "an integrating, scala-wagging, carpet-bagging, race-mixing, bald-face liar"[77] who should be given a "barbed-wire enema")[78] and others, as well as threats to Johnson's family such as the bombing of his mother's house, Johnson could say with authority that judges "do not relish making such hard decisions and certainly do not encourage litigation on social or political problems." The difference between the critics' regard for judicial passivity and the approach taken by Johnson and others was that the exercise of discretion was "measured not by the end result, but how and under what circumstances the result is achieved." Thus decision making was the outcome of a process conditioned by context. For Johnson, the "basic strength of the federal judiciary" was "its independence from political and social pressures, its ability to rise above the influence of popular clamor." Ultimately, he believed this removal from immediate popular influences gave the American people the basis for a sufficiently detached judgment "that decisions of the federal judiciary . . . [became] accepted and revered as monuments memorializing the strength and stability of this nation."[79]

Johnson's trust in the judicial process engendered a primary concern about issues of access and relief. Accordingly, he was an early and active supporter of publicly funded legal aid for the poor and other dispossessed groups, but he believed the basic factor controlling access was whether a sufficient fee incentive existed for lawyers to take on what were otherwise unremunerative suits. In addition, Congress and the judiciary itself liberalized standing and joinder requirements so that lawyers could effectively represent, and courts adjudicate, the "multiplicity of competing if not conflicting interests among members of the same class, among different classes, and among other parties and interveners,"[80] which increasingly characterized litigation during the decades following World War II. Traditional code pleading involved one party suing another with the winner taking all. Judges employed this procedure principally in business or economic litigation, and the result was usually a simple award of damages and a pro-hibitory injunction. The parties in complex litigation that became increasingly common after World War II were social welfare or civil rights litigants whose suits required more than merely a prohibitory injunction to achieve appropriate relief. As a result, Johnson and others developed the structural injunction, a form of equity relief tailored to the needs of the particular case. Usually this type of remedy required the court to monitor compliance, often over a long period of time. In addition, the court often relied on experts and "citizens commissions" whose members were drawn from the community. Citizen involvement in the ongoing implementation of the remedial order further legitimated the process.

Access to, and remedies within, the new process imposed wider social imper-atives upon lawyers. Johnson's overriding deference to the supremacy of law re-quired that lawyers "must be vigilant in keeping our institutions responsive to claims of injustice and voices of dissent." American lawyers were "not only legal technicians, but also . . . social generalists." Especially with regard to "combat-ing emotionalism and demagoguery, lawyers have an educational function with respect to laymen. They must clarify and illuminate the distinction between the constitutionally-protected rights of expression and violation of the law."[81] The "most fundamental of social virtues" was "respect for law," the alternative to which was "violence and anarchy." And it was the lawyer's duty to proclaim "that the heart of our American system rests in obedience to the laws which protect the individual rights of our citizenry. No system can endure if each citizen is free to choose which laws he will obey. Obedience to the laws we like and defiance of those we dislike is the route to chaos."[82]

Johnson had neither sympathy nor respect for lawyers who abdicated their sol-emn duty. "In times of riot and disrespect for judicial decisions, the lawyer must speak. To remain silent is not only a violation of his oath but is tantamount to cowardice and is a grievous injustice to the free society which men of law by con-science and sworn duty, are bound to maintain," he asserted. It was essential that the "voice of moderation" prevail over the "cries of the far left and far right." Both extremists favored "social and political freedoms, individual liberties and states' rights, [but] they were driven by fanaticism. They invariably espouse democracy, but do not begin to understand its very heart: supremacy of and respect for the law—whether we like it or not."[83]

At least initially, Johnson's position toward professional obligations placed lawyers in a difficult position. Even lawyers who defended publicly funded or other fee structures to increase legal aid to poor or dispossessed groups noted that the factors working against the realization of Johnson's views were very powerful.

Most lawyers in Alabama belonged to small firms whose business depended significantly on personal recommendations from satisfied clients. Middle-class and propertied individuals constituted the principal market for those firms' services, and that market was competitive; a lawyer's reputation might easily determine whether potential clients would choose his or her firm and then recommend it to friends, associates, or contacts. As a practical matter, people from the more lucrative client market often distrusted lawyers identified with the representation of indigent individuals or controversial groups such as civil rights activists. At the same time, this more marginal client market was usually insufficiently remunerative to offset a firm's loss of traditional clients.

Ultimately, Johnson's views prevailed because of, rather than despite, market considerations. The growth of public law litigation that changed the federal judiciary's relationship to societal issues was rooted in the social and institutional conflicts that dominated the half-century following World War II. Though far-reaching, these conflicts did not generate a client market to rival the scale of the more traditional one; but the market that did emerge was grounded on such basic tensions that it was more likely to grow than diminish. As federal judges and Congress enlarged access through procedures, fee structures, and legal aid funding, there were sufficient market incentives to encourage even smaller firms to develop this class of suits as part of their wider practice. Thus, by the 1980s, a moderate number of firms throughout Alabama had beaten the odds and achieved the goals Johnson and others had for so long advocated. Also, in conjunction with these changes, Alabama's state law and judicial establishment were increasingly more supportive of "public interest" litigation, enhancing further what nevertheless remained a secondary client market.

Meanwhile, two extremes threatened the law's supremacy and the lawyer's role in sustaining it. The first was the "conduct of those leaders, both political and social, who are busily engaged in the frustration of the law for personal gain." Johnson's criticism extended not only to the self-serving obstructionism of certain elected public leaders such as George Wallace; it also included the corruption of public authority identified with the Watergate crisis in which so many lawyers were found to have committed extensive violations of the law. "When persons with public responsibility make a mockery of law by prostituting legal process and stultifying the forms of law in defiance of their sworn duty to uphold the Constitution and the laws of the land," Johnson said, "the attorney of integrity has a positive duty to intercede." Wallace and Watergate represented a "brutal attack . . . launched against such fundamentals of a democratic society as the administration of justice by impartial courts and the consensus of acceptance and respect for judicial decision." It was the legal profession's "sacred and unique responsibility . . . to quietly illuminate the path of reason and to loudly proclaim the supremacy of law."[84]

Civil disobedience, the other extreme, raised more complex challenges. If lawyers provided dispossessed and exploited groups adequate access to legal institutions, the "condition for justifiable civil disobedience [would] rarely, if ever, exist," Johnson believed. He thus distinguished between legitimate civil disobedience and revolution. Advocates of both broke the law, but proponents of civil disobedience strove to change the established legal order, whereas the revolutionary worked for the "total eradication of the existing legal system." The latter was fundamentally inconsistent with the supremacy of law. Under certain circumstances and to a point, however, civil disobedience and the legal order were reconcilable. The only legitimate form of civil disobedience was "an open, intentional violation of a law concededly valid, under a banner of morality or justice by one willing to accept punishment for the violation."[85]

He also conditioned his acceptance of civil disobedience on several pragmatic considerations. First, "a serious extensive, and apparently enduring breakdown in the responsiveness of our institutions must be a necessary condition of justified civil disobedience." In the "recent history" of America "only the persistent and flagrant denial of the rights of our Negro citizens in certain sections of our country could be cited as an example of this kind of breakdown." Second, demonstrators employing a strategy of peaceful disobedience should gauge the risk of it turning into a "violent confrontation. One who is responsible for violence loses all possible justification for civil disobedience," Johnson said. Third, "basic principles must be at issue, the provocation must be extreme, and the evils likely to endure unless most vigorously combated." Finally, he distinguished between the conduct of individuals and that of groups. The lone protester acted as the result of "a private assertion of personal conviction," whereas "large dissident groups" employed civil disobedience as a "tactic of political protest." The latter was more controversial than the former. American tradition sanctioned by the First Amendment's free exercise clause "defer[red] to the mandates of individual conscience," which had "virtually no risk of violence and the effect on attitudes toward law [was] likely to be slight." The nation "inherit[ed]" this "tradition of civil disobedience from men of the moral stature of Socrates, Jesus Christ, and St. Thomas More."[86]

Circumscribed change attained through the adversarial process was central to Johnson's essentially conservative faith. Critics attacked Johnson's uses of judicial discretion, primarily because he employed the remedial process (particularly injunctive relief) to vindicate rights by compelling public officials to act in policy areas where previously they had declined or refused to do so. Inferentially, Johnson's detractors also recognized that the process legitimated the rights of traditionally excluded groups. As a description of judicial activism, however, both criticisms obscured the comparatively moderate results Johnson's injunctive innovations actually achieved. Making rights the basis of remedies meant that inhuman and tragic institutional conditions improved, but the problems underlying these conditions often were not permanently solved. And that was exactly the point: Johnson applied institutionally autonomous judicial authority to force elected and appointed policy makers to confront on an ongoing basis social issues that had little or no ultimate solution. Rather, like crime or the maintenance of highways, such social issues required continuous policy-making attention so that the system of which they were now part might function to a reasonably effective degree. Ultimately what Johnson did was to get and hold public officials' attention on matters they preferred to ignore.

Thus Johnson's professed rationale for what others described as boundless judicial activism was fundamentally conservative. His expression of core values emphasized a patriotic vision of Americanism resting not on pervasive social or class amalgamation or individualistic libertarianism but on basic equality under law and equality of opportunity. Johnson defined rights guarantees enshrined in the Constitution and Bill of Rights as being contrary to the mass social and political conformity imposed by "totalitarian arrogance," the opposite of which was a brand of individual liberty characterized by the fundamental right to personal security, opportunity, citizenship, and freedom of expression and conscience. Americans achieved this vision of equal rights through legal institutions, particularly an independent judiciary and access to the adversarial process depending on fair and effective representation by lawyers. Fundamental fairness secured through judicial autonomy protected individual rights and deflected social and political struggle. Thus did Judge Frank Johnson defend constitutional rights.

Tony A. Freyer

Notes

Introduction: Johnson's Unusual Origins and Early Career

1. The leading biographical works on Johnson's life are Jack Bass, *Taming the Storm: The Life and Times of Judge Frank M. Johnson, Jr., and the South's Fights Over Civil Rights* (Doubleday, New York, 1993); Tinsley E. Yarbrough, *Judge Frank Johnson and Human Rights in Alabama* (University of Alabama Press, University, 1981); Robert F. Kennedy Jr., *Judge Frank M. Johnson, Jr.* (G. P. Putnam's Sons, New York, 1978); Frank Sikora, *The Judge: The Life and Opinions of Alabama's Frank M. Johnson, Jr.* (Black Belt Press, Montgomery, Ala., 1992). See also Tony A. Freyer and Timothy Dixon, *Democracy and Judicial Independence: A History of the Federal Courts of Alabama, 1820–1994* (Carlson Publishing, Brooklyn, 1995), and Tony A. Freyer, *Individual Rights, Judicial Discretion, and Judge Frank M. Johnson, Jr.*, 39 *Saint Louis University Law Journal* (Winter 1995): 523–66.

2. In addition to the biographical studies listed in note 1, see references to Johnson in Taylor Branch, *Parting the Waters: America in the King Years, 1954–63* (Simon & Schuster, New York, 1989); Dan T. Carter, *The Politics of Rage: George Wallace, the Origins of the New Conservatism, and the Transformation of American Politics* (Simon & Schuster, New York, 1995); David J. Garrow, *Bearing the Cross: Martin Luther King, Jr., and the Southern Christian Leadership Conference* (William Morrow, New York, 1986); Juan Williams, *Eyes on the Prize: America's Civil Rights Years, 1954–1965* (Viking Penguin, New York, 1987).

3. In addition to the biographical works given in note 1, see the leading study by a legal academic, Larry W. Yackle, *Reform and Regret: The Story of Federal Judicial Involvement in the Alabama Prison System* (Oxford University Press, New York, 1989); and references in Theodore Eisenberg and Stephen C. Yeazell, *The Ordinary and the Extraordinary in Institutional Litigation*, 93 *Harvard Law Review* (January 1980): 465–517; and Peter Charles Hoffer, *The Law's Conscience: Equitable Constitutionalism in America* (University of North Carolina Press, Chapel Hill, 1990). See also Freyer, *Individual Rights, Judicial Discretion, and Judge Frank M. Johnson, Jr.* A major general work that locates in a broad historical and theoretical context Johnson's mental health facilities and prisons cases is Malcolm M. Feeley and Edward L. Rubin, *Judicial Policy Making and the Modern State: How the Courts Reformed America's Prisons* (Cambridge University Press, Cambridge, 1998).

4. Representative journalistic commentary is found in Steven Brill, "The Real Governor of Alabama," *New York Magazine*, April 26, 1976, 37–41; and "Federal Judge Frank M. Johnson, Interpretor on the Front Line," *Time*, May 12, 1968, 72–78. The Supreme Court citations are given in this volume's conclusion.

5. Unless otherwise stated, the following text and quotations are from interviews Johnson gave Jack Bass, which Bass then published in *Taming the Storm.*

6. *Brown v. Bd. of Edu.*, 349 U.S. 294 (1955).

7. For Rives, see John M. Spivack, *Race, Civil Rights and the United States Court of Appeals for the Fifth Judicial Circuit* (Garland, New York, 1990), 139–45.

8. As quoted, Bass, *Taming the Storm*, at 17.

9. As quoted, Bass, *Taming the Storm*, at 19.

10. As quoted, Bass, *Taming the Storm*, at 20.

11. As quoted, Bass, *Taming the Storm*, at 32.

12. As quoted, Bass, *Taming the Storm*, at 37.

13. As quoted, Bass, *Taming the Storm*, at 28.

14. As quoted, Bass, *Taming the Storm*, at 23, 44.

15. As quoted, Bass, *Taming the Storm*, at 462.

16. As quoted, Bass, *Taming the Storm*, at 41.

17. As quoted, Bass, *Taming the Storm*, at 46–47.

18. As quoted, Bass, *Taming the Storm*, at 52, 55.

19. As quoted, Bass, *Taming the Storm*, at 52–55.

20. As quoted, Bass, *Taming the Storm*, at 60–61.

21. As quoted, Bass, *Taming the Storm*, at 74.

22. Spivack, *Race, Civil Rights and the . . . Fifth Judicial Circuit*, 139, 145.

23. As quoted, Bass, *Taming the Storm*, at 82.

24. As quoted, Bass, *Taming the Storm*, at 83, 84.

25. As quoted, Bass, *Taming the Storm*, at 85.

26. As quoted, Bass, *Taming the Storm*, at 81.

27. As quoted, Bass, *Taming the Storm*, at 105.

The Attorney and the Supremacy of Law

1. The duty of public service by representation of indigent defendants has exacted significantly more effort from the legal profession since the decision of *Gideon v. Wainwright*, 372 U.S. 335 (1963). See also *Escobedo v. Illinois*, 378 U.S. 478, 492 (1964); *Douglas v. California*, 372 U.S. 353 (1963); *Alden v. Montana*, 234 F. Supp. 661 (D.C. Mont. 1964). However, in federal courts financial remuneration for such cases has been provided the attorney by statute. See 19 U.S.C. I 3006A (1964). Designated the Criminal Justice Act of 1964, this legislation furnishes counsel for indigent defendants charged with felonies or misdemeanors other than petty offenses at every stage in the proceedings from his initial appearance before the United States commissioner or court through any appeal. The act provides compensation for the attorney at a rate of fifteen dollars per hour for time expended in court or before a commissioner and ten dollars per hour for time reasonably expended out of court, in addition to reimbursement for expenses reasonably incurred. Except in extraordinary cases, total reimbursement is limited to $500 in felony cases and $300 in misdemeanor cases. The same rates and limitations are applicable for representation in an appellate court. Attorney General Robert F. Kennedy explained the need for compensation of attorneys ap-

pointed to represent indigents: "Far more often, however, the assignment will go to a young and inexperienced lawyer, unable to finance the careful search for witnesses and evidence and the time consuming preparation and trial which an adequate defense may demand. Representation so limited—in time, lacking in money, and short on experience—is representation far short of that contemplated by the framers of our Constitution." H.R. REP. Co. 864, 88th Cong., 1st Sess. 6 (1963).

2. Canon 22 of the ABA Canons of Professional Ethics sets forth the requirement of candor and fairness in dealing with the courts, providing in part: "It is not candid or fair for the lawyer knowingly to misquote the contents of a paper, the testimony of a witness, the language or the argument of opposing counsel, or the language of a decision or a textbook: or with knowledge of its invalidity, to cite as authority a decision that has been overruled, or a statute that has been repealed. . . . These and all kindred practices are unprofessional and unworthy of an officer of the law charged, with the duty of aiding in the administration of justice." ABA Canons of Professional Ethics No. 22 (1963).

3. "The lawyer owes entire devotion to the interest of the client, warm zeal in the maintenance and defense of his rights and the exertion of his utmost learning and ability to the end that nothing be taken or withheld from him, save by the rules of law, legally applied." ABA Canons of Professional Ethics No. 37 (1963).

4. See ABA Canons of Professional Ethics No. 22 (1963).

5. ABA Canons of Professional Ethics No. 1 (1963).

6. ALA Code of Ethics, Reprinted in 2 Ala. Law. 259, 260–261 (1941).

7. Mill, Considerations on Representative Government 3 (peoples ed. 1865).

Civil Disobedience and the Law

1. *Hamm v. City of Rock Hill*, 379 U.S. 306, 328 (1964)(dissenting opinion).

2. *Forman v. City of Montgomery*, 245 F. Supp. 17, 24–25 (M.D. Ala. 1965).

3. *Williams v. Wallace*, 240 F. Supp. 100 (M.D. Ala. 1965).

4. See Greenberg, *The Supreme Court, Civil Rights and Civil Dissonance*, 77 Yale L.J. 1520 (1968).

5. Compare *Cox v. Louisiana*, 379 U.S. 536 (1965), which involved a demonstration on the public streets of Baton Rouge, Louisiana, with *Adderley v. Florida*, 385 U.S. 39 (1966), a case dealing with a protest on the grounds of a county jail.

6. In *Cox v. Louisiana*, 379 U.S. 536 (1965), the Court observed at page 555: "We emphatically reject the notion . . . that the First and Fourteenth Amendments afford the same kind of freedom to those who would communicate ideas by conduct such as patrolling, marching, and picketing on streets and highways as . . . to those who communicate ideas by pure speech."

7. 391 U.S. 367 (1968).

8. *Id.* At 388–89 (concurring opinion).

9. *Williams v. Wallace*, 240 Supp. 100, 106 (M.D. Ala. 1965).

10. See Black, *The Problem of the Compatibility of Civil Disobedience with American Institutions of Government*, 43 Texas L. Rev. 492 (1965); see also Marshall, *The Protest Movement and the Law*, 51 Va. L. Rev. 785 (1965).

11. See H. Thoreau, Walden, *On the Duty of Civil Disobedience*, 295–300 (Rinehart ed. 1948).

12. T. Hobbes, Leviathan 84 (A. Waller ed. 1904).

13. 240 F. Supp. 100 (M.D. Ala. 1965).

14. 42 U.S.C. § 1973 (Supp. III, 1968).

15. See *Rights in Conflict: The Walker Report to the National Commission on the Causes and Prevention of Violence* 4 (Bantam ed. 1968).

16. *Id.* at 2; see generally *id.* at 59–75.

17. See p. 8 *supra.*

18. 296 F. Supp. 188 (M.D. Ala. 1969).

19. 245 F. Supp. 25 (M.D. Ala. 1965).

20. *Id.* at 28–30.

21. Address by Chief Justice Earl Warren, Cambridge, Mass., in Trial, Oct.–Nov. 1968, at 40.

School Desegregation Problems in the South: An Historical Perspective

1. 347 U.S. 483 (1954).

2. *Id.* at 495.

3. *Id.* at 496 n.13.

4. *Brown v. Board of Educ.*, 349 U.S. 294 (1955)(*Brown II*).

5. *Id.* at 298–300.

6. *Id.* at 299.

7. 231 F. Supp. 743 (M.D. Ala. 1964).

8. *E.g.*, No. 42, [1956] Ala. Acts Spec. Sess. 70.

9. No. 894, [1953] Ala. Acts 1201.

10. No. 201, [1955] Ala. Acts 492.

11. *E.g.*, No. 555, [1954] La. Acts 1036.

12. No. 201, [1955] Ala. Acts. 492.

13. See note 8 *supra.*

14. *Shuttlesworth v. Birmingham Bd. of Educ.*, 162 F. Supp. 372, 381 (N.D. Ala. 1958).

15. ALA. CODE, tit. 52 § 61(13) (Supp. 1969).

16. ALA. CODE, tit. 52 § 61(16) (Supp. 1969).

17. No. 528, § 5, [1957] Ala. Acts 724.

18. ALA. CODE, tit. 52 § 61 (11) (Supp. 1969).

19. *Johnson v. Yielding*, 267 Ala. 108, 100 So.2d 29 (1958).

20. 377 U.S. 218 (1965).

21. *Monroe v. Board of Commr's of the City of Jackson*, 391 U.S. 450 (1968).

22. See, e.g., Joyner & Thames, *Mississippi's Efforts at Industrialization: A Critical Analysis*, 38 Miss. L.J. 433, 477 (1967).

23. See Comment, *Judicial Performance in the Fifth Circuit*, 73 Yale L.J. 90 (1963).

24. *Borders v. Rippy*, 247 F.2d 268, 271 (1957).

25. 132 F. Sup. 776, 777 (E.D.S.C. 1955) citing *Avery v. Wichita Falls Ind. School Dist.*, 241 F.2d 230, 233 (5th Cir. 1957).

26. *Id.* at 777.

27. *Gibson v. Board of Pub. Instruction of Dade County*, 246 F.2d 913 (5th Cir. 1957); *Holland v. Board of Pub. Instruction of Palm Beach County*, 258 F.2d 730 (5th Cir. 1958).

28. *Covington v. Edwards*, 264 F.2d 780 (4th Cir. 1959).

29. *Bradley v. School Bd. of City of Richmond*, 382 U.S. 103 (1965).

30. *Shuttlesworth v. Birmingham Bd. of Educ.*, 162 F. Supp. 372 (N.D. Ala. 1958).

31. *Lee v. Macon County Bd. of Educ.*, 231 F. Supp. 743 (M.D. Ala. 1964).

32. *Employment Discrimination — Procedural Problems in Title VII Cases*, 1 Race Rel. L. Survey 235 (1970).

33. *United States v. Jefferson County Bd. of Educ.*, 372 F.2d 836, 860 (5th Cir. 1966), aff'd on rehearing en banc, 380 F.2d 385 (1967).

34. *Brewer v. Hoxie School Dist. No. 46*, 238 F.2d 91 (8th Cir. 1956); *Kasper v. Brittain*, 245 F. 2d 92 (6th Cir.), cert. denied, 355 U.S. 834 (1957); *Bullock v. United States*, 265 F.2d 683 (6th Cir.), cert. denied, 360 U.S. 909, 932 (1959).

35. N.Y. Times, May 25, 1965, at 1, col. 4, cited in Note, *The Courts, HEW and Southern School Desegregation*, 77 Yale L.J. 321 n. 38 (1963).

36. *Stell v. Board of Pub. Educ. For City of Savannah*, 387 F.2d 486 (5th Cir. 1967).

37. S. 952, 91st Cong., 1st Sess. (1969). (Passed Senate June 23, 1969).

38. *United States v. Jefferson County Bd. of Educ.*, 372 F.2d 836 (5th Cir. 1966), aff'd on rehearing en banc, 380 F.2d 385 (1967).

39. *Bivens v. Board of Educ.* No. 24754 (5th Cir., May 24, 1967) *Richard v. Christ*, 377 F.2d 460 (5th Cir. 1967).

40. *Id.*

41. *Bivens v. Board of Educ.*, No. 1926 (M.D. Ga., June 29, 1967).

42. Gozansky, Gignilliat & Horwitz, *School Desegregation in the Fifth Circuit*, 1968 Houston L. Rev. 946, 959 n. 100.

43. 419 F. 2d 1211 (Cir. 1969).

44. 221 F. Supp. 297 (M.D. Ala. 1963).

45. *United States v. Wallace*, 222 F. Supp. 485 (M.D. Ala. 1963).

46. *Lee v. Macon County Bd. of Educ.*, 231 F. Supp. at 749.

47. *Id.* at 754.

48. No. 16, [1966] Ala. Acts Spec. Sess. 32.

49. No. 252, [1966] Ala. Acts Spec. Sess. 372.

50. *Lee v. Macon County Bd. of Educ.*, 267 F. Supp. 458 (M.D. Ala. 1967).

51. *Lee v. Macon County Bd. of Educ.*, 283 F. Supp. 194 (M.D. Ala. 1968).

52. Birmingham Post Herald, January 12, 1970.

53. 380 F.2d. At 389 n. 1.

Observation: The Constitution and the Federal District Judge

1. See, e.g., L. Levy, Judgments 33–57 (1972); Mason, *Judicial Activism Old and New*, 55 Va. L. Rev. 385, 394–426 (1969).

2. See, e.g., Griswold, *The Judicial Process*, 31 Fed. B.J. 309, 321–25 (1972).

3. See The Federalist Nos. 47, 48 (J. Madison).

4. U.S. Const. Amend. X.

5. *Cumming v. Richmond County Bd. of Educ.*, 175 U.S. 528, 545 (1899); *Crews v. Cloncs*, 432 F.2d 1259, 1265 (7th Cir. 1970).

6. *Hoag v. New Jersey*, 356 U.S. 464, 468 (1958); *Threat v. North Carolina*, 221 F. Supp. 858, 860 (W.D.N.C. 1963).

7. *Ohio ex rel. Popovici v. Agler*, 280 U.S. 379, 383 (1930); *Morris v. Morris*, 273 F. 2d 678, 682 (7th Cir. 1960); *Ainscow v. Alexander*, 28 Del. Ch. 545, 550, 39 A.2d 54, 56 (Super. Ct. 1944).

8. *Adkins v. Curtis*, 259 Ala. 311, 315, 66 So. 2d 455, 458 (1953); *Beck v. Buena Park Hotel Corp.*, 30 111. 2d 343, 346, 196 N.E.2d 686, 688 (1964); *Collins v. State Bd. of Social Welfare*, 248 Iowa 369, 375, 81 NW.2d 4, 7 (1957).

9. See, e.g., *Marbury v. Madison*, 5 U.S. (1 Cranch) 137, 170 (1803).

10. See, e.g., *Brotherhood of Locomotive Firemen v. Chicago, R.I. & P.R.R.* 393 U.S. 129, 136–37 (1968).

11. *Brown v. Board of Educ.*, 347 U.S. 483 (1954).

12. *Marable v. Mental Health Bd.*, 297 F. Supp. 291 (M.D. Ala. 1969).

13. *Washington v. Lee*, 263 F. Supp. 327 (M.D. Ala. 1966), aff'd, 390 U.S. 333 (1968).

14. *Gilmore v. City of Montgomery*, 176 F. Supp. 776 (M.D. Ala. 1959), modified, 277 F.2d 364 (5th Cir. 1960), rev'd in part, 417 U.S. 556 (1974).

15. *Browder v. Gayle*, 142 F. Supp. 707 (M.D. Ala.), aff'd, 352 U.S. 903 (1956).

16. *Lewis v. Greyhound Corp.*, 199 F. Supp. 210 (M.D. Ala. 1961).

17. *United States v. City of Montgomery*, 201 F. Supp. 590 (M.D. Ala. 1962).

18. *Cobb v. Library Bd.*, 207 F. Supp. 880 (M.D. Ala. 1962).

19. *United States v. United Klans of America*, 290 F. Supp. 181 (M.D. Ala. 1968).

20. *Harris v. Board of Educ.*, 259 F. Supp. 167 (M.D. Ala. 1966); *Lee v. Board of Educ.*, 231 F. Supp. 743 (M.D. Ala. 1964).

21. *Sims v. Frink*, 208 F. Supp. 431 (M.D. Ala. 1962), aff'd sub nom. *Reynolds v. Sims*, 377 U.S.

22. *Sims v. Amos*, 336 F. Supp. 924 (M.D. Ala), aff'd 409 U.S. 942 (1972).

23. *Weissinger v. Boswell*, 330 F. Supp. 615 (M.D. Ala. 1971) (per curiam).

24. *Wyatt v. Stickney*, 324 F. Supp. 781 (M.D. Ala. 1971), enforced 344 F. Supp. 373 (M.D. Ala 1972) (mentally ill) *and* 344 F. Supp. 387 (M.D. Ala. 1972), modified sub nom. *Wyatt v. Aderholt*, 503 F.2d 1305 (5th Cir. 1974) (mentally retarded).

25. *Lynch v. Baxley,* 386 F. Supp. 378 (M.D. Ala 1974).

26. 349 F. Supp. 278 (M.D. Ala. 1972) aff'd in part, 503 F.2d 1320 (5th Cir. 1974), cert. denied, 421 U.S. 948 (1975).

27. *Id.* at 285.

28. *Id.* at 286–88.

29. *Id.* at 286.

30. *Id.* at 287.

31. *Id.*

32. *Id.* 325 F. Supp. 781 (M.D. Ala. 1971), enforced, 344 F. Supp. 373 (M.D. Ala. 1972) and 344 F. Supp. 387 (M.D. Ala. 1972), modified sub nom. *Wyatt v. Aderholt,* 503 F.2d 1305 (5th Cir. 1974)(affirming constitutional "right to treatment").

33. *Id.* at 782.

34. *Id.* at 784.

35. *Wyatt v. Aderholt,* 503 F.2d 1305, 1310 (5th Cir. 1974).

36. *Wyatt v. Stickney,* Civil No. 3195-N (M.D. Ala., Mar. 2, 1972)(emergency order). This order preceded the final order.

37. *Wyatt v. Aderholt,* 503 F.2d 1305, 1310 (5th Cir. 1974).

38. See *Wyatt v. Stickney,* 325 F. Supp. 781, 785–86 (M.D. Ala. 1971).

39. *Wyatt v. Stickney,* 344 F. Supp. 387, 391 n. 7 (M.D. Ala. 1972).

40. 344 F. Supp. at 395–409 (Partlow State School); 344 F. Supp. at 379–86 (Bryce Hospital).

41. Reese, *Things Unbelievably Better at Partlow, Director Says,* Alabama Journal, Feb. 20, 1976, at 13, cols. 3–4.

42. *McCray v. Sullivan,* Civil. No. 5620-69-H (S.D. Ala., Feb 10, 1976); *James v. Wallace,* 406 F. Supp. 318 (M.D. Ala. 1976).

43. *Holt v. Sarver,* 309 F. Supp. 362 (E.D. Ark. 1970), aff'd, 442 F.2d 304 (8th Cir. 1971).

44. *Costello v. Wainwright,* 397 F. Supp. 20 (M.D. Fla. 1975), aff'd, 525 F.2d 1239, rehearing en banc granted, 528 F.2d 1318 (March 3, 1976)(No. 75-2392).

45. *Collins v. Schoonfield,* 344 F. Supp. 257 (D. Md. 1972).

46. *Inmates of Suffolk County Jail v. Eisenstadt,* 360 F. Supp. 676 (D. Mass. 1973), aff'd, 494 F.2d 1196 (1st Cir.), cert. denied, 419 U.S. 977 (1874).

47. *Gates v. Collier,* 349 F. Supp. 881 (N.D. Miss. 1972), aff'd, 501 F.2d 1291 (5th Cir. 1974).

48. *Morales v. Turman,* 383 F. Supp. 53 (E.D. Tex. 1974).

49. *Id.*

50. *James v. Wallace,* 406 F. Supp. 318 (M.D. Ala. 1976); *Costello v. Wainwright,* 397 F. Supp. 20 (M.D. Fla. 1975), aff'd, 525 F.2d 1239 (5th Cir. 1976).

51. *Novak v. Beto,* 453 F.2d 661, 671 (5th Cir. 1971); *Newman v. Alabama,* 349 F. Supp. 278, 280 (M.D. Ala. 1972), aff'd in part, 503 F.2d 1320 (5th Cir. 1974), cert. denied, 421 U.S. 948 (1975).

52. *Washington v. Lee,* 263 F. Supp. 327, 331 (M.D. Ala. 1966), aff'd per curiam, 390 U.S. 333 (1968).

53. 406 F. Supp. 318 (M.D. Ala. 1976).

54. Recently courts have recognized that prisoners retain all their constitutional rights except those necessarily diminished as an incident of incarceration. See *Pell v. Procunier*, 417 U.S. 817, 822 (1973); *Jackson v. Godwin*, 400 F.2d 529, 532 (5th Cir. 1968); *James v. Wallace*, 406 F. Supp. 318, 328 (M.D. Ala. 1976).

55. Record, vol. II, at 357. The eighth amendment prohibits "cruel and unusual punishments." U.S. CONST. Amend. VIII.

56. 406 F. Supp. at 325.

57. *Id.*

58. *Id.* at 323–24.

59. *Id.* at 325.

60. *Id.*

61. Montgomery Advertiser, Feb. 6, 1976, at 1, cols. 5–8.

62. *Id.*

63. Alabama Journal, Feb. 6, 1976, at 13, cols. 5–6.

64. 406 F. Supp. at 322, 327.

65. *Id.* at 332–35.

66. U.S. CONST. Amend. XIV.

67. *Id.*

68. *Duncan v. Louisiana*, 391 U.S. 145 (1968).

69. See U.S. CONST. Art. VI, § 2.

70. See *Mitchum v. Foster*, 407 U.S. 225, 238–39 (1972); *Zwickler v. Koota*, 389 Li.S. 241, 248 (1967); *England v. Louisiana State Bd. of Medical Examiners*, 375 U.S. 411, 415 (1964).

71. McCormack, *The Expansion of Federal Question Jurisdiction and the Prisoner Complaint Caseload*, 1975 WIS. L. REV. 523, 536 (footnotes omitted).

72. *Dent v. Duncan*, 360 F.2d 333, 337–38 (5th Cir. 1966).

The Role of the Judiciary with Respect to the Other Branches of Government

1. 142 F. Supp. 707 (M.D. Ala. 1956), *aff'd*, 352 U.S. 903 (1956).

2. 347 U.S. 483 (1954).

3. 292 F. Supp. 363 (M.D. Ala. 1968).

4. In re Wallace, 170 F. Supp. 63 (M.D. Ala. 1959).

5. *U.S. v. Alabama*, 171 F. Supp. 720 (M.D. Ala. 1959) (dismissed case against registrars and state because registrars had resigned), aff'd, 267 F.2d 808 (5th Cir. 1959), rev'd 362 U.S. 602 (ordered reinstatement of State of Alabama as defendant); 188 F. Supp. 750 (M.D. Ala. 1960) (overruled motion to dismiss by State of Alabama); 192 F. Supp. 677 (1961) (granted injunction against refusal to register black voters).

6. *U.S. v. Duke*, 332 F.2d 759 (5th Cir. 1964).

7. Pub. L. No. 89-110, 79 Stat. 437 (1965).

8. *Williams v. Wallace*, 240 F. Supp. 100 (M.D. Ala. 1965).

9. *Sims v. Frink*, 208 F. Supp. 431 (M.D. Ala. 1962). The first order of the District Court,

asserting its willingness to review the apportionment rules of the Alabama constitution and statute, is reported at 205 F. Supp. 245 (M.D. Ala. 1962).

10. 377 U.S. 533 (1964).

11. *White v. Crook*, 251 F. Supp. 401 (M.D. Ala. 1966).

12. *Frontiero v. Laird*, 341 F. Supp. 201 (M.D. Ala. 1972).

13. 411 U.S. 677 (1973).

14. 340 F. Supp. 703 (M.D. Ala. 1972).

15. 344 F. Supp. 387 and 344 F. Supp. 373 (M.D. Ala. 1972), enforcing 325 F. Supp. (M.D. Ala. 1971), modified on appeal sub nom. *Wyatt v. Aderholt*, 503 F.2d 1305 (5th Cir. 1974).

16. Comment, *Wyatt v. Stickney and the Right of Civilly Committed Mental Patients for Adequate Treatment*, 86 HARV. L. REV. 1282 (1973).

17. 349 F. Supp. 278 (M.D. Ala. 1972).

18. 406 F. Supp. 318 (M.D. Ala. 1976).

19. New York Tribune, May 1861, quoted in C. WARREN, THE SUPREME COURT IN UNITED STATES HISTORY 370 (1932).

20. 5 U.S. (1 Cranch) 137 (1803).

21. See, e.g., 1 L. BOLIE, JOHN MARSHALL: A LIFE IN LAW (1974) for reproductions of newspaper comments criticizing Marshall.

22. 17 U.S. (3 Wheat.) 316 (1819).

23. Despite this traditional attribution to Spencer Roane, recent scholarship suggests that the Amphictyon Essays were authorized by Judge William Brockenbrough, a member of the "Republican Junto" with Roane and Thomas Ritchie, editor of the *Richmond Enquirer.* See JOHN MARSHALL'S DEFENSE OF MCCULLOCH V. MARYLAND, 13 (G. Gunther ed. 1969 [hereinafter cited as JOHN MARSHALL'S DEFENSE].

24. Roane, *"Amphictyon" Essays II*, in JOHN MARSHALL'S DEFENSE, supra note 23, at 64.

25. *Id.* at 71.

26. Letter from John Marshall to Bushrod Washington, June 17, 1819, quoted in JOHN MARSHALL'S DEFENSE, supra note 23, at 16.

27. Marshall, *"A Friend to the Union" Essays I*, in JOHN MARSHALL'S DEFENSE, supra note 23, at 78–79.

28. Roane, *"Hampden" Essays I*, in JOHN MARSHALL'S DEFENSE, supra, note 23, at 108–12.

29. Roane, *"Hampden" Essays IV*, in JOHN MARSHALL'S DEFENSE, supra note 23.

30. Richmond Enquirer, June 11, 1819, quoted in JOHN MARSHALL'S DEFENSE, supra note 23 at 106.

31. 369 U.S. 186 (1962).

32. See, e.g., *Griggs v. Duke Power Co.*, 401 U.S. 424 (1971); *Brown v. Board of Educ.*, 347 U.S. 483 (1954); *Weeks v. Southern Bell Tel. & Tel. Co.*, 408 F.2d 228 (5th Cir. 1969).

33. See *Wyatt v. Aderholt*, 503 F.2d 1305 (5th Cir. 1974).

34. See *Pugh v. Locke*, 406 F. Supp. 318 (M.D. Ala. 1976) (appeal pending).

35. ARTICLES OF CONFEDERATION, art. IX (1777) sets out limited powers of the federal government congress.

36. Address by James Madison to the U.S. House of Representatives, June 8, 1789, quoted

in Cahn, *Brief for the Supreme Court*, in THE SUPREME COURT UNDER EARL WARREN 31–2 (L. Levy ed. 1972).

37. A. DE TOCQUEVILLE, DEMOCRACY IN AMERICA 103 (P. Bradley ed. H. Reeve trans. 1948).

38. *Id.* at 151.

39. Hand, *Sources of Tolerance*, 29 U. PENN. L. REV. 1, 12 (1930).

40. See *Sheppard v. Maxwell*, 384 U.S. 333 (1966); *Estes v. Texas*, 381 U.S. 532 (1965) In re Oliver, 333 U.S. 257 (1948).

41. See *Griswold v. Connecticut*, 381 U.S. 479 (1965).

42. Quoted in THE SUPREME COURT UNDER EARL WARREN, supra note 36 at 10.

43. See *Warren & Brandeis, The Right of Privacy*, 4 HARV. L. REV. 193 (1890).

44. 381 U.S. 479 (1965).

45. See *Gideon v. Wainwright*, 372 U.S. 335 (1963).

46. 369 U.S. 186 (1962).

47. *Id.* at 270 (Frankfurter, J., dissenting).

48. *Rochin v. California*, 342 U.S. 165, 172 (1952).

49. Quoted in H. BLACK, JR., MY FATHER: A REMEMBRANCE 236 (1975) (without attribution to a printed source).

50. 347 U.S. 483 (1954).

51. Quoted in R. KLUGER, SIMPLE JUSTICE 685 (1965) (from an unpublished memorandum to the other Supreme Court Justices in discussion of the *Brown* decision, found in Justice Frankfurter's papers at Harvard University).

52. *Dred Scott v. Sandford*, 60 U.S. (19 How.) 393 (1856).

53. 163 U.S. 537 (1896).

54. 347 U.S. 483 (1954).

55. *Fisher v. Cockerell*, 30 U.S. (5 Pet.) 248, 259 (1831).

56. See *Calhoun v. Cook*, 362 F. Supp. 1249 (N.D. Ga. 1973), aff'd, 522 F. 2d 717 (5th Cir. 1975).

57. 344 F. Supp. 387 and 344 F. Supp. 373 (M.D. Ala. 1972), enforcing 325 F. Supp. 781 (M.D. Ala. 1971), modified on appeal sub nom. *Wyatt v. Aderholt*, 503 F.2d 1305 (5th Cir. 1974).

58. 325 F. Supp. at 785.

Equal Access to Justice

1. See generally *Critical Legal Studies Symposium*, 36 STAN. L. REV. 1 (1984).

2. 416 U.S. 134, 206 (1973).

3. See *Arnette*, 416 U.S. at 217–27.

4. See *id.*

5. 207 U.S. 142, 148 (1907).

6. 192 F. Supp. 677 (M.D. Ala. 1961), aff'd, 304 F.2d 583 (5th Cir.), aff'd, 371 U.S. 37 (1962).

7. *Dallas Makes History*, The Montgomery Advertiser, Jan. 16, 1989, at C1, col. 1.

8. 251 F. Supp. 401 (M.D. Ala. 1966).

9. Nizer, *Verdict on Women as Jurors*, N.Y. TIMES MAG., Mar. 11, 1962, at 85.

10. 476 U.S. 79 (1986).

11. *Batson*, 476 U.S. at 89.

12. 863 F.2d. 822 (11th Cir. 1989).

13. *Fludd*, 863 F.2d at 828–29.

14. See *Wyatt v. Stickney*, 325 F. Supp. 781 (M.D. Ala. 1971). Numerous subsequent decisions were issued in this case. See *Wyatt v. Stickney*, 334 F. Supp. 1341 (M.D. Ala. 1971); *Wyatt v. Stickney*, 344 F. Supp. 373 & 387 (M.D. Ala. 1972), aff'd in part, sub nom. *Wyatt v. Aderholt*, 503 F.2d 1305 (5th Cir. 1974).

15. See *Newman v. Alabama*, 349 F. Supp. 278 (M.D. Ala. 1972), aff'd in part, 503 F.2d 1320 (5th Cir. 1974), cert. denied, 421 U.S. 948 (1975).

16. *Wyatt*, 503 F.2d at 1310–11.

17. *Newman*, 503 F.2d at 1323–24.

18. See Powell, *Review of Capital Convictions Isn't Working*, CRIM. JUST., Winter 1989, at 10.

19. 306 U.S. 19, 26 (1939).

20. Unpublished findings from report commissioned by the Honorable John C. Godbold, former Chief Justice of the Eleventh Circuit.

21. Robinson, *An Empirical Study of Federal Habeas Corpus Review of State Court Judgments*, Fed. Just. Res. Program (1979).

22. *Id.* at 59.

23. *Id.*

24. *Id.*

25. 250 F. Supp. 208 (M.D. Ala. 1966).

26. See *Gideon v. Wainwright*, 372 U.S. 335 (1963); *Douglas v. California*, 372 U.S. 353 (1963).

27. A. HAYS, CITY LAWYER 63 (1942).

28. FED. R. CIV. P. 23.

29. *Dallas Makes History*, The Montgomery Advertiser, Jan. 16, 1989, at C1, col. 1.

30. See R. POSNER, ECONOMIC ANALYSIS OF LAW § 21.9 (3d ed. 1986).

What Is Right with America

1. I make this statement with an acute awareness that, when the Constitution was first written, it excluded a large part of the people in America—blacks and women. Today, "We the People" includes all citizens. Credit for this cannot go to the framers. It must go to the Congress (Thirteenth (1865)), Fourteenth (1868), Fifteenth (1870), and Nineteenth (1920) Amendments) and to the courts that have, with a few egregious exceptions (e.g., *Dred Scott v. Sanford* (1856) and *Plessy v. Ferguson* (1896)), effectively and fairly interpreted our Constitution.

2. *Forman v. City of Montgomery*, 245 F. Supp. 17 (M.D. Ala. 1965), aff'd, 355 F.2d 930 (5th Cir. 1966), cert. denied, 384 U.S. 1009 (1966) (Individuals seeking to publicly demonstrate have no constitutional or statutory right to engage in sit-downs on streets and sidewalks, thereby blocking vehicular and pedestrian traffic.).

3. *Williams v. Wallace*, 240 F. Supp 100 (M.D. Ala. 1965) (Selma-Montgomery march allowed and state officials ordered to give protection to marchers).

4. *Cottonreader v. Johnson*, 252 F. Supp. 492 (M.D. Ala. 1966) (civil rights demonstrators allowed to peacefully demonstrate and picket but required to give officials reasonable notice of their plans in order that officials might provide for the demonstrators' safety); *Johnson v. City of Montgomery* 245 F. Supp. 25 (M.D. Ala. 1965) (civil rights demonstrators, just as Alabama officials, are required to obey the law); *Forman v. City of Montgomery, supra; United States v. United States Klans, Knights of Ku Klux Klan, Inc.*, 194 F. Supp. 897 (M.D. Ala. 1961) (Ku Klux Klan and local officials enjoined from interfering with passengers in interstate commerce. In addition, local officials required to provide protection to travelers).

5. *Hulett v. Julian*, 250 F. Supp. 208 (M.D. Ala. 1966) (declaring unconstitutional the Alabama statutory scheme whereby Justices of the peace could sit in criminal cases in which they had a monetary interest in convicting).

6. *United States v. Wallace*, 218 F. Supp. 290 (M.D. Ala. 1963) (neither king nor governor is above the law).

7. *Pugh v. Locke*, 406 F. Supp. 318 (M.D. Ala. 1976), aff'd as, modified and remanded sub nom. *Newman v. Alabama*, 559 F.2d 283 (5th Cir. 1977), cert. denied in relevant part, 438 U.S. 915 (1978), rev'd in nonrelevant part sub nom. *Alabama v. Pugh*, 438 U.S. 781 (1978) (striking state and state board of corrections from list of defendants on Eleventh Amendment grounds) (conditions in Alabama's prisons held to be violative of prisoners' constitutional right not to be subjected to cruel and inhuman treatment).

8. *Wyatt v. Stickney*, 325 F. Supp. 781; 334 F. Supp. 1341; 344 F. Supp. 373; 344 F. Supp. 387; 344 F. Supp. 408 (M.D. Ala. 1971–72) (conditions in Alabama's mental institutions held to violate patients' constitutional rights).

9. *Sellers v. Trussell*, 253 F. Supp. 915 (M.D. Ala. 1966) (Johnson, J. concurring) (past history of systematic, invidious and intentional discrimination against blacks provides ample evidence that local bill to extend terms of present commissioners who were elected at time when blacks were deprived of their right to vote was racially motivated); *White v. Crook*, 251 F. Supp. 401 (M.D. Ala. 1966)(neither black males nor women (black and white) may be systematically excluded from juries).

10. *United States v. State of Alabama*, 252 F. Supp. 95 (M.D. Ala. 1966)(Alabama poll tax held unconstitutional); *White v. Crook*, 251 F. Supp. 401 (M.D. Ala. 1966)(neither black males nor women (black and white) may be systematically excluded from juries); *United States v. Penton*, 212 F. Supp. 193 (M.D. Ala. 1962)(voting registrars' actions which favored white applicants and discriminated against black applicants held unconstitutional); *United States v. State of Alabama*, 188 F. Supp. 759 (M.D. Ala. 1960), aff'd, 304 F.2d 583 (United States may come into federal courts to protect state citizens' rights to vote); *Gomillion v.*

Lightfoot, 167 F. Supp. 405 (M.D. Ala. 1958), aff'd, 270 F.2d 594 (5th Cir. 1958), rev'd 364 U.S. 339 (1960)(state may not rearrange boundaries of city so as to disenfranchise blacks).

11. *NAACP v. Allen*, 340 F. Supp. 703 (M.D. Ala. 1972), decree continued in effect sub nom. *NAACP v. Dothard*, 373 F. Supp. 504 (M.D. Ala.), aff'd, 493 F.2d 614 (5th Cir. 1974)(racial discrimination found in hiring of state troopers; state ordered to hire certain percentage of blacks to remedy past discrimination).

12. *Entertainment Ventures, Inc. v. Brewer*, 306 F. Supp. 802 (M.D. Ala. 1969)(Johnson, J. concurring)(seizure of films held unconstitutional); *Brooks v. Auburn University*, 296 F. Supp. 188 (M.D. Ala.), aff'd, 412 F.2d 1171 (5th Cir. 1969)(college may not prohibit students from inviting speaker because the speaker would present views in conflict with those of the administration); *Dickey v. Alabama State Board of Education*, 273 F. Supp. 613 (M.D. Ala. 1967), judgment vacated 402 F.2d 515 (5th Cir. 1968) (state may not force a college student to forfeit his or her constitutionally protected right of freedom of expression as a condition to attending a state supported institution).

13. *Parducci v. Rutland*, 316 F. Supp. 352 (M.D. Ala. 1970)(ordered to show either that story assigned to junior high school English class was inappropriate for such students or that it created a significant disruption to the educational processes, dismissal of teacher for assigning such reading matter violates the First Amendment); *Poulos v. Rucker*, 288 F. Supp. 305 (M.D. Ala. 1968)(materials held not obscene for adult readers).

14. *Shaffield v. Northrop Worldwide Aircraft Services, Inc.*, 373 F. Supp. 937 (M.D. Ala. 1974)(employer may not fire employee who was a member of the Seventh Day Adventist Church because he refused to work after sundown on Friday because of religious beliefs); *Wallace v. Brewer*, 315 F. Supp. 431 (M.D. Ala. 1970)(state statute requiring members of the Black Muslim faith to register violates First Amendment rights).

15. *Lee v. Macon County Board of Education*, 267 F. Supp. 458 (M.D. Ala. 1967), 317 F. Supp. 103 (M.D. Ala. 1970), order stayed, 453 F.2d 748 (5th Cir. 1973) (state is under an affirmative duty to provide equal educational opportunities for all); *Carr v. Montgomery County Board of Education*, 253 F. Supp. 306 (M.D. Ala. 1966), further relief granted, 289 F. Supp. 647 (M.D. Ala. 1968), *modified*, 400 F.2d 1 (5th Cir. 1968), district court order reinstated, 394 U.S. 913 (1969), plan 377 F. Supp. 1123 (M.D. Ala. 1974)(schools ordered to take specific action to eliminate segregated school system); *Franklin v. Parker*, 223 F. Supp. 724 (M.D. Ala. 1963), modified, 331 F.2d 841 (5th Cir. 1964)(state university could not refuse to admit blacks into graduate program because they had not graduated from an accredited institution when state-operated colleges for blacks were unaccredited).

16. *Hadnott v. Prattville*, 309 F. Supp. 967 (M.D. Ala. 1970)(city ordered to desegregate city facilities and to equalize facilities in predominantly black areas).

17. *Newman v. Alabama*, 349 F. Supp. 278 (M.D. Ala. 1972), modified, 522 F.2d 71 (5th Cir.), cert. denied, 421 U.S. 948 (1975)(state must provide adequate medical treatment to its prisoners).

18. *Gilmore v. City of Montgomery*, 176 F. Supp. 776 (M.D. Ala. 1959), aff'd as modified, 277 F.2d 364 (5th Cir. 1960)(modifying judgment to direct that district court retain jurisdic-

tion), on remand, 337 F. Supp. 22 (M.D. Ala. 1972), aff'd in part, rev'd in part and remanded, 473 F.2d 832 (5th Cir. 1973), aff'd in part, rev'd in part and remanded, 417 U.S. 556 (1974)(reversing court of appeals' reversal of district court and remanding for further factual development)(a city may not maintain separate facilities for blacks and whites).

19. *Lewis v. The Greyhound Corp.*, 199 F. Supp. 210 (M.D. Ala. 1961)(racial segregation on buses and in bus facilities enjoined).

20. *Scott v. Opelika City Schools*, 63 F.R.D. 144 (M.D. Ala. 1974)(treating maternity disability differently from other causes of sick leave, absent rational relationship to some legitimate state interest, constitutes impermissible sex discrimination); *Drake v. Covington County Board of Education*, 371 F. Supp. 974 (M.D. Ala. 1974)(Johnson, J. concurring) (teacher reinstated where board fired her for having become pregnant while unmarried); *Frontiero v. Laird*, 327 F. Supp. 580, 341 F. Supp. 201 (M.D. Ala. 1972)(Johnson, J. dissenting), *rev'd*, 411 U.S. 677 (1973)(district court dissent adopted)(woman Air Force officer entitled to same benefits for her "dependent" husband as her male counterparts received for their wives); *Weeks v. Southern Bell Telephone & Telegraph Co.*, 408 F.2d 228 (5th Cir. 1969)(Johnson, J.)(sex not a legitimate basis on which to base refusal to hire woman in a switchman's position); *Cheatwood v. South Central Bell Telephone & Telegraph Co.*, 303 F. Supp. 754 (M.D. Ala. 1969)(requirement that commercial representatives be males not a bona fide occupational qualification for that position).

Conclusion

1. Throughout all four sections only the citation to cases and to direct quotations are given. The leading sources regarding Johnson's role in all the fields of law discussed below, including the civil rights struggle, are given in the Introduction to this volume. To explore the constitutional and legal issues more directly, see the works cited by Bass, Yarbrough, Sikora, Kennedy, Yackle, and Freyer, in the Introduction, considered in conjunction with the following more general constitutional and legal histories, including Mark Tushnet, ed., *The Warren Court in Historical and Political Perspective* (University Press of Virginia, Charlottesville, 1993); Michael Les Benedict, *The Blessings of Liberty: A Concise History of the Constitution of the United States* (D.C. Heath and Co., Lexington, Mass., 1996), especially, 284–387; and G. Edward White, *The American Judicial Tradition* (2d ed., Oxford University Press, New York, 1988); Bernard Schwartz, *The Ascent of Pragmatism: The Burger Court in Action* (Addison-Wesley, Reading, Mass. 1990); Stanley H. Friedelbaum, *The Rehnquist Court* (Greenwood Press, Westport, Conn. 1994).

2. *Browder v. Gayle*, 142 F. Supp. 707 (M.D. Ala. 1956); overturning *Plessy v. Ferguson*, 163 U.S. 537 (1896). For extended discussion, see Mark V. Tushnet, *Making Civil Rights Law: Thurgood Marshall and the Supreme Court, 1936–1961* (Oxford University Press, New York, 1994), 233, 283, 289, 302–5.

3. *Browder v. Gayle*, 142 F. Supp. 707 (M.D. Ala. 1956).

4. Moyers's PBS Interview.

5. Ibid.; Tushnet, *Making Civil Rights Law*, 305.

6. *U.S. v. Wallace*, 222 F. Supp. 485 (M.D. Ala. 1963); *Lee v. Macon County Board of Education*, 267 F. Supp. 458 (M.D. Ala. 1967), *aff'd sub nom. Wallace v. United States*, 389 U.S. 215 (1967); *Lee v. Macon County Board of Education*, 453 F.2d 524 (5th Cir. 1971).

7. *Carr v. Montgomery County Board of Education*, 289 F. Supp. 647 (M.D. Ala. 1968), modified, 400 F.2d 1, rehearing denied, 402 F.2d 782 (5th Cir. 1968), rev'd modification of Court of Appeals, 395 U.S. 225 (1969); *Carr v. Montgomery County Board of Education*, 377 F. Supp. 1123 (M.D. Ala. 1974); aff'd 511 F.2d 1374 (5th Cir. 1975), cert. denied, 423 U.S. 986 (1975); for Justice Black's assessment see *U.S. v. Montgomery County Board of Education*, 395 U.S. 225, 236 (1969).

8. Johnson, as quoted, Bass, *Taming the Storm*, at 231.

9. Johnson, as quoted, Yackle, *Reform and Regret*, at 18.

10. *Gomillion v. Lightfoot*, 167 F. Supp. 405 (M.D. Ala. 1958), aff'd, 270 F.2d 594 (5th Cir. 1959), rev'd, 364 U.S. 339 (1960); *U.S. v. Alabama*, 192 F. Supp. 677 (M.D. Ala. 1961).

11. *U.S. v. K.K.K.*, 194 F. Supp. 897 (M.D. Ala. 1961).

12. *Forman v. Montgomery*, 245 F. Supp. 17 (M.D. Ala. 1965), aff'd per curiam, 355 F.2d 930 (5th Cir. 1966), cert. denied, 384 U.S. 1009 (1966).

13. Doar, as quoted, Kennedy, *Judge Frank Johnson*, at 24.

14. 251 F. Supp. 401 (M.D. Ala. 1966).

15. Patterson, as quoted, Yarbrough, *Judge Frank Johnson and Human Rights*, at 223.

16. Bond, quoted in Williams, *Eyes on the Prize*, at XIV.

17. April 16, 1963, in Martin Luther King Jr., *Why We Can't Wait* (1964).

18. Fredrickson, *Comparative Imagination*, at 183–84.

19. *Paradise v. Shoemaker*, 470 F. Supp. 439 (M.D. Ala. 1979); *NAACP v. Allen*, 340 F. Supp. 703 (M.D. Ala. 1972), aff'd, 493 F.2d 614 (5th Cir. 1974).

20. *Palko v. Connecticut*, 302 U.S. 319 (1937).

21. *U.S. v. Carolene Products Co.*, 304 U.S. 144 (1938).

22. For the transition from the Warren Court to the Burger and Rehnquist Courts, see Tushnet, ed., Benedict, White, Schwartz, and Friedelbaum, cited in full, note 1.

23. *United States v. Wilson*, 159 F. Supp. 149 (M.D. Ala. 1957); *United States v. Germany*, 32 F.R.D. 343, 421 (M.D. Ala. 1963). Quotations infra.

24. *Washington v. Holman*, 245 F. Supp. 116 (M.D. Ala. 1965), *modified 364 F.2d 618 (5th Cir. 1966).

25. 372 U.S. 335 (1963).

26. *Escobedo v. Illinois*, 378 U.S. 478 (1964).

27. *Colegrove v. Green*, 328 U.S. 549 (1946).

28. 369 U.S. 186 (1962).

29. 364 U.S. 339 (1960).

30. *Sims v. Frink*, 208 F. Supp. 431 (M.D. Ala. 1962) (three-judge court (per curiam), aff'd sub nom. *Reynolds v. Sims*, 377 U.S. 533 (1964).

31. Bass, *Taming the Storm*, 276.

32. Note 22.

33. *Brooks v. Auburn University,* 296 F. Supp. 188 (M.D. Ala. 1969), aff'd, 412 F.2d 1171 (5th Cir. 1969).

34. *Everson v. Bd. of Educ.,* 330 U.S. 1 (1947).

35. Jesse Choper, as quoted in Tony A. Freyer, *A Precarious Path: The Bill of Rights After 200 Years,* 47 *Vanderbilt Law Review* (April 1994), at 783.

36. *Lemon v. Kurtzman,* 403 U.S. 602 (1971).

37. *Jager v. Douglas County School District,* 862 F.2d 824 (Eleventh Cir. U.S.C.A., 1989).

38. 408 F.2d 228 (Fifth Cir. C.A. 1969).

39. *Frontiero v. Laird,* 341 F. Supp. 201 (M.D. Ala. 1972), (three-judge court) (Johnson, J., dissenting), rev'd, 411 U.S. 677 (1973).

40. *Jones v. Metropolitan Atlanta Rapid Transit Authority,* 681 F.2d 1376 (11th Cir. 1982).

41. *Griswold v. Connecticut,* 381 U.S. 479 (1965).

42. *Roe v. Wade,* 410 U.S. 113 (1973); *Planned Parenthood v. Casey,* 114 Supreme Court Reporter 909 (1994).

43. *Hardwick v. Bowers,* 760 F.2d 1202 (Eleventh Cir. CA. 1985), reversed, 478 U.S. 186 (1986).

44. Johnson, as quoted, Bass, *Taming the Storm,* 424.

45. "Sodomy Ruling Stems from 1905 Case," *Tuscaloosa News,* November 27, 1998.

46. *Furman v. Georgia,* 408 U.S. 238 (1972); *Gregg v. Georgia* 428 U.S. 153 (1976).

47. Mark V. Tushnet, *Making Constitutional Law: Thurgood Marshall and the Supreme Court, 1961–1991* (Oxford University Press, New York, 1997), 146–78.

48. 696 F.2d 940 (Eleventh Cir. CA. 1983).

49. *Dix v. Kemp,* 763 F.2d 1207 (Eleventh Cir. CA. 1985).

50. Kennedy gave this explanation to Professor Freyer during a visit to the University of Alabama School of Law.

51. Steven Brill, "The Real Governor of Alabama," *New York Magazine,* April 26, 1976, at 37.

52. Eisenberg and Yeazell, *The Ordinary and the Extraordinary in Institutional Litigation,* 93 HARV. L. REV. (1980), at 467.

53. Hoffer, *Law's Conscience,* at 8.

54. As quoted, Bass, *Taming the Storm,* at 21.

55. Robert F. Nagel, *Controlling the Structural Injunction,* 7 HARV. J.L. & PUB. POL'Y (1984), at 335.

56. Owen Fiss, as quoted, Bass, *Taming the Storm,* at 90.

57. Bass, *Taming the Storm,* 251–52, and quoted text, *Williams v. Wallace,* 240 F. Supp. 100 (M.D. Ala. 1965).

58. 240 F. Supp 100 (M.D. Ala. 1965).

59. As quoted phrases, Bass, *Taming the Storm,* 251, 252.

60. *Wyatt v. Stickney,* 344 F. Supp. 373 and 344 F. Supp. 387 (M.D. Ala. 1972), aff'd sub nom. *Wyatt v. Aderholt,* 503 F.2d 1305 (5th Cir. 1974).

61. Eisenberg and Yeazell, *The Ordinary and the Extraordinary in Institutional Litigation*, 93 Harv. L. Rev. (1980), at 468.

62. *Newman v. Alabama*, 349 F. Supp. 278 (M.D. Ala. 1972), aff'd in part, 503 F.2d 1320 (5th Cir. 1974), cert. denied, 421 U.S. 948 (1975); *Pugh v. Locke*, 406 F. Supp. 318 (M.D. Ala. 1976), aff'd in part sub nom. *Newman v. Alabama*, 559 F.2d 283 (5th Cir. 1977).

63. As quoted, Yackle, *Reform and Regret*, at 395.

64. Yackle, *Reform and Regret*, at 20, 259.

65. As quoted, Bass, *Taming the Storm*, at 90.

66. Feeley and Rubin, *Judicial Policy Making and the Modern State*, at 25.

67. Owen Fiss, as quoted, Bass, *Taming the Storm*, at 90.

68. William Dickinson, Alabama congressman, as quoted, Yarbrough, *Judge Frank Johnson and Human Rights*, at 124.

69. Garrow, *Bearing the Cross*, at 404, see also pp. 383 and 401.

70. As quoted, Bass, *Taming the Storm*, at 248.

71. Martin Luther King Jr., *Letter from Birmingham Jail* (April 16, 1963), in *Why We Can't Wait* (1964). J. L. Chestnut, an NAACP–Legal Defense Fund lawyer involved in representing the protesters in Selma, affirmed that King supported pursuing a settlement strategy in Johnson's court because he (King) had never defied a federal court order. Also, the NAACP lawyers sued Wallace in order to establish jurisdiction in Johnson's court. J. L. Chestnut Jr., phone interview by Tony A. Freyer, July 20, 2000.

72. Hoffer, *Law's Conscience*, at 196.

73. "What Is Right with America," 2, 3, 4.

74. "With a Juvenile Delinquent, a Youth Offender, or a Young Adult Offender?," 30 F.R.D. 258, 259, 260 (1962).

75. *"The Role of the Judiciary with Respect to the Other Branches of Government,"* 11 Geo. L. Rev. (1977), 455, 469.

76. Ibid., 469, 474.

77. Wallace, as quoted, Bass, *Taming the Storm*, at 194.

78. Wallace, as quoted, Yackle, *Reform and Regret*, at 105.

79. All other references in this paragraph are Johnson, as quoted, Yackle, *Reform and Regret*, at 474–475.

80. "The Role of the Judiciary," 11 Geo. L. Rev. (1977), 470.

81. "Supremacy of the Law," The Alabama Lawyer, July 1969, at 295.

82. "The Attorney and the Supremacy of Law," 1 Geo. L. Rev. (1966), 41, 42.

83. Ibid.

84. Ibid., 41 and 42 n. 164.

85. *Civil Disobedience and the Law*, 44 Tulane L. Rev. (1969) 2, 12.

86. Ibid., 8, 9.

Index

Cases

Subjects